ROLLS-ROYCE HEI

CW01020545

ROLLS-ROYCE ON THE FRONT LINE

The life and times of a Service Engineer

Tony Henniker

HISTORICAL SERIES No 29

Published in 2000 by the
Rolls-Royce Heritage Trust
P O Box 31 Derby England DE24 8BJ

ISBN: 1 872922 17 1

The Historical Series is published as a joint initiative by the Rolls-Royce Heritage Trust
and the Sir Henry Royce Memorial Foundation.

Previous volumes published in the Series are listed at the rear, together with volumes
available in the Rolls-Royce Heritage Trust Technical Series.

Cover Picture: Tony Henniker, from a painting by Flight Officer Veronica Burleigh, RA

Books are available from:
Rolls-Royce Heritage Trust, Rolls-Royce plc, Moor Lane, PO Box 31, Derby DE24 8BJ

Origination and Reproduction by Neartone Ltd, Arnold, Nottingham
Printed by Premier Print, Glaisdale Parkway, Bilborough, Nottingham

INTRODUCTION

As a long-time member of the Trust's Derby Branch, I have always looked forward to the next issue of our excellent Branch magazine, 'Archive': whenever a Tony Henniker reminiscence was included, this turned to excitement. A chance meeting with Tony at the Sir Henry Royce Memorial Foundation in Paulerspury in 1998 offered the opportunity to congratulate him on the content and easy, self-deprecatory style of his contributions. As had been suspected, these were only snippets from a full and fascinating career looking after the Company's products, some literally in the field, where resource, skill and diplomacy are at a premium.

Luckily, it did not take a great deal of cajoling to persuade Tony to share more of his story with us at greater length, and here it is. As a bonus he has also included about one hundred photographs, depicting strange and also well-known aircraft and characters, many from his extensive personal library as well as those of the Trust and the Company. Another plus is the Appendix. The very young men Tony rubbed shoulders with include what must be a roll-call of many of the Allied fighter 'aces' and it indicates the victories they notched up in their careers, their Decorations and the ranks they eventually attained.

It has been most enjoyable working with yet another of those exceptional individuals the Company seems to nurture, and so help illustrate an activity which has not had much attention in the Historical Series to date. I am sure you will get as much enjoyment from this account as I have done.

Ian A Neish
September 2000

CONTENTS

ROLLS-ROYCE ON THE FRONT LINE

CHAPTER ONE

Early days

I suppose it all started as a disappointment, though this was not to last long. Before leaving school I had decided the RAF was the career for me, but my powerful Granny said "No, the Royal Engineers was to be my destiny", whilst my parents did not take kindly to the idea that their only child should go flying and inevitably get himself killed. Memories of the 'square bashing' endured in the school Cadet Force were enough to strengthen my resolve against the first counter-proposal, but the second, more general one, prevailed. Perhaps as a sort of compromise, Father first explored an obvious local alternative career. I had made my first model aeroplane at the age of five, so the prospect of building the real thing for the RAF was much more alluring than building bridges for the Army. He therefore contacted the Bristol Aeroplane Company at nearby Filton. However, their lack of enthusiasm for this idea rather put him off. Next, the *Magic of a Name* and encouraging noises coming from Derby, convinced him that Rolls-Royce had no future without his seventeen year old son.

Thus it was that on 12 August 1929, I and two other would-be Premium Apprentices presented ourselves at No 1 Gate, Nightingale Road. My companions were Rod Gratton and Wendell Holmes. Rod learned to fly with No 504 (City of Nottingham) Squadron, Auxiliary Air Force (AAF). He also became a Service Engineer and was posted to Canada in the combined role of engineer and pilot. He eventually took up residence there and became involved in hair-raising sub-arctic adventures with a Buzzard-engined Ju52 at one stage. Years later he came over to Derby and gave a most interesting account of that period to the Heritage Trust shortly after its formation. Wendell found himself a more conventional career, progressing the issue of test reports for Jock Burns in the Contracts Department. This activity helped expedite the progress payments due from the Ministry on our development contracts. Unfortunately, he is no longer with us, having died some years back.

To get back to 1929, the 'Glorious Twelfth' meant little to me then, but must have been significant, as most of my subsequent career was spent 'trouble shooting'. It turned out that I was the first of this type of trainee to have expressed a preference for aero work rather than the car side. For this reason, they despatched me to what was called the 190 Shop, after the 190hp engines erected there in the 1914-18 war. It was to be a one-month probationary spell under the legendary Bill Smithdale, to find out if I would make it as an engineer.

A thumbnail sketch of the background to the young man just entering his first employment may help explain some of the directions taken by my career and recounted herein. There are Irish connections on both sides of the family, and going back five generations there was a First Baron Henniker of Stratford-on-Slaney, County Wicklow, whilst his grandson was a Rear Admiral, RN. There was a marked military bias through both families, as my maternal grandfather, a Rahilly, was a doctor in the RAMC, serving many years on postings to India. On his retirement, he and Granny settled in Weston-Super-Mare with a large brood. Father had been in the Army before emigrating to Tasmania to farm, and on a trip to England in 1910, had met and married Mother. She went back to Tasmania with him, and I was born there in 1912. Came the War, they returned to England so Father could rejoin his old regiment, while Mother and I joined the 'family' in Weston. This did not last long, and 1921 found us back in Tasmania to try to rescue the farm which had been allowed to deteriorate in Father's absence. The rescue operation could not have been a great success because by 1926 we were all back with Granny. It was only after the last move that a disjointed education

A young Tony Henniker with Father in 1916.

Kestrel engines undergoing strip, inspection and assembly. After passing exacting endurance tests the engines are stripped down to the smallest component for inspection and reassembly. From left to right: Pat Bate (later manager of Hucknall), the author, Jim Lomas, Harry Nixon and Wat Moreton. Extreme right is Bert Millward. Ties were worn by everyone.

was put on a formal footing by my despatch to Blundell's School at the age of fourteen.

The current production engine in 1929 was the 22-litre Vee-12 Kestrel and this was built and erected in the 190 Shop. I was put with several of the fitters in turn and given simple tasks to assess what sort of a job I could make of them. In those days there was no set tuition as we have today. You learned the hard way, joined the then Amalgamated Engineering Union, and if you were keen, nearly everyone was willing to teach you what you needed to know. Bill Smithdale was the Superintendent. He was a great help and we became good friends over the years, as he thought I had a future in the Company. He even maintained this opinion after I had managed to scrap a Kestrel cylinder block by drilling the dowel hole for a sparking plug adaptor through into the combustion chamber. Bill wore a trilby hat on the back of his head all day and when stirred to wrath, which happened regularly, he would tear it off and throw it on the floor. His men were rumoured to so enjoy this scene that once in a while suitable provocations were deliberately engineered.

At seventeen I felt rather lonely, far from home in a Midlands town where people's accents were strange, and local expressions heard at work were difficult to understand at first. Private life was entirely your own affair; there was no friendly hostel for apprentices and you had to find your own 'digs'.

I had six in the first eighteen months, and a total of eleven in four years. The total apprentice strength would have been about twenty and (except for me) all were learning about the manufacture of 'the best car in the world', which of course was the major function of the Company in those days. We didn't see much of each other at work or at play and there was no social life, nothing in the way of a room or club where we could meet for reading or games or discussing our work, nor was there an opportunity to voice any problems or suggestions for improvements. Possibly circumstances kept me from joining in the fun – through lack of cash – and so spending a great deal of spare time at the Derby Technical College. Perhaps I was not the poorest apprentice, but I must have been very near it. Rolls-Royce paid the lowest legal wage – one shilling per day, from which twopence ha'penny was deducted per week 'for widows and orphans', leaving five and ninepence ha'penny spending money, to which my father added half a crown per week. This gave me a total of eight shillings and threepence ha'penny, or forty-two new pence per week, and on this I ran a motorcycle! It seemed strange, even in those days, but apprentices were not encouraged to go to the Derby Technical College, though if you did want to go, you were excused one morning per week to attend. The remainder of our classes were held in the evenings – the evenings the three of us who attended had left out of a week, which had to include homework. Rolls-Royce wanted to train managers who knew the business of manufacturing from A to Z; universities could train and supply the design, research and development specialists.

One exception to our 'apartheid' was an organised trip, which was enjoyed by all and took place roughly once a month. These 'Works Visits' were always on a Saturday morning and consisted of being conducted round other motorcar manufacturer's factories – generally in Coventry and Birmingham, or a steel works in Sheffield; even on one occasion Players cigarette factory at Nottingham. There was no coach laid on of course, and we were expected to get there by our own transport. I always went with someone who had a nice car – nearly everyone had a four-wheeled vehicle of some kind, with the exception of Dick Buckle and 'Lousy' Henry who had 'Aero Morgans'. We were always given a good lunch and after the visit the race back to Derby was always won by Buckle or Henry, with their snarling twin-cylinder JAP motorcycle engines on three wheels.

After the one-month probationary period I was launched on a four-year journey through the twenty or so departments in the factory, all varying in size, importance and interest. Most combined aero and motor car work, and as I spent some time in all, I was able to get a good insight into both sides of the business. The first group, in which I include the foundries, drop forge and pattern shop, were the worst in which to work, and just as well they were dispensed with in the first year. They were very interesting but the working conditions were atrocious. This did not apply so much to Bill Walker's pattern shop, a glorified carpenters' paradise. Everything that had to be sand cast – in iron, brass or aluminium – was first made in wood (sometimes strengthened with metal) in the exact shape and size allowance as required for the finished article. The atmosphere was a little dusty but nothing worse. The brass foundry was bearable as it was small, and only comparatively small articles were made in it, but the iron and aluminium foundries were dreadful.

In winter there was some compensation but in the summer, with the heat of the furnaces and the atmosphere of smoke and fumes, it was all I could do to survive for the scheduled two months in each. How men could spend their working lives in such places, and survive, never ceased to amaze me. The aluminium foundry was the worst as it was some way from the Main Works and, being isolated, there was no getting out of the building between 7.55am and the lunch break at 12.30pm. In between casting the atmosphere cleared a little but there were always fumes coming from the furnace of molten aluminium. Perhaps die-casting was the very worst, where molten aluminium was poured into hot steel dies and allowed to harden enough to become solid and be released from the die, when the whole process would be repeated until that batch of liquid aluminium had been used. Sand casting for large items like engine crankcases was a much slower process as after each flow of metal the sand mould had to be broken up to release the cast article and a new mould made (with the help of the wooden pattern) out of sand. This gave one a breather or at least the illusion that you were on the beach at Blackpool or Skegness. The iron foundry was slightly better as it was in the main factory and one could slip outside for a breath of fresh air or to feed the cupola with pig iron. Also, casting (in sand pits) was only done twice a week. Actually, cast iron was used mostly for making car cylinder blocks and exhaust manifolds, not in aero engines but it was all part of the training. With the wooden pattern made in the pattern shop and the sand mould formed with the brass tools I had made in the brass foundry, I produced what was to emerge after my machining, grinding and fitting shop experience – a small cast iron surface or marking-off table.

Father used to tell me (I suppose with a farmer's outlook) that motorcar manufacturers were really only sophisticated blacksmiths! Had he compared the dropforge with the smithy, his analogy would have been more accurate. Actually the smith's hammer and anvil had been replaced by large steam-operated hammers or larger drop hammers with hollowed out dies interposed between them and the anvils to form the shapes of connecting rods, valves, crankshafts and gear wheel blanks. The 'real' blacksmith was the man who, with a pair of tongs, would start with a large oblong ingot of near white hot steel and manoeuvre it under a large steam hammer cleverly controlled by his mate until they had beaten it into some shaft of several different diameters and three times its original length.

All these items which I had now seen made in the rough were followed through to their various cleaning-up processes – castings having all the unnecessary 'runners', 'risers' and 'flash' cut off, then being wire-brushed or sandblasted before being machined and drilled to receive their moving parts, which were usually made from the forgings. Before being allowed into the machine shops, gear cutting, milling (nothing whatsoever to do with making flour!) and broaching, or the hardening, plating and enamelling shops, I was sent to the tin and coppersmiths (known as the 'tin bashers') which I enjoyed. There, I was able to do some useful work by myself, and after a while even help with the production of parts for cars and aero engines. Many of the skills practised here have today been taken over by the machine; not only computer-controlled, but in some instances, robots, making the human being less and less necessary. Who would believe that the old Rolls-Royce car radiator cores were made from hundreds of small brass tubes soldered together and the matrix so formed contained in a 'box' of sheet brass which had thin sheets of solid nickel soldered on all the outside surfaces – and you couldn't see any joins at the corners – and finally polished? I still have one of the very large soldering irons used for this work. This was before the general use of chromium plating or stainless steel, although the latter material had already appeared as parts of the car exhaust systems. Working in copper was fascinating, and as in practically everything in those days, there was no formal tuition – you learned by working with, and watching, the skilled men and if you were willing there was always somebody ready to help. Of course, if you were not keen or interested enough, you got no help at all. My coppersmith friends told me that once I had passed The Test I was one of them. The Test was being able to turn a piece of copper tube one inch in diameter and one inch in length, inside out; no easy job and it took days of hammering and continually annealing (softening) the copper by heating it red-hot, expanding one end and contracting the other until you had a flat disc with a tiny hole in the middle. You then simply reversed the process until you finished up with the short length of tube with which you started. Perhaps I never became a coppersmith but I did make quite a nice small copper jug. It was while learning to weld that I had my first brush with authority.

Welding was also carried out in this same shop and of course you found you suddenly had lots of friends who wanted little private jobs (foreigners) welded, and in this respect you were very vulnerable to the other apprentices. In those days it was very fashionable to have a fishtail on the end of the exhaust pipe of your car or motorcycle and I had, in fact, progressed far enough to weld together the two stainless steel pressings which, when finished, made the standard 'fishtail' of the Silver Ghost of the time. For your private vehicle, however, the larger the fishtail, the more sporting you were. One day another apprentice – Peter Barr (who in later years found himself as a Lieutenant Commander on Lord Mountbatten's staff in India), brought me a large fishtail. It was at least twelve inches wide and he had had it made up for his MG Midget and wanted it welding together. This was a little large to conceal and sure enough, Jimmy Bowers, the shop superintendent, must have seen it and Jimmy hated everybody – especially apprentices. The next thing I knew, I was sent for by 'Wor' (Arthur Wormald – the Director and General Works Manager) who gave me a lecture and a severe reprimand, which I considered rather unfair, as 'foreigners' were not new in the Works. Later, I understood the sub-text: the crime was in being caught! As I was leaving his office, still quaking in my oily welding shoes, Wor called me back and in a different tone of voice explained that he had broken his coal tongs and would I call at his office in the morning to collect them and weld them up for him, and he wanted a good job made of them! Then came the punch line, *"and if you are caught or anyone finds out who they belong to, I'll sack you, and I mean it!"* I trembled all the way back to the shop, my hands being much too shaky to do any more that day. Was I in luck? Jimmy Bowers was taken ill the very next day and was whipped off to hospital. I was never thanked for doing the job, but neither did I get the sack. When Jimmy Bowers returned a few weeks later (less whatever it was he had had removed from his person) he seemed a different man – he even gave me a smile or two, which I returned as I had learned an interesting and valuable lesson while he had been away.

Nowadays, working in a factory is very much safer than it was over half a century ago. Accidents are less frequent and under today's Factory Acts strict safety precautions and improved working conditions are implemented. This is thanks in no small measure to the persistent pressure of trades unions. During my apprenticeship any contingency, from a minor laceration to the loss of a limb, was dealt with by the nearest First Aid post. Getting a steel splinter in the pupil of my right eye called for a cycle trip down to the Derbyshire Royal Infirmary with my eye bandaged to have the offending bit removed. Medical facilities improved over the years and some quarter of a century later an elaborate medical centre was built actually inside the old brass foundry at the original factory at Nightingale Road. The capacious general surgery, X-ray room, operating theatre and several rest and therapy rooms were staffed by two doctors, a sister and a number of trained nurses. Much later I became acquainted with the senior doctor, Tim Langdon, and Sister Ellis, as for many months I attended the centre for treatment. Listening to the medical talk and discussions Tim and Sister had over patients – lacerations, burns, and occasionally a few grisly stories, gradually lulled me into thinking that I could face up to anything, and blood had little fear for me. That was until the morning I came along for my usual appointment and found Tim peering at something in a white enamel bowl, which was occupying his full attention. *"Come and sit down Tony and give me a hand"*, said Tim – which on reflection was an unfortunate remark. Besides his own two, there was a third hand in the bowl. I felt the blood draining from my face as it had from the hand, which approached the whiteness of the bowl. Tim presented me with a pair of forceps and at intervals asked me to turn the severed hand over slowly while he made copious notes and verbal observations on points of interest. I persuaded myself that I was not going to be sick and, perhaps encouraged by the knowledge that the firm's photographer had long since passed out, the colour gradually returned to my cheeks. Sweet dreams were not for me that night, and the memory now reminds me of the barbaric law (still practised in some climes) when the punishment for stealing was the removal of the right hand. As if to confirm the righteousness of this practice, in Derby at least, the severed hands were buried in a corner of the cathedral – so a verger told my wife one day.

Of the six or so departments dealing exclusively with cars, I spent some time in four. These included gearbox and back-axle assembly and test (we quietened gears by hand lapping in those days and went out on the road with a 'sound-box' wooden body on a chassis to magnify any slight noise), chassis erection and the electrical department, where girls wound the coils of the electric starters and dynamos, which were made in-house. This experience meant that I also got a pretty good grounding in the art of making hand-built motorcars. After many more informative but not very exciting experiences, it was natural that the Test Department, in which one got to grips with the finished article be it aero engines or motorcar chassis (Rolls-Royce didn't make their own bodies in those days), was the most interesting. On the aero engine side the work consisted of first endurance testing an engine after its completion. It then went back for complete strip, inspection and rebuild, then back for a final test on the beds. This work I loved, though it was noisy, cold and unhealthy. Running the engine on the ground was akin to the working environment of its final destination – the aeroplane. It required concentration and a certain amount of intelligence – working out what performance the engine should be giving under the particular barometric pressure and air temperature of the day, at certain running conditions and fuel consumption and at simulated varying altitudes etc. The possession of a slide rule was useful and very much the 'in thing', as pocket calculators had not been dreamt of. The tester and his assistant were also left very much alone to get on with the job with only an occasional visit from the superintendent or the AID Inspector (the Aeronautical Inspection Directorate were Air Ministry officials placed at all aircraft and engine factories) when an engine was on final test. It was a tough life standing behind an engine running flat out, to read the instruments in a howling gale of cooling air mixed with exhaust gases. The expression Endurance Test applied as much to the tester as it did to the engine.

The test beds – there were about twelve of them – were built side by side, similar to two rows of large lock-up garages with sliding doors at either end. Each had its cast iron base on which to mount the engine to be tested and a coupling-shaft to the Heenan and Froud water brake for absorbing and measuring the power output of the engine. While there were two large silencers outside each bed to keep the noise down a little, there was also a large propeller-like fan blowing a gale of air over the engine while it was running. To read the instrument panel which, with the controls, was situated right up against the rear of the engine, one had to stand in the icy cold blast

R' type engine being passed off final test in 1929 on a typical open test bed. The carburettor in this photograph has been airbrushed out to confuse the competition at the time!
Left to right: Charles Conway, Ray Dorey (who became a Director and General Manager of the Motor Car Division) and George Parkin (who became Chief Production Test Engineer).

15

– and in mid-winter at 6.00am on the early shift, I really do mean icy blast. There was none of your modern clinically clean, soundproofed and heated first floor gallery from where testers gaze down on the screaming monster through thick double-glazed unbreakable glass, waiting perhaps for a system malfunction or even for an engine to blow up – from which they could gather valuable data. No, testers were not even given protective clothing but we did get three shillings above the rate and half a pint of fresh milk per shift to compensate for the fumes, and – oh yes, I nearly forgot, there was also a pair of (useless) ear defenders. Of course you could always warm your hands on the near red-hot exhaust pipes!

Each tester had his regular mate – they were called 'labourers' which was grossly unfair, as they had to know what they were doing when controlling the dynamometer but they also did the heavy, and I suppose, labouring work. Test crews were a happy gang – they had to be, working under such conditions. They didn't spend their time moaning although compared to today's working environment they had every justification. During my four years as an apprentice I cannot remember a single day being lost through strikes but during that period the Company's name was being upheld and history was being made. In later years that sense of commitment was never fully reciprocated. The endurance test was a bit boring, as once one had the engine rigged and running at the correct load, and the petrol, oil and water flows, pressure and temperature etc were stable, there was really nothing to do for the remainder of the two hour run, except gaze upon the new-born mechanical baby and take its temperature now and then. An occasional visit from Len Packham, the superintendent, broke the monotony and sometimes we had a party of visitors or prospective buyers of military aircraft with the Kestrel engine. I was with Joe Ash, the tester on No 10 bed, long enough to know him and his labourer pretty well. To while away the time and to help keep reasonably warm, the three of us had got together a simple routine chorus girl type dance act with various steps in unison including high kicks with arms linked across our shoulders. In the noisy surroundings – the din was too much for us to talk to each other – one felt a kind of isolation from the world – perhaps a false sense of security, but we were never caught! As already indicated, engines came back to the test beds for their half hour 'final', which was much the same exercise as before. The real fun came at the end of this second run when the engine was 'passed off' ready to be prepared for despatch. The exhaust silencers were removed and the final running was carried out with short, open exhaust stubs on each of the twelve cylinders. The engine would then have to respond to rapid throttle opening and back down to tick-over without hesitation, and within so many seconds. This was a pretty hairy experience – having the flames and noise from the twenty-two litres and twelve cylinders – six on either side – burst on you in a sudden roar, the vibration seemed to go right through you. The big reward came when visitors approached, you waited until they were fairly near, and then opened up: the effect was most satisfying!

After several months I was thought to be responsible enough to stand in for anyone who was away ill and was entrusted with the running of a bed. I only had one close shave of wrecking an engine – partly because of an inexperienced mate who forgot to open the bed coolant cock to the engine before starting. Luckily, we noticed before it was damaged. Although a few repair Condors went through Harold Fisher's bed while I was there, the engine of the day was the Kestrel. Harold seemed synonymous with the Condor; they were both getting on a bit and of the old school. The Condor was the last of the engines with twelve separate cylinders bolted to the crankcase. Harold, a great character, always finished an engine test by flipping a ball bearing out of each ear (better than ear plugs, he said) and catching it before it reached the ground. This was followed by one of his latest jokes, which were always funny – but for the wrong reasons. He suffered from a very bad stutter which increased as his joke reached its climax, by which time we were in fits of laughter. Harold would curtail the punch line, concluding that we were laughing because we had heard the joke before. He never realised that we were laughing at him, not his joke! Without the experience gained on the 22-litre Kestrel there would have been no Merlin (27 litre), which was very similar but twenty-three percent larger in capacity and well over twice the power output. The Buzzard (36 litres) –

Early Condor with epicyclic reduction propeller shaft.

Condor III incorporating A J Rowledge changes i.e. fork and blade rods, spur reduction gear and main bearing lateral bolts.

A normally-aspirated Kestrel engine.

an overgrown Kestrel – sired the racing 'R' engine of the same size, which powered the Schneider Trophy seaplanes and subsequently the land, water and air record-breaking machines. To come down to earth, so to speak, each of the Buzzard's twelve cylinders was twice the capacity of the whole engine of today's average motorcar. I was still not quite twenty-one when I was asked to join three fitters, whom I shall never forget, to go to No 4 Stores Depot, Ruislip, and carry out certain modifications on a quantity of Kestrel engines in storage. I suppose it was considered that if I survived my first outside job I would have had a good grounding and should be capable of facing anything the aircraft world could throw at me.

Just before my twenty-first I had written to Wor (Arthur Wormald, Director and General Works Manager) asking him whether he thought the Company had a future without me and he replied that … *"I have taken the matter up with Mr Platford (EP) and after receiving his report am pleased to inform you that we are prepared to employ you on Aero Work… according to future requirements"*. Delightfully vague, I thought, but at least I had a job. Now was the time to look at what the future held in store for me. From what I had heard I was now to be trained for 'outside work' which meant travelling and this was very attractive. It would be disappointing not being able to go further with the Technical College but as the work there got harder, I found that it was becoming increasingly difficult to study while living in digs. It would have been so different had I been living at home that I wondered whether I would be able to make the necessary progress; assuming I could find a job at the factory. I decided that four years of this had been enough, so the decision was made. The only real disappointment during those four years was none of Rolls-Royce's doing. Not having the time to join No 504 (City of Nottingham) AAF Squadron, I had arranged to join the Nottingham Flying Club at Tollerton, through the good offices of Cyril Lovesey. Cyril was not only a member, but he had his own Tiger Moth, and had promised to give me some dual instruction. Cyril was probably the best development engineer the Company had ever seen, and was a keen pilot at the time. All this had been agreed with my father as, of course, he would have to finance me. At the very last moment Father called it off, saying he now realised he couldn't afford the outlay – or was it family pressure? At the time it nearly broke my heart and took a lot of living down and I'm afraid I let my father know how I felt. Of course I later realised it might be a blessing in disguise, as it probably was. Perhaps in my early days with Rolls-Royce the impressive and stirring saying of Sir Henry Royce ('R' to his immediates) would have given me the final spur to go out into the world to continue the great tradition. It was not until years later that I read those now famous words; *"Whatsoever is rightly done, however humble, is noble"*, spoken by the great man at a luncheon he was giving, and which were translated into Latin, the more to express the sentiment of the time. In later years I became less starry-eyed, maybe even a little cynical.

Before leaving my second Alma Mater (or my seventh would be more accurate!), I must mention an unusual – and on the whole – pleasant weekend spent with my uncle, Franklin Ratsey RN, in order to watch the 1931 and last Schneider Trophy Race. I was halfway through my apprenticeship at this time and the justification I made to my boss for a few days leave was that as the first premium apprentice to study the aeronautical (as opposed to the motorcar) side of the business, it would be educational to see the Rolls-Royce 'R' engines perform in the two Supermarine S6B seaplanes. As I was prepared to travel to Portsmouth and back on my motorcycle, my superior, Arthur Wormald, seemed convinced that I was a keen lad and should be encouraged. I doubt whether great grandfather, Vice Admiral Henniker, would have had much time for me as, lacking nautical experience or salt in my veins, my knowledge of matters maritime was, and still is, very limited. Uncle provided ample opportunity for this fact to become apparent in the few days that followed but most of what I had learned has long since been forgotten.

During World War II uncle had one thick gold ring round his sleeve (I understand the Admiralty has since ditched the rank of Commodore) and was involved in Atlantic convoys, but when we met for the Schneider Trophy Race his job sounded something like Portsmouth Harbour Master and a couple of boats seemed to go with the job. This was where my lack of seafaring knowledge began to show. I could identify the general run of things but of fighting ships I knew little, and of specific details – nothing. I mean I knew that there were differences between a coracle and a corvette: I had been in the former and understood its functions and the latter was also small for its class of ship, but I had no idea what its real duty was or the size or number of guns it mounted. I was pretty sure it was correct to be IN and not ON a boat or ship, and yet it sounded right to be ON board. When was a boat not a boat, but a ship, and were they not both vessels? – a word which surely should be reserved for tankers as liquids are the latter's cargo. One is tempted to wonder if the confusion is intentional.. Uncle Franklin had all the answers, of course, but we had many friendly arguments over the rights and wrongs of nomenclature. With tongue in cheek I persisted with comparing a cabin cruiser with a cruiser, and as all sea or water-going craft were referred to as 'she', surely a man-o-war or a merchantman should have a sex change! Were he alive today I would like to ask his views on machines like the hovercraft or the hydrofoil which have partially taken to the air, and whether the nomenclature of gunboat and gunship adequately describes their respective functions. Uncle was uneasy about flying boats and airships merely, I suspected, to have a dig at my line of business. I thought an airship was so named because of its size; an airboat would be something smaller, while a flying-ship would sound as though it should be much larger than a flying boat. He did not agree, and an airship looked neither like a ship or a boat. I knew he was really interested in air only when it filled the sails of his yacht (or was it a sloop, barge, or yawl?), but was it not the Royal Navy that played about with airships before anyone else in this country? In 1911, eleven years after the first Zeppelin, Vickers built the first rigid airship, the R1, in this country for the Admiralty. It had the unfortunate or optimistic name of 'Mayfly'. It didn't! The non-rigid North Sea class (or Class B – limp; hence 'Blimp') did fine work with the Royal Naval Air Service during World War I. I just remember seeing the R34 and well remember the R100 of Barnes Wallace and Nevil Shute fame. Both these craft successfully flew the Atlantic, the latter using six Rolls-Royce Condor engines, ably watched over by Tony Hunt, who for a time joined me in France during World War II. The crash of the government-sponsored, botched up R101 at Beauvais in October 1930 put paid to airships in this country for five decades.

An early scrapbook of mine has Blundells School printed on the outside and the inside cover announces that it is for Latin Exercises. I cannot for the life of me remember how it got filled up with pictures of Parry Thomas,

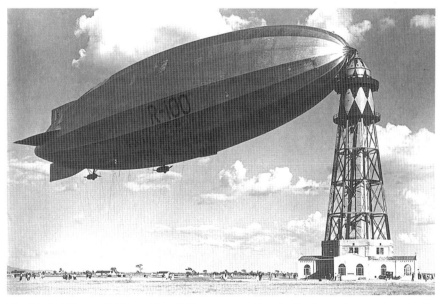

The R100 of Barnes Wallis and Nevil Shute powered by six Condor engines made a double Atlantic crossing with Service Rep Tony Hunt, who was with me in France in 1940.

Miss England II with two 'R' engines which crashed killing Seagrave and Helliwell, the Rolls-Royce Service Rep.

Segrave, Lockhart and Lee Bible (both Americans), together with their record and (neck) breaking cars or how they made a connection with Latin. Then there were cuttings of *Miss England*, not the half-naked girls synonymous with today's title, but the motorboat which killed Segrave (and the Rolls-Royce man E Halliwell) trying to capture the record on Windermere and Kaye Don with the rebuilt boat. Finally, I had some of the history of the Schneider Trophy in pictures from our first win before World War I as well as those beautiful and graceful seaplanes made by Italy, America and for this country – Glosters and Supermarines. Having won the 1927 contest (Supermarine S5, Napier Lion) and the 1929 race (Supermarine S6 Rolls-Royce 'R'), I was now going to see the final race for myself. One of uncle's craft was a speedboat in which we made our trips to his yacht club at Cowes and to the larger boat which served as a hotel (in which I cooked breakfast every morning, and the real reason for my visit) then out to one of the official timing ships for the actual race. We had already seen several practice flights made by the English and Italian seaplanes (the American Mercury had crashed during practice in the States) but now my scrapbook was about to come to life and I was to see the real thing and from the best possible vantage point.

Uncle Franklin seemed to know everyone on board, so once I had made fast alongside (provoking the most interesting curses from uncle, some I had never heard even on the shop floor at Derby), we were greeted by the Captain who was on Christian name terms with my nautical relative. Several pink gins later we were told that the Italian aeroplane would not be competing, so the race was a bit of an anti-climax and our entry had only to complete the course to win the Trophy outright. However, the Supermarine S6B was impressive if only for the noise the Rolls-Royce 'R' engine made pushing out its – for that era – terrific 2300 bhp, propelling the aircraft round the triangular course as many times as necessary at an average speed of 340 mph. The Sound Barrier wasn't talked about in those days but the noise of the engine arriving after the aircraft had passed impressed upon me that the

The 'R' engine was developed from the Buzzard specifically for the 1929 Schneider Trophy Race. The surplus of engines built powered record-breaking cars and boats. Note, the characteristic inlet trunking is not in place in this photograph.
Mr Charles Conway (left) and George Parkin (right) watch a 1929 engine coming off test. Eric Platford and Cyril Lovesey can be seen behind Conway's shoulder.

speed being reached was approaching that of sound. The distance from the aircraft to the timing ship as it passed must have made up for the difference between 340 mph and the over 600 mph speed of sound.

While many felt it was unsporting of Great Britain not to call the race off, this was in fact the last effort that any country could afford due to the tremendous outlay and we only managed to compete in this last race thanks to a gift of £100,000 by Lady Houston. If excuses are needed for motor racing, apart from advertising the car manufacturers or the products of the backers who put up the money, improving the breed for the benefit of the family car is a genuine one. Jacques Schneider established his Trophy because he felt that the development of the seaplane was being neglected, while both aero engine and aircraft manufacturers claim that they learned a great deal from building these beautiful racing seaplanes. Rolls-Royce certainly learned a lot from their 'R' engine, and R J Mitchell incorporated many ideas from the Supermarine S6 seaplanes in the design of his Spitfire, so all the effort and expense was well worth it. No doubt Italy and America were also able to make technological advances in their Macchi and Curtiss aircraft of later design but it is hard to see what Glosters gained from their sleek looking Golden Arrow seaplanes which stuck to the Napier engine which was less powerful than the 'R' engine. In 1936/7 it must have been

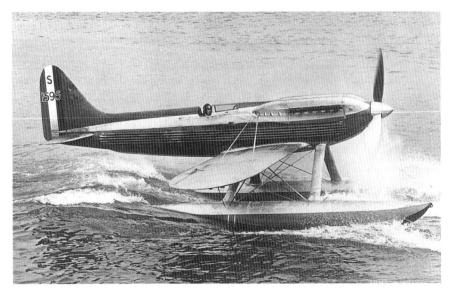

F/O Atcherley taxiing on S1595, one of two Supermarine S6B seaplanes at Calshot during the 1931 races.

frustrating for Gloster's design team to know that even with the built-in drag of two large floats their 1929 seaplanes had reached some 350 mph and yet with a war looming, they were still producing biplane fighters (Gladiators) to AM requirements which were at least 130 mph slower. Perhaps H P Folland, their designer, put his experience into the Gnat. His pretty little fighter first flew in 1954/5 but took a further twelve years before entering service. I wonder where Willie Messerschmitt obtained his 'know-how'? Not from participating in the Schneider Trophy!

CHAPTER TWO

Released onto the outside world

Although I was still an apprentice and had not started earning a wage, my first outside job was in fact a working holiday. If I had known what the future held with the Company I probably would have waited a further six months or so to achieve the objective of getting among the aeroplanes. In the spring of 1932 I just couldn't wait and this enthusiasm persuaded someone at Rolls-Royce to arrange for my ten days summer holidays to be spent at the Westland Aircraft Company at Yeovil. This amounted to a very short 'apprenticeship' in which I would at least have a chance to get some idea of how aeroplanes were built. All that Westlands (they were still part of Petters diesel engine makers in those days) required was that I should obey the same rules and regulations as applied to all their employees – 'clock on' in the morning etc. If, for instance, I did not keep regular hours they would ask me to leave.

In order that my parents would see something of me, I lived at home and motorcycled over to Yeovil and back each day, a round trip of some 90 miles. It was rather a long way for a day's work without pay but the weather was perfect and it was all a thrill, and I certainly did no work. The firm was turning out Westland Wapitis (based on the de Havilland DH9A) and this was the new world I had been looking for. After three and a half years of engine making it was time to see how the 'other half' was made. It was fairly easy to scrounge a lift in the gunner's rear cockpit during test flights, and this was to be my first experience of cross-country flights of any length. I flew with the chief test pilot, Captain Louis Paget, who, even in those days, was convinced that flying was safer than driving a car. No doubt he was busy taking figures all the time – even noting the readings of the Bristol 'bunch of carrots', stuck out in front that seemed to propel us successfully, whereas I treated each flight test as a joy ride.

One day we flew over Cheddar Gorge and noticed an unusual amount of activity concentrated in one short stretch. The road seemed unusually white and what appeared to be a horse-drawn carriage was making return trips up and down, watched by a crowd of people on either side of the road. We reduced height and circled several times, whereupon many faces were turned skywards. It was most strange! That evening the local paper reported the filming of a scene from *The Maid of the Mountains* (starring Harry Welchman), and apparently the 'white' road was chalk put down to create the illusion of dust stirred up by the carriage. The proceedings had been interrupted by some 'wretched' aeroplane, which had come over and attracted the attention of the locally hired extras who had looked up, so retakes had to be made when the aircraft had gone!

We often made for the South coast and one afternoon we flew over Dorset and Portland Bill. There under the calm sea we could see the stricken submarine M2, laying in seventeen fathoms of water on the sandy bottom some three miles west of the Bill. She was an old vessel, having been made by Vickers and completed in 1918, but instead of mounting a large 12" battleship's gun, she had been fitted with a hangar to house a small two-seat seaplane with folding wings. This Parnell Peto could be catapulted from the deck of the submarine and after carrying out its reconnaissance, return and land beside the M2, which would lift it back on deck by means of a crane. These trials had apparently been successful but on 26 January 1932, the M2 dived at about 10.30am and no further communication was received. Presumably water had flowed through the hangar doors, which had not closed correctly, and here we were six months later and she was still on the bottom. As far as I can remember she was never raised and her sixty officers and ratings never surfaced again.

Early in 1933, after the Yeovil holiday, I was sent to Brooklands. This was famous for its motor racing circuit but in its centre was an aerodrome which was used by two equally famous aircraft manufacturers, Vickers and Hawkers, and it was to the latter that I had been sent to join two other Rolls-Royce men. The Vickers factory was conveniently situated on the Weybridge-Byfleet road at the side of the track, so every completed aeroplane could be pushed out onto the concrete for engine runs and then straight onto the grass aerodrome for flying. However, Hawkers had to

The Parnell Peto being catapulted from the deck of the ill-fated submarine M2.

transport all their aircraft, less wings and undercarriage, by road from their factory (the old Sopwith and Hawker Engineering Company) at Kingston-on-Thames. The aeroplanes were then assembled for flight testing and dispatch from their hangars at the far side of the aerodrome.

Vickers had built some quite large twin-engined aeroplanes in the past. The most famous must be the Vimy with its war-like name. Actually it was too late to be used as a bomber in 1918 but in 1919, in a converted form, it made the first non-stop Atlantic crossing and the first flight from England to Australia. A year later one made the first flight from England to South Africa, all naturally with Rolls-Royce engines! It was just as well that Hawkers built only single-engined aircraft as they all had to be transported through a tunnel under Brooklands track, which did not have much headroom but was the sole entrance for vehicles to the aerodrome itself. It was from this tunnel that I emerged and suddenly found myself in this exciting arena – this new scene of aeroplanes and motor cars, where many

Eric Platford (EP), my boss for many years, inspecting an Eagle engine of the transatlantic Vickers Vimy in 1919. He was the first of two Premium Apprentices to join Henry Royce at Manchester and was his first car engine tester.

28

Brooklands was often used for testing the Company's motor cars such as the streamlined lightweight Embericos 4.5 litre Bentley, driven here by Captain George Eyston in 1939.

of the famous learnt to fly – A V Roe in 1908, T O M Sopwith in 1919, who in turn taught Harry Hawker and the future Lord Trenchard. There must have been a race in progress for the sight, sound and indeed, smell of cars (Castrol 'R') roaring round the track, with the occasional aeroplane overhead was something completely new to me. I was just twenty-one and the atmosphere of this thrilling environment confirmed that this had to be my future world, the bottom rung of the right ladder. Later on, once settled into the job and the routine of things, I grasped the opportunities which presented themselves during that very interesting and enjoyable year, with both hands.

I certainly could not afford to join the very expensive Brooklands Flying Club and the entrance fee to get onto the track for a Saturday race meeting was also beyond my reach. So the form was that one arrived for work on a Saturday morning as usual, getting in with a works pass, attended to any jobs that required completion that weekend and then spent the remainder of the morning in the small Rolls-Royce office making out one's expense sheets for the week and rolling a quantity of cigarettes on the then popular Rizla machines. After a snack lunch one would casually wander across the aerodrome to the other side and the Brooklands Racing Drivers Club building. There, one was among the pits and the racing cars, and could see all the action for nothing. There were meetings of some kind nearly every Saturday and sometimes Rolls-Royce or Bentley cars would come down from Derby to be belted round the track for hours on end as the drivers tried to blow them up.

It didn't take long to get used to this new life, which was so very different from working in a factory. I had sold the old Douglas motorcycle and acquired JV1925, a brand new Austin 7 four-seater tourer, with the money that an embarrassed family solicitor had put in trust for me when I was born. I had, of course, heard of Brooklands and knew it was synonymous with motor racing in this country, but had never imagined what it was really like, so I wasted no time in looking up its interesting history. Wealth has a habit of making news one way or another. Perhaps a rich American by the name of James Gordon Bennett was facilitated in so doing, as he was also in the publishing business as the Paris-based proprietor of the *New York Herald*. From the keen motorist's point of view he has gone down in history as the man who, at the turn of the century, inaugurated the first truly international motor car road race, which became known as the Gordon Bennett Cup. Continental enthusiasts were lucky in having sympathetic governments which allowed sections of public roads to be closed for racing, but not so the British government which would not hear of such carryings-on. The first RAC Tourist Trophy race had to be held in the Isle of Man when a Rolls-Royce was beaten into second place by a Napier and in the same year, 1905, Vincenzo Florio established the Targa Florio in his native Sicily, having first inaugurated the Coppa Florio in Brescia five years before. Britain was by now at a disadvantage and when it came to her turn to stage the Gordon Bennett Cup, the only possible venues were the Isle of Man and Ireland.

The lack of racing facilities in England did not go unnoticed by one keen motorist and Surrey land owner and he was determined to rectify this situation. Mr H F L King had already given permission to the agents for Itala, his favourite motorcar, to build an assembly factory on his estate called Brooklands, near Weybridge. After an abortive attempt to reach Brescia for the 1905 Coppa Floria, he decided to build his own motor racing track. Work started late in 1906 on this three-mile circuit, banked to permit cars to reach 120 mph. It was completed eight months later; too quickly perhaps, as the bankings were not allowed to settle down and frost cracked a lot of the 200,000 tons of concrete surface. It was the first ever purpose-built track of its kind and become one of the wonders of the world. The level ground in the centre became the first aerodrome in England. In 1914 the Royal Flying Corps (RFC) took over the aerodrome and soon the hangars were built which were now occupied by Hawkers, while in 1915 the Itala works was pulled down to make way for the Vickers factory – or the 'Vickers Sheds' as they became known locally. The history of Brooklands is a subject in itself. It produced all the famous British racing drivers of the age, the Graham Hills, Jackie Stewarts and Nigel Mansells of the day. Names of great deeds and achievement – Malcolm Campbell, Henry Seagrave, John Cobb, Kay Don, Earl Howe, Parry Thomas, Tim Birkin, Woolf Barnato, Goldie Gardner

Terence Henry beating hell of out an unsuspecting unsupercharged Kestrel while the author enjoys the noise from the rear cockpit.

A line-up of Hawker Audax army co-operation aircraft at Brooklands before being handed over to the test pilots.

and more. Many lost their lives for the sport or for the improvement and safety of the motorcar whilst at the same time flying the flag for this country.

My job consisted of learning how the Kestrel engines – the then current end product of some six thousand hard working people in Derby – were installed in airframes to create a complete aeroplane. It was our job to ground test and make any adjustments necessary before clearing the aircraft for flight and handing over to the test pilots. We lived in a little world of our own – all hands couldn't have amounted to more than fifteen or twenty, including the three Rolls-Royce men and a couple of AID inspectors. Numbers would be supplemented by an occasional visiting engine representative on the rare occasion when the client was misguided enough to want an engine other than the Kestrel. The Persians, for instance, wanted Pratt & Whitney Wasps in their Furies and one day a man who was to be my future boss turned up. W P Calvert (Cal) was working for Napier at that time and had the installation of an air-cooled Napier Dagger to cope with.

While Hawkers had a superintendent who ran the works, the three test pilots, P W S (George) Bulman, P E G (Gerry) Sayer and Lucas were looked upon as the senior staff, while our senior man was Bob Smith, who was replaced by Jim Lomas when the former was sent to Japan – I think to look

Author with Hawker Audax and his first motorcar, JV 1925.

32

after a Shorts-designed flying boat order. Alf Fodem was the superintendent while Olive, the only girl, ran the office and was also our typist and telephone operator. Amongst her attributes was a useful pair of lungs, which she used to shout "Rolls-Royce" at the top of her voice when we were wanted on the 'phone. She was in love with our resident tinsmith and you could tell when they had had a bad night out; he would beat hell out of sheets of inoffensive aluminium the next morning!

Every gallon of petrol that went into the aircraft was poured in from two-gallon petrol cans by 'Albert' perched on the top of a pair of steps. He unloaded the cans himself from the delivery lorry, stacked them in a store and brought them out two at a time, when required. Sometimes when I drove JV1925 home in the evening my petrol gauge showed FULL when it had no business to be. Happy days!

It was at Brooklands that I had the idea of joining the Auxiliary Air Force. Later I realised the relocations involved in my future job would have made this impossible – apart from any other shortcomings – like a severe and perpetual shortage of cash. However, at that time Ron Harker put my name up and arranged an interview with the adjutant of either No 600 or 601 Squadron at Hendon. They were situated fairly near but I realised later when I knew the RAF a little better that you are unlikely to find any paupers in even a provincial AAF Squadron, let alone the two most expensive ones in the country, both County of London Squadrons! By the time I had reached Colindale Avenue I had become a little apprehensive. On entering Hendon and navigating the Austin 7 through the ranks of Bentley, Aston Martin, Lagonda, Invicta, Alfa Romeo, MG, Delahaye and other similar vehicles, it dawned on me that I might be making a big mistake. The adjutant was at first polite until he looked out of the window and saw JV1925. The interview ended abruptly. Another mistake might also have been made during my time at Brooklands. The Asiatic Petroleum Company had asked Rolls-Royce if they had a likely lad who would be willing to join their Aviation Department, which handled the foreign sales of Shell. I duly had the offer of a job there as a technical assistant. Perhaps this was one of those great opportunities one misses in life through a wrong decision but having made up my mind I never had any nagging thoughts in later years. Had I accepted the offer, I would have had to work in an office in London with an occasional visit to Paris. Come to think of it, it sounds most attractive!

Visiting aeroplanes there were in plenty; private ones to the flying club and military ones to Hawkers or Vickers. Sir Alan Cobham's Airspeed Ferry, called *The Youth of Britain II* turned up one day and it was nice to see G-ABSI again, as this was the first aeroplane in which I flew – along with the other 36,000 passengers it had taken up for five shillings. I am proud that that was the only time I ever paid for a seat in any of the twenty-five or so

Sir Alan Cobham's Airspeed Ferry, G-ABSI, the first aircraft in which I flew – five minutes for five shillings.

different types of flying machine in which I have flown.

As a stepping stone towards being capable of working on my own, when Vickers had a subcontract to build a batch of Hawker Harts under licence, I was given the job of passing the engines off. Towards the end of 1933, the Vickers contribution to Air Ministry (AM) contract M1/30 was ready for intensive flight tests. This was interesting, as it was the first Buzzard installation I had come across; an engine about half as big again as the Kestrel. The aeroplane looked very much like a large Hawker Hart and its duty was in the Torpedo Spotter Reconnaissance role. It was a lovely hot sunny Sunday afternoon when Mutt Summers, the Vickers test pilot, took it up while I lay on the grass watching the aeroplane getting smaller and smaller as it climbed over the aerodrome, waiting for it to return. I must have dozed off for a few seconds, for the next thing I heard was the roar of an accelerating engine, a few seconds of silence and then a dull thud. Looking up I saw an opened parachute slowly descending and at about the same speed, bits of aeroplane floating down at what seemed at the time, an extraordinarily casual rate of descent. These were bits of fabric and sections from the wings and fuselage; the heavy bits had already spread themselves over the countryside. The thud I had heard was the engine with what remained of the fuselage, burying itself in Weybridge cemetery, an appropriate spot no doubt but a bit disturbing for the inhabitants thereof! Mutt at this time in his life had not learned how to pull strings, so landed slap on the track instead of the grass, doing one ankle a spot of no good. Vickers had got their sums wrong and made the aeroplane too light and the wings just came off. Hawkers said it served them right for copying the Hart. This was the first time I had witnessed an aeroplane fold-up in the air and it suddenly seemed a more serious business.

On leaving Brooklands I had no thoughts of when or if I would ever return but when the occasion did occur, over half a century had slipped by. This was the Royal Aeronautical Society's (RAeS) Hurricane 50th Anniversary Symposium, being held at the old Vickers', then a British Aerospace, factory. Hurricane PZ835, *The Last of the Many*, was flown in for the occasion and put on show. I suppose when it took off to fly out the next day its Merlin was the last Rolls-Royce engine to take off from what remains of Brooklands aerodrome. In May 1949 Vickers Armstrongs was granted planning permission for the use of the entire site as an industrial or housing estate but at the time no action was taken. Today, with the shortage of land, no doubt sooner or later the inevitable will happen and a dormitory area will be created. When it does, its occupants will sleep with the ghosts of Brooklands – and the original occupiers – the Ancient Britons.

The Vickers Type 207 (MI/30), Torpedo Spotter Reconnaissance, which I saw break up in the air.

CHAPTER THREE

Messing about in flying boats

"Where is Bert Millward?" was my greeting on arrival at Short Brothers, Rochester in March 1934. Even, *"Why have they sent you?"* failed to dampen my youthful eagerness for my first solo outside job. I knew other reps had preceded me over the years; Charles Conway and Harold Green could have been no strangers to Shorts when they accompanied Alan Cobham on his 23,000 mile flight round Africa in 1927 with their 'Singapore 1' (two Condors). Then, some three years later, I think it was Bob Smith who worked on a Shorts-designed prototype for the Japanese, called the Kawanishi KF1 (three Buzzards) at Rochester before going to Japan to look after the four production models made there under licence. I do not know who covered the many Eagle installations in the float-planes, flying boats and bombers – not forgetting the R31 and R32 airships built by Shorts at Cardington (five Eagles apiece). What is certain is that the first member of the Company to be involved with the three brothers Short was C S Rolls. The Shorts had moved their balloon factory from (of all places, Derby) to Battersea by the time he flew the balloons they made for him ('Brittania' and 'Imp' for instance) at Battersea. Later, Rolls saw a Wright Flyer on a visit to America, and when Shorts obtained a licence to build six at Leysdown, Isle of Sheppey, in February 1909, he offered to buy the first one. Shorts are credited with creating the first aircraft production line in the world, when building these Flyers under licence. Since Rolls bought what is believed to be the first one, it can be said that he was perhaps the first to fly the first aircraft off the first ever aeroplane production line. One imagines the recent (1906-08) building of the new Rolls-Royce factory in the brothers' hometown of Derby was a subject of conversation between them.

It seems that 1912 was a vintage year for water-borne aircraft. Jacques Schneider donated his Trophy to encourage seaplane development; Avro were the first in this country to have an aeroplane on floats; Sopwith's Bat Boat was the first successful flying boat in Europe but the American, Glenn Curtiss won the accolade for his boat, which was the first to rise above the waves – the year in which the Titanic sank beneath the them. At the outbreak of World War I the Marine Aircraft Experimental Establishment (MAEE) at Felixstowe, was the centre of what little flying-boat activity there was, and the Establishment equipment was gradually increased by the purchase of Curtiss H-12 and H-14 boats from America on the advice of Sqn/Cdr John Porte. Porte was an accomplished engineer officer, operating within this Government experimental factory and had worked with Curtiss before the war. When the Rolls-Royce Eagle went into production (backed by the Admiralty and with the encouragement of a certain Lt W O Bentley RNAS), Porte installed it in the larger H-14 as well as the successful 'F' (for Felixstowe) series of boats which he produced by improving the design of the Curtiss hull. This culminated in the F-5 (two Eagle VIIIs).

The end of the war saw a number of single-engined civil boats made by Supermarine and Vickers, using Eagle IXs. It took the latter company two months to build an amphibian boat in an old Weybridge dance hall and while several of the subsequent production run of 30 or so Vikings used Eagle IXs, the prototype G-EAOV was powered by a Falcon III. To fly the Atlantic in 1919 was magnificent; to cross the English Channel four months later and get yourself killed by hitting a tree on landing was tragic. G-EAOV was being flown to the Paris Air Show by Vickers' test pilot – Sir John Alcock.

Despite being one of the world's most successful flying boat makers, Horace Short was really a seaplane enthusiast, and originally saw no future in flying boats. However, by 1919 the Rochester factory on the Medway had been enlarged for the full production of the F-3 and F-5 boats, some 34 of the latter being built before orders were curtailed. For the next five years Shorts reconditioned F-5s for the RAF.

My main reason for being at Shorts was to cover the first production order of four Singapore IIIs (four Kestrel VIII/IX), which was probably the best RAF flying boat of its day. The evolution of the Singapore series from the Cromarty of 1920/21 (two Condor IIIs) for which Shorts had an order for three, would have come to nothing but for the enthusiasm of Oswald Short. When the original Cromarty wooden hull was damaged beyond repair, the Air Ministry (AM) lost interest, nor did they encourage Oswald in his determination to build a metal hulled boat, even after he had made the unique Silver Streak, the first all-metal aeroplane in the world, which flew in 1920. Four years later, however, Shorts were allowed to build a metal hull for an F-5 and this proved to be lighter and stronger than the old water-absorbing wooden ones. The Cromarty, now with a metal hull, was duly resurrected and emerged still with two Condor IIIs, as the Singapore I. In 1926 the RAF organised the 'Scandinavian Cruise', an evaluation exercise to show the flag and widen their search for further new equipment, but the performance of the four contenders proved little. The Supermarine Southampton and the Saunders-Roe (or Saro) Valkyrie (three Condor IIIs) – the two wooden hulled boats – both gave trouble; both sank in a storm, while Short's Singapore was first back to Felixstowe, followed by the Blackburn Iris, the flagship. The result was that production of the Iris (three Condor IIIs), with the Southamptons continued, while the Singapore's prize was to remain at Felixstowe on slave duties. That might well have been that, had Cobham not suggested his African flight. This epic expedition used the 'borrowed' Singapore and was sponsored by Wakefield (Castrol), Shorts and Rolls-Royce, with no government backing. Even after those achievements, on being handed back to the RAF, it spent the rest of its days as a test bed for Buzzard engines.

A year later AM Spec R5/27 was revised into R32/27, calling for a faster boat with a longer range than the Iris or Southampton. Saro and Supermarine submitted sesquiplanes (biplane layout, having the lower wings shorter than the uppers), each with three Jupiters, while the Blackburn entry was the Sydney (three Kestrels), a monoplane conversion of the Iris. Each of the three contenders was given a contract for one boat, but the Short offering of a much modified and improved Singapore I (the three Condors being replaced by four Kestrels) was rejected. Oswald Short was not pleased. Presumably after some heavy arm-twisting, an order for one, (now known as Singapore II), was given. This was justice indeed, as it proved to be superior to the Southampton X, the Saro A7 and the Sydney, although only faster by 10, 16 and 17 mph respectively. The Saunders-Roe boat, however, did make a limited appearance as the London. After modifications and trials both at Rochester and Felixstowe (positioning radiators above or below engine nacelles, Buzzard type of greater capacity from the Singapore I tests, etc), Shorts obtained an order for four Mk III boats under AM Spec R3/33 (later R14/34) and production commenced in March 1934.

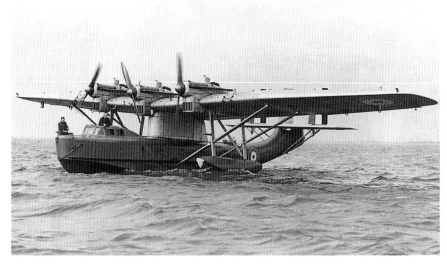

The Blackburn Sydney monoplane flying boat powered by three Kestrel engines.

A total of 37 Short Singapore Mk III (4 Kestrel) boats were built.

Staggered batches of orders caused a slow production rate and by July 1936 I was quite glad to hand over to Pat Bate, having by then covered some 25 of the total production of 37 boats and even the novelty of flying in many of them had worn off! During the production runs there were 'visiting firemen' aplenty (it was a nice run out from Derby!), fitters for mods, George Farmer for auto boost controls and finally, EP when he came down to tell Shorts that they had had my services for too long! Most of the production was delivered straight to the Squadrons but one or two early boats were sent to Felixstowe where rep George Moseley had a habit of complaining about the inaccuracy of my boost control settings. Boost gauges varied, so on one occasion I set up the four engines using a mercury 'U' tube. Unfortunately I throttled one engine back too rapidly and mercury shot out of the open end of the tube and disappeared into the bilge. As mercury and duralumin hate each other, panic action had to be taken to prevent a hole being 'eaten' through the hull!

There was always plenty of work in between production batches, such as visits to Supermarines to ground test 'Scapa' boats. Their Southampton started life as it finished – with Rolls-Royce engines. The prototype was in effect the Swan (two Eagle IXs), while the last was the Southampton Mk IV (two Kestrel VIIIs), its name being changed to Scapa when going into production. It had a redesigned hull and with its two Kestrels neatly mounted beneath the upper wing, seemed an adequate replacement for the Southampton IV having double the range and an increase in speed and ceiling of some 50%. However, only 13 were made and the AM decided a new spec was required (R24/31). This resulted in Super's successful Stranraer, 45 alone being made for the RAF. Shorts' competitor to the same spec was in fact my first interest when arriving at the Seaplane Works. It was a more modern looking gull-winged monoplane with a Goshawk mounted on each of the wing knuckles – hence Knuckleduster – but its good looks were rather spoilt by two large condensers mounted atop of each nacelle. As far as I can remember, this was one evaporative cooling system that actually worked; though I know of one engine John Lancaster Parker managed to cook. Parker, by the way, must have been the supreme boat pilot of the age: he seemed to have flown nearly everything that Shorts ever made.

I don't imagine the Knuckleduster was ever intended for production but a vast amount of data was gathered on flight performance, both at Rochester and MAEE. Early in 1934 the boat returned from the MAEE for an engine change and twin rudder application to secure better control for single engine flying. To prove the point, and while demonstrating to VIPs, the port engine died! Rain or sea spray had entered the magneto distributors and even after drying out, severe tracking could not be prevented. That afternoon an Austin 7 could be seen streaking up to St Pancras to meet the Derby train – and the guard - with a new magneto under each arm! An evening in March with a stiff breeze causing a choppy Medway is not the best of conditions for fitting and timing mags, and certainly did not deserve the rebuff from Harold West (Wst) of the Electrical Lab, who told EP *"If your Tester Inspector had cleaned up the magnetos they would have been perfectly serviceable".* What nerve!

Apparently the huge German 12-engined Dornier DoX of 1928 had inspired Oswald Short to design a similar but more efficient boat. This initially failed to interest the Directorate of Technical Development (DTD), but with the backing of Lord Trenchard, Spec R6/28 was issued. Supermarine's tender the 'Giant', was a monoplane with six Buzzards mounted on top of the wings and was only half built when cancelled in 1932, while Shorts received an order for one boat, a biplane, also with six Buzzards but mounted in three nacelles. It was in effect a larger version of the Singapore II, called the Sarafand, and it made its first flight in June 1932 and during 1934 returned to Rochester from the MAEE for repairs and to have six uprated Buzzard IIIMS installed. Once the engines were installed there was little room for control setting or maintenance and I found synchronising all six engines was a bit of a handful when all on my own.

It was on the Sarafand at Felixstowe that I lowered the fuel levels in the six wretched carburettors as a way of curing persistent flooding and at Shorts where I had a little impromptu taxiing experience. One day I was running the front starboard engine on the river at TO boost when the fore anchoring buoy burst with a loud bang and the Sarafand swung round into midstream moored only by the aft buoy. With the wind, tide, current, or all three, the boat seemed held in this position, a little too near the barge traffic. By starting the port engine I managed to bring the boat on station and by throttle juggling both engines, to keep it facing upstream. This entertained many of the Short staff who had appeared on the towpath to watch the fun!

The Air Ministry's thoughts for a new Sarafand were contained in Spec R2/33, calling for a slightly smaller four-engined (equivalent to six Buzzards) boat with the Sarafand's performance. It was fortuitous that a few months later Imperial Airways required a similar spec, as a replacement for their Kent boats. This gave Shorts the opportunity to cut development costs for one basic boat, and resulted in the long-running production of the Sunderland/Empire boats.

210 Squadron was one of the first to receive Singapore IIIs. Past Squadron members included an ex-Imperial Airways boat captain, later known as 'Pathfinder', Don Bennett, and a Commanding Officer (CO) called 'Bert' Harris who became better known as 'Bomber' Harris. Their home base was Pembroke Dock (PD) at the head of Milford Haven. My first visit, in September 1934, was to rectify a Kestrel problem by changing all the valve springs on boat K3593; an easy job – said quickly. You just lift eight cam/rocker shafts and replace more springs than there are days in a year! The boat was due to fly Sir Phillip Sassoon on a 20,000 mile trip around the Far East and as if to guarantee my work, I was invited to fly with it as far as Calshot, where the VIP was to embark. On arrival I was dumped on the quayside in the rain, with a pocket full of spare valve springs and no transport! My second visit to PD was in December to 'put out fires'. The rear engines of K3595 were the worst offenders and starting – or 'firing up', was a little too literal, with exhaust flames long enough to more than blister the white paint on the wooden propellers. In this installation, the rear engines were slightly inclined down at the reduction gear end. My suggestion to Derby that the triple gear oil scavenge pump oil system design was at fault, allowing the oil level in the sump to rise till the big ends churned it, was not only met with disbelief, but I collected a rocket from EP into the bargain *"You can't tell Rolls-Royce that their scavenge pumps ...... etc"* To prove this diagnosis, a length of boiler sightglass tubing was found in the adjacent shipbreaker's yard and connected by suitable plumbing to the sump of one

The 'universal test bed' at Derby for running engines at any desired angle of inclination.

of the offending engines through a spare compressor drive blank, the tube being fixed vertically to the side of the nacelle at the appropriate height (roll over Heath Robinson). Sure enough, the gradual rise in oil level in flight could then be seen from the dorsal gunner's position. Some time later, while passing the universal test bed at the Works, I noticed Ted Gibson running a Kestrel VIII with its nose inclined down a few degrees. Ted told me that some flying boat Squadron had complained of oil build-up and he had just run a check and proved it to be justified. I was never told of these results and all enquiries received evasive answers.

Normally December would not be the best of months for a shake-down cruise around the British Isles but the Squadron was due to take up duty in Singapore early in 1935 so we had little choice. I was invited to join K3595 – if only to see that 'my' glass tube did not fall off and let all the oil run out. The water was rough, even when taxiing the four miles down the Sound before TO, and it seemed an age before the four boats formed up and headed north. The weather was foul and, having just avoided being airsick, landing on rough water at Stranraer (no Simple Harmonic Motion!) was enough to make most of us seasick before leaving the boat, a messy business. An airman had to stay aboard each boat during the night in case it dragged anchor and of course oil filters had to be dropped to drain unscavenged oil on the rogue engines each morning to prevent the oil/petrol fires on start-up. The weather had abated slightly by Oban, the next night stop, and rather than call at Inverness, the Commanding Officer (CO) decided to fly non-stop to Felixstowe. This leg became monotonous at 100 mph cruise, so to liven things up a little, 'George' (autopilot), was cut out and I was allowed to fly K3595 for a period. Felixstowe saw George Moseley waiting with the news that EP was very annoyed not having heard from me. The four boats gave Rochester a gentle formation beat-up, so giving Shorts a chance to be proud of their product before we went on to land at Calshot. Here, we were over-welcomed by Wing Commander (W/Cdr) Gaskell-Blackburn, the 'station master' (the only serving RAF officer, apart from the King, with permission to grow a beard) and little breakfast was taken the following morning! F/Lt Beatty (half brother of Earl Beatty) was K3595's captain and had been out with Jeffery Quill the night before and decided to show Calshot how a flying boat could be thrown round the sky. With the over-revving of the four Kestrels I could almost hear the 'pinging' of breaking valve springs but after one further stop all four boats made PD.

The Squadron left for Singapore in mid-January 1935, and by the end of the month I found myself at Brough, nothing to do with the Sydney or Perth (Iris V) but looking after the Goshawk in the abortive Blackburn F7/30 (Day and Night fighter), so releasing Jack Osbourne to join No 210 in Naples. *"What for, and why not me?"* was my first reaction. No doubt I was too

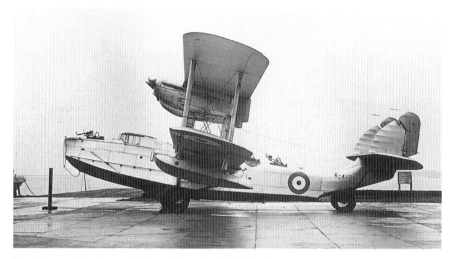

The Supermarine Scapa (2 Kestrels) replaced the Southampton.

young – or stupid. Three weeks later Reg Holt was sent to relieve me for another Singapore III contract. The day after getting back to Rochester I was shocked to read in the morning papers that on 16 February K3595 had crashed into a mountain in Messina with the loss of all lives. Having mostly flown with that crew I assumed that had I gone in place of Osbourne I would have been on board, but with relief saw that the civilian passenger was not Jack. The *Daily Telegraph* of 18 February 1935 reported the sympathy shown by the Italian authorities; Messina was in civic mourning, Italian sailors firing a volley over the nine gun carriages. Two Italian warships escorted HMS Durban to Malta for the funeral in Valetta where the nine victims were to be buried. Five years later, on 11 June 1940, the Italians sent 10 Cant aircraft to drop bombs on Valetta.

Rolls-Royce was well represented in the flying boat world at that time, from single to a one-off five-engined (Felixstowe Fury) and even the six-engined Sarafand; Condors were powering no less than seven different named boats including the Vickers Valencia, Fairey N4 and Rohrbach Rocco.

The Singapore III was really the end of the Rolls-Royce involvement in flying boats except for two Supermarine Seagulls (Griffon RG14SM), to Spec S14/44 and last but not least, a few years later when Ivan Waller chose a spectacular way of severing Rolls-Royce's association with flying boats, by departing from the one and only R1/36 Blackburn B20 (two Vultures) in a hurry – by parachute!

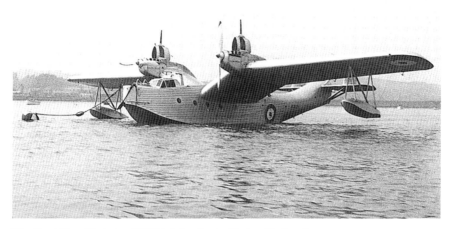

The Short Knuckleduster R24/31 flying boat with two Goshawks.

The Short Sarafand R6/28 powered by six Buzzards was sponsored by Sir Hugh Trenchard.

Blackburn's ill-fated B20 flying boat with retractable hull with two Vulture engines. Ivan Waller, the Rolls-Royce service engineer, had to take to his parachute to leave it for the last time.

CHAPTER FOUR

Junkers Flugzeugwerk A G, Dessau

Croydon was coming to the end of its many years as London's airport when in November 1936 I caught the 1.00pm flight for Berlin. The KLM Douglas DC-2 aeroplane looked very modern beside the Imperial Airways HP42 biplane (four Jupiters), yet we took all of two hours to reach Amsterdam (Schipol), where I transferred to a Lufthansa Ju52 to complete the journey. Next day a train took me to Dessau, Junkers' home.

Being the capital of the small principality of Anhalt, Dessau had lost its importance when in 1870 Bismark amalgamated the separate states into a federal Germany. However, the industrial revolution saw the district (Saxony), turn to mechanical engineering and Dessau became important again with the expansion of the vast Junkers Flugzeugwerk complex. Dessau happened also to be the birthplace of Hans von Ohain, whose gas turbine reputation has been drowned by that of our Frank Whittle.

On arrival in Dessau I found my way to the best hotel in town – as recommended by Junkers. It seemed proud of its name 'Hotel Goldener Beutel' but any resemblance to a 'money bag' or purse escaped me. We visitors called it The Bottle. However, it was quite comfortably warm and the food was a great improvement on that enjoyed by the average citizen, as I was to discover later. The hall porter-cum-receptionist looked very like my idea of Hindenburg and never smiled, but he was able to find me a small room at the top of the hotel with – luxury compared to English standards – a wash basin with H&C and the H was always hot. The bathrooms were kept tightly locked and a bath with a pat of soap was extra on the bill, although the quality of soap suggested 'guns before soap' as well as 'guns before butter'.

The following morning I was surprised to find a large Mercedes from the factory was waiting and I was whisked off in style and deposited at the main entrance of 'Jfa' – pronounced 'Ifa' – the local name for Junkers. After much signing of visitors books, forms and a factory pass, my passport and letter of introduction from Rolls-Royce were taken away and I was put in the charge of an armed factory policeman who led me into the multi-storey office block. Eventually we reached 'TK' – short for the technical office – where I met Herr Libertz and Herr Bolton with whom I would be dealing on all technical subjects throughout my six-months stay on this exercise. Both spoke English well and I thought Bolton sounded more English than my own name.

Junkers was an old established firm and I suppose the most famous aircraft they had produced was the Ju52/3m, a rugged, three-engined fixed

ROLLS-ROYCE LTD.

DERBY.

TELEGRAMS:
"ROYCAR, DERBY"

TELEPHONES: -
DERBY 1320 (6 LINES)

IN YOUR REPLY PLEASE
QUOTE

EP/Thn12/MH

13th November, 1936.

Messrs.Junkers Flugzeugwerk-AG,
Dessau (Anh),
GERMANY.

Dear Sirs,

         The bearer of this letter is our
Tester-Inspector Mr.A.T.M.Henniker, who is
being sent out by arrangement to advise on
the installation of the Kestrel XVI engines
in Junkers JU-86 aircraft which are going to
South Africa.

         It is understood that he will fly
with the first machine to South Africa, and will
remain there for a period to advise on the
maintenance and upkeep of this engine in service.

      We are,
        Yours faithfully,

For & on behalf of ROLLS-ROYCE LTD.

TEST DEPARTMENT

The letter of introduction from Eric Platford to be presented on arrival at Junkers.

undercarriage passenger/freight carrier with the Junkers patent wing and fuselage construction of corrugated sheet aluminium. Large numbers of these aeroplanes were used extensively as bombers in the Spanish Civil War, and well into WWII for parachute dropping, troop carrying, glider towing and communication. I was soon to learn with some astonishment that the factory was in full production with the Ju86 twin-engined bomber (Junkers Jumo diesel engines) and they were coming off the production line in large numbers. I tried to get some idea of the output by checking the serial numbers but the prefix letters were altered from time to time making it impossible to form any accurate estimate. What became of all these aircraft I know not, as they did not appear as the main German bomber force at the outbreak of war in 1939, though some were used for photographic or high altitude bombing purposes. Elsewhere the Dornier Do17 and Heinkel He111 were also being made in large numbers and these were used initially as the two main German bombers, while the He111 even survived the war. With Merlin engines installed, it became the main bomber in the Spanish Air Force. (They were loaned for the making of the *Battle of Britain* film). When I left Germany in May 1937 I had not seen what were to be two of Junker's most successful wartime aeroplanes, namely, the Ju88 and later, the Ju288. What I had seen was a rather odd-looking fighter with fixed undercarriage and exaggerated gull-shaped wings. This was none other than the Ju87, Stuka dive-bomber, probably the most feared aircraft in Europe in the early days of the war. When one dived straight into the ground at the far end of the aerodrome making a rather large hole, it gave a clue as to what type of aircraft it really was.

The exception to all this military activity and the reason for my presence at Junkers, was that six civil passenger versions of the Ju86 bomber had been ordered by the Union of South Africa Government for South African Airways, and Kestrels had been specified. These aircraft could be taken over by the South African Air Force (SAAF) in time of war, and converted back to bombers. Various Hawker military aircraft were already being built under licence in the Union, with Kestrel engines installed, so it was logical to keep a common engine type for – after conversion – all military aircraft.

Rolls-Royce welcomed the possibility of re-entering commercial aviation (it was a long time since the 1919 custom-built three passenger single Rolls-Royce Falcon III engined Westland Limousine I). Meanwhile, Junkers were hoping to gain experience in installing high power liquid cooled engines, on which their knowledge proved to be limited at that time. I was to fly out to South Africa on a delivery flight with the first three of the six aircraft and stay for a period of two months to look after Rolls-Royce aviation interests. South African Airways offered me a two-year contract with a possible extension, which I turned down. The man who took the job has now been there for over forty years and reached the rank of major in the SAAF. This was my first overseas job and it was to prove a tough one; I was certainly thrown in at the deep end. As all the installation work on marrying the Kestrel engines to the German airframe (and radial engine type bulkhead) was of Junker design, it was completely untested by Rolls-Royce, and the initial job was clearly one for an Installation Engineer – which I was not. Actually, Terence Henry from the Installation Department at Hucknall came out with me for about ten days or so. I knew Terence well as we had attended Derby Technical College together, so there were no problems in working with each other. As time passed however and troubles mounted, I began to realise that nobody in Rolls-Royce had found it possible to take a firm hand with Junkers over the design of their equipment. To add to my woes, Terence made no secret of the fact that he was becoming more and more reluctant to visit Dessau. I was going to find myself 'holding the baby'!

I flew home to England for Christmas 1936 and had a few days with my parents in Somerset but most of the nine days stay was spent in Derby depressing my boss EP (Eric Platford) with my bad news. I departed from Croydon again in January in a KLM Douglas DC2 to Holland where again I transferred to a Lufthansa Ju52 and joined the other eight passengers making for Berlin. The weather was foggy before we left Schipol but by the time we arrived over Templehof (Berlin) it was dark with thick fog and visibility was nil. Knowing the aerodrome was practically in Berlin and therefore surrounded by buildings, I was pretty certain we would not land in such weather, so when the pilot throttled back I became distinctly uncomfortable. The cabin had an illuminated notice which told one to 'Fasten your seat belts' and the only other object of attention was an altimeter. The former was already flashing and the latter showing practically zero metres, all causing me some concern. In those days the crew consisted of first and second pilots only, with no nice little stewardess to hold one's hand. It was with some relief and amazement that we hit nothing but the ground and that quite gently. On climbing out of the aircraft into thick fog somewhere on the aerodrome, we were led to the terminal building by a luggage porter carrying an Aldis-type lamp. The blind landing equipment used was the Lorenz system, which was most impressive for 1937, but I was wrong to think the old flare path had become a thing of the past, as was proved on many RAF airfields throughout the war which was to come.

I had already had experience with the installation of Rolls-Royce engines in some ten different types of British aircraft but had never seen anything quite like what was to occupy most of my daylight and quite a lot of my night thoughts for over six months. It was now time to get down to detailed assessment of this new project for myself. The first thing that made me doubt my eyes when I saw this installation was a substantial length of wire hawser

50

secured to each of our engines and I felt the explanation had to be good. Apparently, during this period, German aeroplanes had a habit of shedding their engines in mid air and one or two of those had fallen on populated areas, which must have been a headache for those people on the ground! German aircraft manufacturers were, therefore, instructed to anchor their engines to the airframe at all costs and by whatever means. The sight of aeroplanes flying with their loose engines dangling does not bear thinking about. However, this edict resulted – at any rate for our Ju86 – in a massive engine mounting reminiscent of the Forth Bridge making our Kestrel look diminutive buried among the 'girders'. The hawser, as thick as your finger, was fixed to the front of the wing on one side, round the front of the engine and back to the wing again on the other side. A large nearly square 'box' slung under each engine nacelle housed a radiator which had a surface area large enough to cool an engine half as big again as the Kestrel. The exhaust system trailed around the engine from one side to the other and by the time all this, plus a large carburettor air filter was covered by a cowling, the resulting size and frontal area was larger than that required by the later Merlin which was to give 50% more power than the Kestrel.

For most of the winter months in bitter cold and with the ground often covered with snow, engine ground tests were carried out ad nauseam, proving that most of the Junkers-made equipment was inefficient. Alterations and modifications suggested by the Company improved matters only marginally and as time went on I was getting tired of the whole project while Junkers got more desperate, yet were still unwilling to take advice.

One interesting innovation on the Kestrel XVI VP (for Variable Pitch) was the application of a Jumo two-position metal-bladed propeller made by Junkers under licence from Hamilton Standard of America. This was the first production Rolls-Royce engine to be so fitted, and so had an additional oil pump to power the changeover. The VP had two positions for the propeller blades – fine and coarse – and this functioned rather like a two-speed gearbox on a motorcar. The aircraft took off in fine pitch (low gear) to obtain high rpm and, therefore, power from the engine, while at low air speed. Having climbed to the desired height, the propeller was moved into coarse pitch (high gear) for lower, or cruise, rpm at higher air speed.

At last ground tests showed that things seemed to be as near right as they were ever going to be so it was decided to start the full test programme. Four of us took off on a clear day with No 1 aeroplane without incident, though I noticed our climb seemed very sluggish. When I remarked on this to Herr Gotshalt (a flight test engineer whom I disliked even more than he disliked me), he said that the propellers were fixed in coarse pitch for some reason he could not, or would not, explain. He said it would not affect the tests and all would be well when we had gained operational height. We continued to climb very slowly and levelled off at about 3000 metres. All went according to plan for half an hour or so until I was urgently called up front to observe that the oil and water temperatures had risen off the clock on the starboard engine. The immediate normal action would be to shut down that engine and return to base on the remaining one. This would have caused no problems had we been able to put the port engine into fine pitch to obtain the extra rpm and power with a larger throttle opening to cope with the increased load and work in keeping us airborne. As things were, we could not maintain height so the pilot turned for home, some eighty miles away, and it should not have been too arduous to select a suitable field. However, from now on Gotshalt decided that he should take command of the situation and started telling the pilot what to do. Somewhat naturally 'der piloten' thought otherwise and an argument started. I did not quite understand what it was all about but gathered that it was a question of whether it was better to make a wheels-up landing, or try a normal one with the undercarriage down. Either way, the argument was getting us nowhere. As I had nothing to lose, save my neck perhaps, I intervened and explained to Gotshalt – who by now I disliked even more – that the pilot must be the captain of the aircraft and any seniority in Junkers was irrelevant in this situation. If the pilot wanted our advice he would ask for it and at the moment he was a very busy man. After a while my 'friend' quietened down but still remained rather excited, speaking to me in German and the German flight engineer in English!

I knew that landing wheels-up would cause quite extensive damage to the propellers and, therefore, the engines and radiators etc, but on very soft ground the belly landing would probably do little damage to the aeroplane itself. To save the aeroplane completely required a wheels-down landing and space but one had to find this nice firm, flat field. The snag was that all the land thereabouts seemed to be cultivated and partly under water due to melting snow, so landing with wheels down didn't appear to be the right thing to do. However, this was what was going to happen, so I retired to midway down the cabin and strapped myself in. Tricycle undercarriages had not come into fashion so with the aircraft's nose well up, the pilot came in holding off with the tail well down. After a run of not more than thirty metres in the soft ground the main landing wheels sank and refused to move any further. Up went the tail, in went the nose on which it seemed to poise for a few seconds trying to decide whether to go right over or return to a normal attitude. The aeroplane decided on the latter and we were relieved to find ourselves the right way up and in one piece. We all sat for a few seconds, feeling a little stupid, and looking at each other. All was very quiet after the sudden stoppage of all the noise, and then someone suggested it would be a good idea to get out. The depth of mud I stepped into grabbed and retained a nice pair of brown shoes I happened to be wearing – and never saw again – so I had to slosh about in my stockings. After the action, the reaction. This seemed to be felt about five minutes or so after we had landed and I was soon to become the most popular member of the crew, being the only one with any cigarettes. The near-new box of 50 Players cigarettes recently brought back from England went in no time at all, though not quite as fast as the shoes had disappeared!

It seemed an age before the Junkers team arrived in three vehicles – which were nearly bogged in the mud – and we were able to proceed with the post-mortem and assess the damage. Both propellers had hit the ground and were bent and the fuselage had a slight ripple on the top, while some rivets had pulled on the bottom, so this particular aeroplane would not see South Africa for a long time. A plus point was they were able to loan me a pair of 'gummibuhts', which they made sure I returned before leaving Germany. It took no time to discover the cause of the starboard engine failure. When the bottom cowling was removed out fell a little water drain cock with its broken Junkers copper pipe, which had obviously vibrated until it fractured. I felt like saying I told you so, but my German was not good enough. We eventually got back to Dessau that evening and I was dropped off at 'The Bottle' feeling a bit dejected as I entered with my (Junkers) gumboots covered in mud.

Following my report of the forced landing, Rolls-Royce suddenly became concerned for my well-being, as the following extract from my boss EP dated 13 January shows.

"We do not think that you should go with the machine when it is making its handling flights – which appears to be all that it is doing at present – but as soon as they (Junkers) are satisfied in this respect, and they consider the aircraft is actually fit for a proper flight test, whereby engine running and conditions can definitely be observed, by all means go with the machine as an observer to satisfy yourself on the various engine features"

Such solicitude was quite unnecessary; I knew they cared! One would assume that after all these trials and tribulations Junkers would have taken more notice of the advice from Rolls-Royce but they never did.

All the time I was at Junkers no mention was made of the fact that it was a Kestrel which had launched the first Stuka (Ju87) on its maiden flight and when its twin fin tail disintegrated in the air, a Kestrel supplied the power for the second prototype. My enquiries into the functioning of this Junkers-made engine installation fell on deaf ears, as no doubt I was not supposed to know any of these facts. At the time I was certainly unaware that the Ju87 had a rival in the Heinkel He118, and that this aeroplane had been despatched into the air for the first time by a Buzzard. Later the Buzzard was replaced by a Kestrel V. I don't think I ever heard of the Messerschmitt Bf109 in 1936, nor did I know that in the previous year it had reached a speed of 290 mph during its maiden flights – also with a Kestrel V. It would seem that Rolls-Royce did the future Luftwaffe a great favour but perhaps the Germans considered that they were only getting a little of their own back. The ultimate engine for these three aeroplanes was the Daimler-Benz DB601 series and Daimler was the parent company of Mercedes. It had been a Mercedes racing car that was towed to Derby at the outbreak of war in 1914 by a certain W O Bentley RN, in order that its advanced aero style engine might be stripped down for Royce to view before he designed the Eagle of 1915!

From a German caption 'Heinkel – Kampfzweisiter He118 (D-UKYM) mit 955 PS Rolls-Royce Buzzard Motor 1936'. It flew in 1937 with a Kestrel V engine.

The prototype Junkers Ju87 Stuka dive-bomber with Kestrel V engine. Note the original twin-rudder tail unit.

The prototype Messerschmitt Bf109 with Kestrel engine. The actual engine used is not known, but presumably was a Kestrel XVI-type VP conversion.

CHAPTER FIVE

Living in Germany

Winter 1936/7 had been cold and miserable as well as lonely in Dessau. It was, therefore, good to greet Terence Henry when he returned for four days for the final installation tests in mid April. Michael Gaze then joined us a few days before the flight to Johannesburg, as he had by now joined South African Airways from Rolls-Royce, the job I had turned down. At 'Ifa' I normally saw only a few people to speak to, such as my police guard and the men working on the aircraft, with an occasional visit to the technical office in the main building to discuss matters with Libertz and Bolton. Both spoke faultless English but conversation with anyone else was very limited as my German was only what I had picked up during my stay. It must be remembered too that Dessau was virtually Junkers and it was not wise for a member of the community to be seen talking to 'the Englishman'. Any suggestion of an invitation into anyone's home was completely out. Chances of learning much German were, therefore, small.

The dark evenings were mostly spent in the hotel with a very occasional visit from Libertz or Bolton – never together. Early in 1937 all visits ceased and, at about the same time, I was informed that the factory could no longer supply transport, so I was reduced to the use of public transport – old single-decker buses whose progress along the cobbled roads contrasted with the all-round independent suspension of the Mercedes. I realised that what was to have been a stay of a couple of weeks was turning into several months and I was outstaying my welcome and from now on it seemed I was to be avoided. I knew my reports to Rolls-Royce were being read and was aware, by setting simple traps, that my hotel room was being searched from time to time.

The hotel still provided a certain amount of comedy. I must have been a bit of a headache for Gustof Bosser, the hotel proprietor, who was forever bailing me out of awkward situations. The dining room was run on restaurant lines and I always insisted on having my regular table, which caused considerable jealousy among the young waiters who were most keen to learn English. They each had their own tables to look after, so I was favouring one waiter. This came to a head one day and the manager was called to sort things out. Using the headwaiter – who spoke a fair amount of English – as interpreter, a new system was agreed which allowed each waiter to move round to a new set of tables every so often. The reason for this enthusiasm for learning English then became clear. The waiters were, without exception, members of the Hitler Youth Movement. Being able to speak English was a great feather in their caps and earned them more marks or badges, or would it be swastikas?

Gustof Bosser also relieved a slightly more serious situation on the occasion when I refused to contribute to the Winter Help Fund. Nearly every Saturday afternoon gangs of Storm-troopers haunted the streets and public buildings, hunting in pairs and rattling their collecting tins. From what I could gather, nobody dared to refuse to contribute at least a few pfennings. On this occasion I had already contributed thrice within the space of one hour when along came another pair into the hotel writing room, where I was attempting to write a report, and rattled their tins under my nose. I felt this was more than enough and all the 'Heil Hitlering' that went with it made me a little sick, so I refused to contribute any more. This created a bit of a stir, the turning of heads and a pregnant silence while I explained in my best English – rather loudly – that I had already done my stint and didn't think I should be called upon to repeat the exercise. Gustof came to the rescue again though his explanations didn't seem to be getting very far. Finally, one of the 'ugly twins' – who I thought looked a bit cold with just his brown shirt and breeches – realised that while they were talking they were losing good collecting time. With the usual clicking of heels and a couple of "Heil Hitlers" they departed, throwing me a dirty look as they went.

Cole, a Marconi man, came over from England for a few days to check the aircraft radio and naturally stayed at The Bottle. One afternoon we were sitting in the hotel foyer minding our own business, when the entrance doors opened with a flourish and in came a dozen or so excited Storm-troopers, all in their lovely uniforms, stamping about the place in their highly-polished jack-boots. To our surprise, the other hotel guests jumped to attention and with their right arms raised, gave the usual salute – that is, all except us. We were made more conspicuous when the man of the moment made his entrance and threw us – still sitting down – a quizzical glance as he passed. Perhaps it was just as well we did not know that it was none other than 'Little Willie', the old Kaiser's son. A very red-faced Gustof explained all this to us in his best attempt at English after the gathering had sealed themselves up in the dining room. We believed him, as we also did when he told us that he had had some hard explaining to do when asked who those two anti-Nazis were in HIS hotel!

The *"Heil Hitler"* and saluting business was very catching, which was only natural since it had replaced *"good morning"* right through the day to *"good night"*, or even *"how do you do?"*, though a compromise of *"auf wiedersehen – Heil Hitler"* was in order for *"goodbye"*. It became quite natural – and only polite – for me to enter a café or restaurant and *"Heil Hitler"* the customers at large, and of course, salute (with the half-bent-arm as opposed to the stiff arm type, the latter being more of a military salute).

One got so used to this type of welcome that the occasional slip on my several short visits to England did not go down at all well!

Food in Berlin was good. In the eating houses of Dessau, including The Bottle, it was passable, while at the Junkers factory – where I lunched nearly every day – it was pretty grim. One large canteen catered for management, white collar and shop floor workers alike, and was run on a cafeteria basis. Every meal – at least every luncheon – consisted of a bowl of Irish (German?) stew, which appeared to consist of a small amount of meat with plenty of potatoes and haricot beans hidden in what looked, and tasted like, pea soup. The alternative to this meal – which only cost three pfennings (just over three pence) – was a stand-up snack at a small outside stall. It consisted of a couple of hot sausages with a dollop of mustard on a small cardboard plate, followed by a banana and a bar of chocolate which tasted like anything but chocolate. This was an exclusive way of eating for several reasons. Firstly, the snack cost about one mark, and secondly, most of the staff made a point of eating in the general canteen with all grades as it was a desirable thing to create an image of working – and eating – together as one big team. Another reason which made for a small clientele was that it was pretty chilly, anyway in the winter, and I never discovered how it survived, catering for so few.

Herr Bolton took me out to lunch in the town on a few occasions, where one could get a reasonable meal. His family came from Hanover with presumably English ancestry somewhere along the line, and he had spent some years in the USA where I gathered he had done pretty well for himself in the aircraft industry. Under some sort of threat he had been forced to return to Germany and give his talents to Das Vaterland. Most of his assets had been confiscated and how or where he lived I was not invited to find out. His only possession of any consequence I was aware of was his ancient and very second-hand car, which looked extraordinarily like an Austin 7. It was, in fact, an Austin 7 built under licence and called Dixi by a German aero engine firm by the name of Bayerische Motoren-Werke which diversified into making motor cars. The badge to this day symbolises a revolving aeroplane propeller surrounded by the initials BMW. Incidentally, a famous car manufacturer on the other side of the world in Yokohama, sometime trading under the name of DAT Automobile Engineering Company, in 1933 also decided to base their new small car on the Austin 7 when they resumed making cars instead of lorries. From son-of-DAT to Datson, and perhaps to add a touch of the 'The Rising Sun' image, it finished up as Datsun, now changed to Nissan.

Otto Libertz was very senior in the Junkers hierarchy and always seemed pleased to see me, but his joie de vivre appeared to me to be rather exaggerated compared with the rather glum Bolton. I felt I couldn't trust him an inch (or centimetre), while the latter I could. Libertz seemed pretty well off, wore nice clothes and drove about in a medium-size Mercedes. It was a little time before I noticed the small red badge he always wore in his lapel with a black swastika on a white background. He was a member of 'Der Partei'. He gave me a lift to Berlin on one occasion and I tried to buy him a drink before the return trip. I had already spent the weekend by myself but it appeared he did not want to be seen with me in a public place in the city.

By this time I had been given a permanent armed works policeman of my very own, as opposed to having the next one for duty whenever I arrived at the factory. He was my constant companion and joined me at the guard room when I arrived and never let me out of his sight – well hardly ever. A simple soul, not speaking a word of English – he seemed to enjoy looking after me each day, which started with a click of the heels extended arm salute, and a *"Heil Hitler Herr Hennik-ere"*. I fooled him one day after I had been at the factory a few months and had got to know the ropes a bit. While the aeroplanes were being built I was continually popping in and out of the fuselages while my guard was content to remain on the floor until I eventually reappeared. When the siren went for lunch on this occasion I remained in one of the aircraft after everyone else had gone, and watched developments through one of the cabin windows. My companion soon became agitated and when I saw him making for the nearest telephone, I thought it was time to put him out of his misery, so casually reappeared as if all was normal and pretended not to understand his muted ticking off!

Hans looked very smart in his green uniform, black Sam Browne and pistol holster – which housed his Mauser – and, of course, the black jackboots. A typical matching German cap, with swept up crown in front with the Junkers 'flying man' badge completed the picture. On Saturdays things became very slack and Hans just wore grey overalls with leather belt and the usual German civilian – or semi-military – black chauffeur-styled peak cap. Nobody did much work and it was obvious that the foreman, at least, only appeared for the overtime pay.

My office – or should I say the office I was allowed to share with the foremen and supervisors – was furnished with tables and chairs, any number of internal telephones and – which seemed most important – several mirrors hanging on the walls. This was an eye-opener to me. All the occupants, almost without exception, looked at themselves in a mirror on entering or leaving the office and combed their hair if necessary. It must just have been because they were a vain bunch, as there were no girls within miles. I soon learned that it was of little use asking my shadow if it would be possible to go and see a certain person in any part of this vast factory. He would hesitate and take some time to make up his mind whether he should refer the request to higher authority, or whether he dare take the responsibility himself. The form was to announce in a commanding voice that you intended to go to a certain place to see so-and-so, when Hans would spring to attention, click his heels and reply *"Jawohl Herr Henniker"*, and off we would march in the appropriate direction. I pushed this ploy a little too far one day by announcing that we were going to the experimental hangar where I knew there were a lot of interesting things going on. Of course, we did not get very far as I could not produce the special pass required and I think my 'shadow' got a slight ticking off for allowing me to get anywhere near the place. I probably saw more of Hans than any other German and we naturally became quite friendly. He occasionally called round to The Bottle to take me out for a drink but would not have one with me in the hotel. Our conversation was limited to the contents of my pocket phrase book but after a few beers we understood each other perfectly.

There were four German youths working on the South African aircraft who could speak English reasonably well; all had worked in South Africa for Suid Afrikaanie Lugdiens on their Ju52 aircraft. Pfifer (Whistler), Warwick (pronounced Varvic) and Kunzel were due to return with the Ju86 aircraft to Johannesburg. At first they appeared reluctant to have much to do with me and for some mysterious reason South Africa, or where they had learnt their English, was not mentioned. The fourth lad turned out to be an Afrikaner who had become a German citizen and was very proud of the fact that he was about to join the Hitler Youth Movement. Pfifer was the most senior, probably what we would call a chargehand. He was always broke and once sold me an English sovereign piece for the equivalent of ten shillings. Kunzel, on the other hand, had a small three-cylinder two-stroke DKW and on just one occasion he called for me and we met Pfifer for a drink, but as the winter progressed I found myself left more and more to my own devices.

One always had to go through Berlin to get to Dassau or return to England and either way it was necessary to spend a night in the city. I generally stayed at the Hotel Der Fürstenhof in the Potsdamer Platz, or the Hotel Esplanade but never seemed to find time to explore much of the City. After all, the Junkers job went on continuously for seven days a week and in those days everyone was conscientious enough to stick to their job – or was frightened of losing it. Work was not easy to come by between the Wars and Rolls-Royce too, like many other companies, was built more on fear than love.

On one occasion Terence came to Berlin for a couple of days and I went up to join him and meet Capel, the South African Airways European representative, to discuss the gloomy position at Dessau. Terence and I had some time to spare before our meeting, so feeling pretty cold, took ourselves to the pictures and saw *San Francisco* in English which we could understand, and German sub-titles which we could not. During the newsreel, scenes were shown of the funeral of King George V and when *God Save the King* struck up, Terence and I jumped to attention and remained standing, in spite of various threatening noises coming from behind us. When the lights went up we felt we were the target for many pairs of eyes; a suitable subject for an H M Bateman cartoon! Capel knew Berlin well, so after our discussions we did the town. This kind of nightlife was completely new to the two lads from Derby; we were stepping into another world. Our first port of call – Haus Vaterland – was an establishment the like of which I was sure did not exist in England. Once inside we found ourselves in a vast central hall with a wide stairway leading up to several floors. In large rooms on either side of the stairs there were restaurants, dance floors (each with its own band), cabarets, floorshows and bars. The décor, dress, music, food and wine all represented different parts of Germany and a few foreign lands such as Canada, with members of bands dressed as Mounties with furniture and background with a pine tree log cabin touch. There was an English pub but, alas, it sold only German beer.

We had not been sitting down for more than a few minutes when three pretty young girls appeared, sat down beside us, and said they would like to entertain us. It was fairly easy to pick out foreigners, as the nationals seldom frequented such an expensive place, and the multi-lingual girls seemed able to register one's nationality from a distance. First the drinks; this was invariably 'champagne' – actually a sparkling Hock from the Rhineland but at champagne prices. It was followed by the procession at decent intervals of other girls, first with a tray of cigarettes, a second with chocolates and a third with roses and carnations. Yes, our new found friends would like a rose each to go with the chocolates and cigarettes we had just bought them. They offered you one of their cigarettes but of course before the packet was opened you politely offered your own, which were accepted. Drinks having been consumed, the girls began to drift away, promising to be back later. They were careful to take their gifts with them, to be returned to their respective trays for further resale to other victims.

Other spots with variations on the same theme were scattered around Berlin's 'West End' where one could be entertained in similar ways. 'Femina' was a typical café where small tables were arranged in a large room all in view of a gallery housing the girls. Each table had a telephone with a number large enough to be seen from the gallery, and each girl also displayed a number large enough to be seen from any table. Having selected your girl, you rang her number and invited her down for a drink. It was no problem if you were shy or a little slow in your selection; it would not be long before a girl would 'phone you and invite herself – in your native language of course. Such places had, no doubt, been around Europe for years but it was all very new and exciting for two lads of twenty-four from England. Later that year Bond – one of the two Marconi representatives who flew with me to South Africa – and I, found ourselves in a similar kind of night club in Rome. Sure enough, along came two 'entertainers' wanting to know whether we would like to buy them a drink. We said we would, provided they drank the same as we were drinking – beer. They were somewhat taken aback but, as one of the girls was English, they agreed to stay for a while and we had a very interesting conversation, learning a little of what was an unusual way of earning a living. Soon the management appeared and wanted to know why beer and not champagne. However, we spun him a yarn about why we were in Rome and we all had champagne – on the house. The girls apparently did very well on a basic wage and a bonus, depending on how much money they could persuade the customers to part with. They moved round Europe perfecting several languages on the way, which often led to a better job and sometimes a husband. It was not their habit or in their contract to let the entertainment extend to the bedchamber, so they said.

Throughout the winter continuous ground and flight tests were carried out, showing marginal, or small improvements, the worst item being the water-cooling system. By March I was pretty sick of the whole affair, so took a long weekend off which I spent with my parents, travelling there and back by train, arriving back in Dessau on the 29th of March.

Terence made a belated visit between 20 and 24 April, and his report on returning to Rolls-Royce was a gloomy summary, as the following few extracts show:

"We consider the system (water cooling) extremely unsatisfactory, and we are unable to get Junkers to make any alterations".

"We hold the view expressed in our previous reports as regards this installation which are confirmed periodically in Henniker's reports".

"The standard of reliability on anything to do with the aircraft is appalling compared with our own ideas of safety".

"The instruments are so unreliable that it seldom occurs that even a ground run can be done on the engines without one or other of the instruments breaking down"

So now, at this late stage in the proceedings, I began to smell panic back home and a bit of buck-passing was about to begin. A letter from my boss dated 28 April contained the following:

"… we do not favour the idea of you… flying with the machines to South

Africa. The time has come when you must make it clear to all concerned that you are acting as a representative of Rolls-Royce Limited and in this capacity you must see that everything is done to obtain successful running of the engines..."

So now at last I knew what I was in Germany for! It seemed to me that when I started receiving these kinds of mixed up letters, some people at Derby were frightened of getting their knuckles rapped.

By May everything was slowly grinding to a halt. Both South African Airways and Junkers had been informed in no uncertain terms that Rolls-Royce was taking no responsibility in any way for the functioning and reliability of their engines and they had advised South Africa not to accept the aircraft. I was most surprised, therefore, when word came through that South African Airways had suggested that they carry out their own acceptance tests from their aerodrome at Germiston after the aircraft had arrived. Junkers readily agreed to this idea, so the work in Germany was virtually finished and the trip was on.

On 7 May I flew to England for a few days holiday at home and a final briefing from Rolls-Royce, leaving Michael Gaze in charge, although by now he had left Rolls-Royce and signed on with South African Airways for a salary of £40 a month (The Company had thought I would be worth £45 to £50 per month, should I be willing to accept the job). Most of my leave was spent in Derby, during which time my boss EP again tried to persuade me to travel to South Africa by sea. By this time the aircraft had gained a well-deserved bad reputation for reliability, even in an era when flying was not quite the mundane event it is today. Despite this, I felt that as I had done all the dirty work and stuck with the aeroplanes right through the piece, I most certainly would not give up now.

If only Junkers had accepted the Company's offer to design and manufacture the whole engine power plant (ie engine mounting, water and oil cooling systems with respective radiators; the whole suitably cowled and finally bench tested with propeller)! Time and money would have been saved, much ill feeling avoided and I would have slept better at night. Perhaps they were just trying to gain the valuable experience and information which they needed the hard way, and the laugh was on us.

Bolton had learned, or perfected, his command of English in the USA whilst Gotshalt acquired his knowledge of our language at school, so was it more than a coincidence that all the other people concerned with the project who conversed with me had learned their English in South Africa? Naturally the people who had any part to play in the order for Ju52 aircraft for the Union some two years previously were naturals for working on this new contract. So there was no real reason for me to conclude that Germany was more than friendly with South Africa. I had no particular knowledge of South African affairs and, except for calling at Cape Town and Durban on voyages to and from Tasmania, I knew little or nothing of the country and its people. Knowing that two RAF pilots had, in 1933, established a World Distance Record of some 5300 miles flying a long range Fairey monoplane from Cranwell to Walvis Bay in German South West Africa, reminded me that the Union controlled that country on behalf of the League of Nations. This may have been a remote 'German Connection', especially as I now remembered overhearing conversations in German when I caught the words "West Afrika". There was more to it than this of course, but what other Government, for instance, would have put up with all the delays and set-backs which had taken place during the past three or four months, without sending their engineers over hot foot to find out what was really going on? I began to think Germany must be making a gift of the aeroplanes in exchange for good relations.

It is impossible to say whether the failure of the enterprise had any bearing on my future with the Company and there is nothing like success for succeeding while failure is never forgotten. Some twenty-five years later, when South African Airways were about to buy Douglas DC8-50 aircraft with American engines we offered the Conway (gas turbine) engine at a lower price, lighter weight and all-round superior economy, yet South Africa went for the American engine. The explanation was long in coming to light but when it did, sure enough, somebody remembered back to 1937 and the story that Rolls-Royce engines were not successful in civil aircraft and this made their minds up for them. Luckily, I could find all the detailed reports to establish the true facts but it was then too late to undo the damage.

I returned to Dessau for the last time on the Coronation Day of King George VI, 12 May, having crossed the English Channel seven times. I had been lucky to find a bed in London the previous night but nearly missed the flight due to the heavy road traffic that day. The taxi ride on that last visit to Croydon was as thrilling as any to be had in, say, Paris. This time I was all packed up for an anticipated stay of two months in the Southern Hemisphere with £5 Sterling and a Letter of Credit in my pocket. Michael reported that all was quiet and no more development work was going to be done on either of the two remaining aircraft out of the first of two batches of three. I shall never know the fate of the other four or even if they were ever completed. 'Our' two were being prepared for delivery and had acquired their South African registration markings – ZS-AGG and ZS-AGF. A *Flight* (or was it *The Aeroplane?*) photographer had been allowed to take photographs of both aircraft flying in formation and remarked that the release of performance figures with the lighter engines (Kestrels) was awaited with interest. Suddenly there was nothing more for me to do until all was ready for departure and this would not be for at least a week or so. Michael and I, therefore, decided to see a little of Germany from the ground. Apart from trips to Berlin and on one occasion when I took myself off to Leipzig to see the Messer, the famous fair, I hadn't really left Dessau. We found that Gustof Bosser also owned a hotel in Wernigerode in the Harz mountains some sixty miles west of Dessau. Our hotel bill could be transferred to the Goldener Beutel – at a reduced rate. Spring was in the air, so Gustov booked us in for a few days stay. The country was awakening from the long winter and the two hours spent on the slow train journey gave us ample time to appreciate the lovely scenery. Nearly all the snow had gone from the ski slopes and with Michael being a keen climber, our walking seemed to be more vertical than horizontal. The common explanation for the climbers' great urge to get to the top of everything did not impress me. With a little help from the small mountain railway, we climbed 'The Brocken' to the hotel sitting on top. This must be the highest hotel in Germany and the views looking down on the forests of pine trees made me realise just how beautiful some of those parts are.

The last of numerous ground runs on ZS-AGG before departure for South Africa. Standing in front, Pfifer, a Junkers inspector.

65

We returned to Dessau a little healthier than when we had left and found that Bond and Barton, the Marconi representatives, had arrived. Also there was Captain Inggs from South African Airways and he was going to fly one of the aeroplanes on our forthcoming trip. The five of us had a few days in which to get to know each other while we did final checks on the machines.

CHAPTER SIX

Delivery flight

The weather on the morning of 27 May 1937 was cloudy but fair when we finally took off from Dessau for the last time. I was flying in ZS-AGG with Bond, Barton (Marconi) and Captain Erhard Rother, a Lufthansa pilot on secondment for the trip. Captain Inggs of South African Airways piloted ZS-AGF and was in command of the flight. We were airborne first, shortly followed by AGF but the latter soon turned back with undercarriage trouble. This was a good start indeed. We arrived over Munich soon after 9.00am in a severe thunder storm and it was not until noon that AGF caught up with us. The leg to Rome involved immediate climbing to cross the Alps. The panorama of the snow-covered mountains seen for the first time was indeed breathtaking – what breath one had at 19,000 feet without oxygen; our pilot was privately catered for.

We landed at Rome in the early afternoon and here we ran into our first spot of bother with bureaucracy. The Spanish Civil War was about to start and there appeared to be some trouble with the Italian authorities; there were doubts as to the real destination of the aircraft. Assuming the Italians and Germans were on the same side, there were rumours going around that our aeroplanes would be diverted to Spain, which seemed a little far-fetched. At all events we were told that we had arrived without an 'International Carnet' and before being allowed to proceed to Africa, one would have to be obtained from the Italian Embassy in Berlin. This resulted in a six-day stay, during which time one member of the crew had to remain on each aircraft night and day, just in case. Hotel arrangements split the crews and I found myself sharing a room with Bond and, as Barton and Michael Gaze spent most of the time with the aircraft, we two saw Rome. We took a train to Ostia one day for a breath of sea air – a popular resort on the west coast, but dared not stay long just in case we received flight clearance. We were always leaving 'in the morning' – which was long in coming. On returning to Rome we found that another delay had been built into the programme.

Without referring the matter to either me or Gaze someone had decided that our fuel consumption had been high, presumably due to climbing over the Alps, and that we would not be able to make Tripoli in one hop. To remedy this shortcoming, most of the passenger seats were removed from both aircraft and in their place 80 gallons of petrol in 20 four-gallon cans were stored on the cabin floor. If it became necessary, we would take it in turns to replenish the main fuel tanks by pumping petrol from each tin with a hand pump – perhaps putting our cigarettes out during the operation!

Leaving Germany with two of the Ju86 Kestrel XVI-engined aircraft for South Africa. I flew in ZS-AGG with a seconded Lufthansa pilot.

Air safety regulations were being broken carrying this lethal cargo; and this was not for the last time. Inggs seemed to be in charge of the trip, but did not want to listen to much advice from me; whilst I was doubtful about who was the actual owner of the aeroplanes at this stage and Michael Gaze felt that he was only responsible for servicing the engines since he was by now an employee of South African Airways. We could have had the aeroplanes grounded if we had so wished but were both eager to get on with the job in hand, so passed the whole thing off as a joke. If there had been any doubts about the range of the aircraft, why could we not have refuelled at Malta which was directly on our route? It would have saved another day's delay in Rome. Perhaps it was that petrol in Malta would have to be paid for in Sterling.

We eventually left Rome on 2 June and headed for Tripoli on a lovely day which made the Mediterranean look very blue. We flew down the coast of Italy very close to, and level with, the snow-covered but smoking crater of Mount Etna. Bearing south we left Italy via the Straits of Messina – reminding me of the Singapore III flying boat disaster in which my friends had lost their lives.

It was while looking down as we flew over Malta that I noticed a quantity of oil had begun to cover the trailing edge of the starboard wing directly behind the engine. I notified Herr Rother and suggested he keep an eye on the oil pressure and temperature of that engine. A small amount of oil makes a large mess and on landing at Tripoli in the late afternoon, we found that there was still plenty left in the tank. The cause of the trouble was a fractured oil cooler and the Junkers man who made up the spares list for the flight must have had a prophetic impulse to include a spare one – a most unlikely failure on a British aeroplane. Needless to say, the extra petrol we had carried in the cabins was not required, so the passenger seats were removed from the luggage compartments and reinstated in their rightful places.

The hotel was modern and comfortable and it was a surprise to find such a fine building on the edge of the desert. Bond and I had a walk round the native bazaars and the motor racing track where the Tripoli Grand Prix was an annual fixture. The city was a mixture of ancient and modern, the influence of Mussolini being very apparent. Colonel Gadaffi's parents were perhaps putting a deposit on their first tent about this time!

An early start was made on the morning of 3 June. We took off first and headed east, shortly followed by AGF. We were now flying over the sea again (the Gulf of Sidia) and heading for Benghazi and it was not long before we realised that AGF was dropping behind. Presumably Rother knew what was happening by radio but the rest of us in AGG were only made aware that something was not as it should be after we had landed and AGF came in on one engine. Inggs had shut down the starboard engine when he noticed an excessively high water temperature reading but the question was, for how long had the engine been overheated before he became aware of the fact? The cause of the trouble was soon discovered – a split header (water) tank but this time we had no spare with us, so either we would have to send for a new one from Germany or attempt a local repair. We were sceptical when the local airport people said they could tackle the job, but surprised at the excellent patching job they carried out as welding thin aluminium is not for amateurs. The real worry was to ascertain the damage done to the engine. In spite of Inggs' assurance that he had shut the engine down straight away, a large quantity of water had been lost and I feared the worst. Michael and I spent most of the morning of 4 June giving the engine a thorough inspection and ground test and found that it had, in fact, overheated and as a result had developed an internal water leak to combustion space in one of the cylinder blocks. This should mean fitting new blocks and probably new pistons and rings. In our circumstances the correct action to take would be to change the engine for a new one. One engine had been wrecked at Dessau already for the same reason (involving the scrapping of big end bearings, crankshaft, etc), and yet to get a new engine out from Dessau and have it installed would cost another ten days or so. I had to decide whether to take a chance and push on or whether to ground the aircraft. It seemed we had reached the point of no return and the whole project was going sour on us, so I decided to do a test flight with Inggs and see where we went from there. As a result of the measured consumption rate I decided we could carry on with our journey, provided we did certain inspections at every stop. Michael went along with this decision and as Inggs was in charge we got his agreement since the engines did not belong to Rolls-Royce.

It was agreed that AGF should take off first, do a couple more circuits and if Inggs was happy to press on to Cairo where I knew we would at least have the facilities of the RAF. In the event we would require further assistance in other directions. Take-off was early in the afternoon and we flew above and behind AGF all the way. We saw a great deal of sand, most of which did not look very flat; it was not the kind of terrain one would choose for a forced landing. I think we were more anxious about the progress of AGF or "Richard King" as she was called, than were her crew, so we were all quite relieved to see her land at Heliopolis while we did a wide approach to have a look at the Giza Pyramids before landing.

After a night at the Heliopolis Hotel – rather Victorian and a bit of a comedown from the Benghazi and Tripoli hotels – but with English food, we could detect no deterioration in our lame engine, but now a new trouble had occurred. Not only had the exhaust system started to crack, but also some securing studs had broken and a number of nuts had vibrated loose. The RAF came to the rescue and did the necessary welding, while Michael worked on the nuts and bolts side of the job. This work was going to take the best part of a day, so Barton and I went into Cairo and bought ourselves khaki shirts and shorts, along with the traditional pith helmet, from a large French store. In the afternoon we had a quick look round the bazaar area before taking the road to the Pyramids, with tea at the Mena House Hotel on the way. I was reminded how this trip to the Pyramids was made by Sir Francis Henniker in 1920 using rather strange means of transport – more of which anon.

The aircraft were now 'serviceable', so after a drink at Shepherds, it was early to bed for a dawn start for Khartoum. Once in the air the following day, and after assuring myself that the red hot exhaust pipes were not falling off, I caught up with some sleep till we made the approach to Wadi Halfa for refuelling. There was a pleasant surprise at the Customs Office when I was handed a letter from my father. He seemed to know the most likely places at which we would call – which was more than I did! We were now in the Anglo-Egyptian Sudan and it was too hot for comfort, so it was a great relief to get into the air again.

We landed at Khartoum at 2.00pm local time, too late to continue to Kisumu after refuelling, so we enjoyed the company of several English people staying at the Grand Hotel, which was also used by Imperial Airways passengers on the Empire flying boat route. We also met a couple of RAF pilots to whom we told our story of carrying petrol in the cabin, but it fell rather flat. Apparently five years previously, No 216, a local RAF Squadron, were flying Vickers Victorias at the time. To enable one of them to make the first non-stop flight from Khartoum to Cairo, the story goes that petrol was pumped into the main fuel tanks from tins carried in the fuselage. We had been beaten to it!

The cool of the early morning saw us leaving Khartoum when again I finished off some sleep of the night before. It had been so hot that I had failed to sleep even with the aid of a large overhead fan and flasks of iced water, which were replenished at intervals by a white-clad native boy creeping through the dark like a ghost. We put down at Juba – still in the Sudan – for more petrol, where it was even hotter. Stepping out of the aircraft was like walking into an oven and how any European could live there I do not know, in fact, the only one we saw was the Shell representative. In such heat it seemed an age before both aircraft were refuelled from four-gallon petrol tins by the team. We now appeared to be free of any more installation troubles and our lame engine was still going strong, so we pressed on to Kisumu on the north-east of Lake Victoria. Our luck – on which we should not have had to rely so much – was out again. Here we had two hold-ups. One has to remember that each night stop all the troubles we had experienced so far on the way – cylinder block leak, oil

Refuelling at Juba was hot, slow and primitive.

71

cooler, header tank and exhaust system failures, had to be checked on each engine in turn for any repetition. Now, when the bottom cowling was removed on one of the engines, down fell a complete air filter with its attached engine air intake. This was bolted back in a bit of a Heath Robinson way and the other engines inspected for any similar trouble. Just another example of Junker inexperience in installation design.

The following morning all was set for departure to Dodoma in Tanganyika (Tanzania), which had belonged to Germany before the 1914-18 war. We in AGG or 'Ryk Tulbagh' arranged to take off first for a change, and Rother taxied to the farthest corner of the rather small airfield of longish grass to get the longest possible run. We were at least 4000 feet above sea level, which would slightly reduce the power of the engines and the direction of the wind that day meant that we would have to clear several high-ish hills soon after takeoff. Unbeknown to him, Rother had chosen the one soft patch at the edge of the aerodrome in which to turn into the wind and the starboard main wheel sunk in up to its axle and refused to move. No tractors were readily available and it took some time to obtain spades, two strong planks and a six-wheeled Foden lorry to pull us out. By now it was midday so we were not going to get any further than Dodoma for the next hop, which had been intended only as a refuelling stage. From the welcome our German contingent received on landing that afternoon, one might have thought that the night stop had been planned! Mostly German was spoken in the hotel and we English were made to feel very much the outsiders. Our mileage for that day was no more than 450 so to try and make up a little Inggs and Rotha had decided on yet another early start and to go straight through to Johannesburg with refuelling stops at Mpika in Northern Rhodesia (Zambia) and Salisbury (Harare). After all, by now we had been no less than twelve days on the trip which must have created an all-time high for cost per passenger mile – not that we were paying! The internal water leak in the sick engine was now getting worse, but we were three-quarters of the way there and though we were lightly loaded, the thought of the loss of power on take-off made me watch the ground run more closely than usual.

Refuelling at Mpika took too long for various reasons, so our arrival in Salisbury was delayed until 12.35pm. It might have been a commonplace thing in that part of the world but another delay we were not expecting was a swarm of locusts which descended on the aerodrome just as the aircraft was being refuelled. If only to prevent the engine radiators becoming completely blocked, we could not take-off again until these animals decided to move on – which they did not do until late in the afternoon, which meant a night stop after all. While enjoying the comforts offered by Meikels Hotel, I read an account in an Imperial Airways journal of a flight made taking a similar route to ours.

"On February 4th, 1920 Wing Commander Pierre van Ryneveld, accompanied by Flt/Lt. Christopher J Q Brand, left Brooklands Aerodrome in a Vickers Vimy biplane fitted with two Rolls-Royce engines to make the first flight to Cape Town. They reached their destination six weeks later, having covered approximately 7500 miles in 109½ flying hours".

"Six weeks later" indeed. So seventeen years on, perhaps we were not doing so badly after all! I was to meet Sir Pierre later in my stay in South Africa. He was then Commander-in-Chief (C-In-C) of the Air Force, and later Chief of General Staff with the rank of Lt General, and I mentioned his epic flight. He explained that the reason they took so long on his trip was that they had to change an engine en route and it took weeks before they could obtain a new one. What bad luck!

The last leg of our journey was without incident; we landed at Germiston at 1.00pm on 10 June, and it was with some relief that we taxied in and cut the engines. The British contingent was not allowed to be relieved in another way however. Whilst Inggs and the Germans were allowed to go straight through Customs, we were kept on the apron at the pleasure of the Excise gentlemen, who spent some time in going through our luggage. There was an unfamiliar flag on the airport building – a tricolour of orange, white and

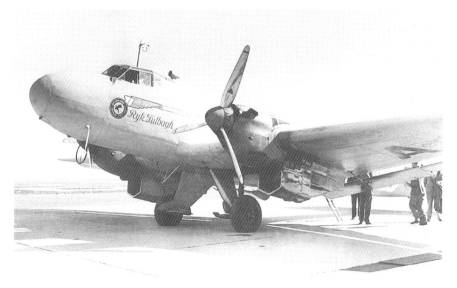

ZS-AGG arrives at Germiston 10 June 1937.

73

blue – so it seemed we were in a foreign country once more. I never saw the German crew again and Bond, Barton and I were left to our own resources. A Shell representative gave us a lift to The Germiston Hotel where we stayed a few days before we split up.

The next day, before I had finished breakfast, I found myself standing in line at the local police station for an identity parade conducted in Afrikaans, of which I understood little. As somebody who had lived in Africa for more than one night had 'done it', I was soon free to go to the airport. There I met Lieutenant Ottley, the chief engineer, and Colonel Holdhouse, the general manager of SAA, with whom I briefly went over the last six months at Dessau and we prepared ourselves for a meeting with Oswald Pirow, the Minister for Railways, Harbours and Airways. I was at first surprised to find what I took to be ex-army people running everything but it became clear when I realised how small the white aviation population was – both military and civil – and that most of the airway's staff and mechanics were reservists in the Air Force. (Michael Gaze became a Major during the war which was to come). Our meeting duly took place with Pirow and a director from Junkers, Herr von Mohl. Colonel Holdhouse expressed his opinion that had Junkers obtained a Rolls-Royce installation, none of the present troubles would have taken place and that SAA would not accept any of the six aircraft until their performance and reliability was up to specification. He went on to tell Pirow and von Mohl that Rolls-Royce installations gave satisfaction in the Air Force where engines were treated much more harshly.

By the end of July the four engines and the wings had been removed from the two aircraft and the whole stored at the end of one of the hangars, all of which looked a sad state of affairs. I had already been in touch with the South African Air Force and as there was nothing left to do at the Rand Airport (Germiston), I removed my domicile to a northern suburb of Johannesburg, Germiston being to the south.

Many years later I discovered that Junkers were part owners of South African Airways – which might explain a great deal.

CHAPTER SEVEN

Life in South Africa

Before leaving England I had collected numerous addresses from friends of my parents who had relations or contacts in South Africa – although I never did find time to visit the Bishop of Pretoria – and it was through one of these that I found a room in The Manor, Winifred Road, Park Town. This was a pleasant establishment run by Mrs McCready and might well have been her family home before its enlargement to hold some twelve to fifteen lodgers.

Johannesburg – 'The Golden City' – was quite a thrill. It had its own particular unexplained fascination, as have many cities around the world. To me, in 1937, it was so modern and easy to find one's way about with the grid pattern streets and skyscrapers; I imagined it to be a New York with no sea. Today, towns and cities all over the world have their high rise buildings but some sixty years ago there were not many outside the Americas that could beat Escom House, or Anstey's Buildings, which boasted twenty-plus storeys and must have been the tallest when I arrived in the country.

Many of the older buildings in more of a Colonial, four-storey style, were more attractive than some of the newer ones; there was the largest hospital in the Commonwealth, which must have rivalled Groot Schuur at the Cape which is more famous today; The Carlton Hotel, almost too expensive to have a drink at the bar; The Rand Club – something like all the big London clubs rolled into one – to which I was invited on one occasion. They all formed a part of this interesting city. But the building, or rather its contents, which I found the most fascinating, was the City Library in the Market Square. I could have spent many an hour there had I had the time; not reading books but looking at photographs. It was hard to believe that here was a modern city of half a million people living on a spot which only 50 years before was in the middle of nowhere, supporting some fifteen farmers who extracted a bare living from a windswept and none too fertile land. What was so interesting to me was being able to follow the development of Johannesburg through the pictorial history that had been built up with the many photographs, which had been contributed by amateur and professional photographers over the years. This is probably unique as most other modern cities were established before the camera was invented and historians have to rely on conjecture, sketches and drawings to augment their writings. Here were the photographs of the first collection of tents and huts, some made from mud, followed a few years later by quite substantial looking stone buildings, there being no timber for miles around. Very few of these photographs were without oxen and ox-wagons as it must have been necessary to transport just about everything that was required, including heavy machinery, which would have to come overland – probably from Durban. In today's life of the jetlag sufferers, thoughts are seldom spared for these beasts of burden without which – who knows – no Vootrekkers and no Johannesburg? Another point I couldn't miss was that in most of the photographs the men seemed to be working in their best Sunday-go-to-meeting suits, complete with watch chains in their waistcoat pockets and that there were virtually no women to be seen.

Life in Johannesburg seemed rather parochial from the point of view of the inhabitants, and there were no easily accessible places to 'get away from it all' unless you made a trip of 400 miles or so to the Kruger Game Reserve, Durban, or a slightly nearer sight of the sea at Lourenço Marques (Maputo) in Mozambique, a mere 300 miles away. There were plenty of local attractions for those who could afford them. Tennis and swimming were the most popular of the outdoor sports as many people had their own tennis courts and swimming pools in addition to the public facilities. There were half a dozen or so public parks – Joubert being the largest and most central – and many golf courses for which you had to put your hand pretty deeply into your pocket to join, as no doubt you did for the two country clubs. Both the flying clubs at the two aerodromes had their dances where you naturally met most people involved in the aircraft world – which was small.

It was at this time that I again became involved with the Kestrel XVI VPs which had brought us to South Africa. Rather before they had thought through how to make use of them, the SAAF had agreed to take on charge the eight engines held by South African Airways, along with the twelve still remaining at Derby and originally intended for the Ju86s which were never delivered. After lengthy talks with the SAAF and correspondence with Hawkers and Hucknall, it was realised that conversion of the existing Hartbees was out of the question, if only on cost grounds, though it would be practicable if done during new airframe manufacture. The alternative, of converting the XVI VP to standard Hartbee type specification, still involved an extensive conversion list; larger radiators and oil coolers, updraught air intakes, return to wooden propellers, stiffer engine mountings, camshaft-driven BTH air compressor and gas starter alterations, deletion of VP oil pump, addition of gun-gear and so on.

Then, out of the blue, Phillips & Powis Aircraft announced the Kestrel RR Trainer at the SBAC Show of 1937. With a Kestrel XVI installed, it was the fastest of its type and would be a very attractive aeroplane for the SAAF since with only a few mods it would be a home for their surplus XVIs. I was asked by Colonel Darby (Db – Sales, London) to put the idea to the SAAF. They became very interested and discussed the purchase of sixteen or eighteen aeroplanes. However, when it came down to specifications, costs and delivery dates etc I could get no information at all from Phillips & Powis (ie Miles). To save time, Db had asked me to deal direct with Miles, but it seemed that they had announced this new aeroplane without any thought as to how they would respond to potential customers! It was also strange that, while all this was going on, the local P&P agents knew nothing of this potential sale.

Meanwhile, EP naturally felt rather out of things and kept telling me to get on with my own job and stop trying to be a fancy salesman! Finally, the SAAF said they could not be expected to buy an aeroplane straight off the drawing board and without firm costings etc. They suggested we could talk again as and when the RAF had some aircraft in service. I was back in England before AM Spec 16/36 was issued for Master Is in June 1938, but with a de-rated engine (Kestrel XXX) installation, and losing 70mph off the top speed compared with the original XVI. By the outbreak of war, only seven of these Kestrel-engined aircraft had been delivered to the RAF. Out of an order totalling 900 Masters, the majority were powered by either Bristol Mercury (Mk II) or Pratt & Whitney Wasp Junior (Mk III) engines. Eventually the SAAF received a large number of Masters, but they were all Mk II or Mk III models.

When it came to diversion, the bioscope (cinema) was the most frequented form of evening entertainment and the Palladium, Colosseum and Empire were large, modern and had it all – organ, resident orchestra and/or stage show which came into their own at half-time. This was necessary as they were run on the live theatre principle, where seats had to be booked in advance for each separate performance. The live theatre itself hardly existed, and apart from visiting companies, mostly from the UK, there was little else worth patronising. There was no such thing as an English-type pub in which to have a drink after an evening show, so it was either go straight home or call at one of the drive-in snack houses where one could have a large variety of sandwiches – toast and fried bacon, or chicken went down very well – with iced or hot drinks of every flavour under the (African) sun – but no alcohol. All this was supplied without moving from your car, a quick and efficient service.

Another sporting facility was the skating rink, which was a leftover from the City's fiftieth anniversary exhibition, and it seemed a little incongruous to be in the hot sunshine one minute and the next in a cool atmosphere surrounded by ice. It was here I learnt how to fall down, but not how to skate, and saw my first ice hockey match between visiting American and Canadian teams. It was then I began to appreciate what a tremendous amount of continuous practice professional skaters had to put in to make it all look so easy and keep at the top.

The Earl Howe motor racing circuit just outside Johannesburg had not

MILES AIRCRAFT

PHILLIPS & POWIS AIRCRAFT LTD

CONTRACTORS TO THE AIR MINISTRY AND FOREIGN GOVERNMENTS

THE AERODROME
READING · BERKSHIRE

TELEPHONE: SONNING 2211
TELEGRAMS: HAWK READING
CODES: BENTLEY'S & A.B.C.

OUR REF
LAH/GEH
Sales

YOUR REF

DATE
January 24th,
1938.

A.T.M.Henniker, Esq.,
The "Manor",
5, Winifred Road,
Park Town,
Johannesburg.

Dear Sir,

      We are in receipt of your letter of
the 12th instant for which we thank you.

      We are very pleased to note the
result of your discussion with the South African
Air Force in respect of the Miles "R.R.TRAINER".

      With regard to your request for a
quotation for fifteen or sixteen machines, we would
inform you that we are not at the moment in a position
to supply this but we are giving the matter our serious
consideration and will indicate a figure at the earliest
possible moment.

          Yours faithfully,
    p.p.PHILLIPS & POWIS AIRCRAFT LTD.,

          Sales Department.

DIRECTORS: F. G. MILES, M.S.A.E. A.F. SIDGREAVES, O.B.E. LT. COL. M. ORMONDE DARBY, O.B.E.

Phillips and Powis' reply to my request about their new trainer.

long been opened and I went to one international meeting which attracted large crowds and famous car drivers. I don't know whether Kyalami, the current South African Grand Prix circuit, is at the same location though modernised, with the usual name change, or whether it is at a new spot with a local name. The driving standards of the general public were a bit frightening at times and when there was a pile-up it was generally a good one. Driving home after that race meeting was terrifying; everyone was a budding Dick Seaman, Caracciola or Nuvolari, the ace racing drivers of the era.

Johannesburg had two daily English language papers – *The Rand Daily Mail*, whose one-time editor was Edgar Wallace, and *The Star*, an evening paper which started life in Grahamstown as the *Eastern Star* and was moved, lock, stock and barrel, by ox-wagon and train to Johannesburg around 1890.

Most people were proud of their lovely country but *"it's the people that's the trouble"* they said, and it was not difficult to understand what they meant. Apart from Native tribes, Cape Coloured, Hottentot, Indian communities, etc it appeared to me that the Whites themselves were their own worst enemies. It seemed that the Boer War had to be kept alive, at least by a large number of the old Afrikaner generation who had made up their minds never to forgive or forget. Whatever it might cost the country, whatever it took and by whatever method thought necessary, the Dutch were going to take over the country to the exclusion of the British. They could then solve the 'Native Problem'! I had no idea whether any of my friends knew what was going on behind the scenes, that the secret society of Afrikaners – the "Broederbund" – drawing its members from all walks of life – was sending key men to Germany to study Hitler's methods for taking over a country by subversion. Did they know that South Africa was letting Germans into the country with a variety of work permits and allowing them to establish themselves in communities around the country? Whatever the Afrikaners' own motives were, it is easy to see in retrospect that it all suited Hitler's book perfectly. To declare war, and should Britain become involved, Germany would immediately take over South West Africa once again, followed by the Union and, of course, The Cape. With Rommel, the master of the Suez Canal, the British Empire would be cut in two. It was then no wonder the Germans had got a better welcome than we did when we arrived at Germiston, but I am glad I had none of these suspicions until much later on, otherwise my stay would not have been so pleasant.

It is still hard to believe that a nation that produced a General Smuts – who is a legend – and a van Rynevelt, who joined the British Army as a private in 1914 and before the cessation of hostilities had commanded No 45 and No 78 Squadrons RFC, could be selling their country in this way. A nation which bred a Denis Reitz, who with his brother, rode out to fight the

British with one of the first Commandos to be formed in Pretoria, who then joined the British Army as a private in 1914 and within two years was a Colonel in the Royal Scots Fusiliers in France. All three Afrikaners, all upright men of integrity. I met some charming Anglicised Afrikaners who had the same outlook as Smuts (Hertzog was then Prime Minister) and thought the present government introspective and short-sighted and that the nation's future would suffer as a result. A small illustration of this amused me one day in Johannesburg's GPO when I heard an Afrikaner women ask for a quantity of postage stamps but would not accept those printed in English, demanding "Suid Afrika" issue only. So, from a large sheet printed alternatively "South Africa" and "Suid Afrika", the man had to spend ages tearing the sheet up just to release the Dutch ones. The next customer was asked to accept a quantity of loose stamps.

Towards the end of July, Michael Gaze invited me to join him and a party of four to spend a long weekend in the Kruger Park Game Reserve, some 400 miles up country on the Mozambique border. The two married couples went in one car, while Michael and I went in his newly acquired Ford V8. We set out on a hot day and the tarmac roads surrounding Johannesburg soon gave way to corrugated dust surfaces. We found that you had to maintain a constant road speed to have a reasonably smooth ride; a few miles above or below that critical speed and you certainly knew the road was composed of ruts equally-spaced out by some magic hand. The road builders had obviously never heard of 'harmonic motion' or natural frequencies. It was on the outward journey that I experienced my first and only case of a car engine cutting out due to the petrol boiling – on the Pontiac, not Michael's Ford. This was due not only to the temperature of the day but the fact that we were between 5000 and 6000 feet above sea level. This held us up for some time as we could only wait until things cooled down a little. One night was spent on the way at Middleburg and two at different camps within the Reserve, sleeping in native style rondaval huts. We were lucky in seeing several prides of lion and hippo, giraffe, springbok, koodoo etc but no elephants. The best chance of getting a good look at the animals is firstly to try and be the first car out of camp in the morning, and secondly, to drive slowly. The uninitiated roar off in a cloud of dust hoping to get to the animals first, but only succeed in frightening them all away so nobody sees a thing. The game are living in their natural home and there is no good reason why they should hang around the tracks just to be gaped at by noisy and dust-raising tourists. Nobody is supposed to leave their car between camps, for obvious reasons, but on one of the days we were there we had to ignore this rule. The Pontiac suddenly ran out of petrol and it seemed a bit of a waste of time to sit there until we were rescued by a warden, which is what happens if all are not in camp by nightfall – whichever camp you have booked in to. The trouble, I discovered by crawling underneath the petrol tank, was caused by a missing drain plug which must have been torn out by hitting a rock in the track. Michael and I drove on to the nearest camp where the only receptacles available for carrying petrol were empty beer bottles. These we filled, found a cork and some rag, bought some chewing-gum from the shop and, with an armed warden, returned to the stranded car. While the rest of the party stayed in the car pretending they hadn't been outside the vehicle, I made a running repair – as they say – while Michael and the game warden stood prepared, eyes skinned and rifle at the ready. This repair not only got the Pontiac back to camp but lasted for the remainder of the weekend and the trip back to Johannesburg.

Our agent was instructed to supply me with my own transport, which he did, but to my disgust it turned out to be a Singer 10 of unknown vintage, yet known condition. It transported me at a steady 50 mph below which speed the wire wheel spokes squeaked, and above which speed the thing protested in various departments – not least the steering. It was a disgrace and I was ashamed to be seen in it. Complaints produced an equally old Chevrolet two-seater, just as dilapidated but reliable. It was a more suitable car for the out of town roads but I didn't like the Chevvy either. It did not feel safe and was like sitting on a blancmange; rolling on corners, while the steering was so low geared you had to wind the wheel round and round like a traction engine. Having stopped the car in the conventional way, it would pitch forward before finally settling back on its heels! I told our agent and Rolls-Royce what I thought of the situation, handed in the Chevrolet, cabled for £200 from Derby (which, to my surprise, arrived without question the following day) and went all British and bought a second-hand Riley 6/15 with a Wilson pre-selector gearbox, the latter making the characteristic whining which planet gears produce when chasing a sun gear for a mate. It was also often of two minds which gear it fancied at any one time, irrespective of the one selected. Despite this, it only let me down once, and this certainly caused some embarrassment. While heading a line of traffic in Eloff Street at the traffic lights, in what nowadays one would call downtown Jo'burg, the engine suddenly stalled just as the lights turned green. As the hooting of the cars behind became deafening, a complete stranger opened the nearside door, jumped into the car saying *"I know this car....... now try"* and sure enough, the engine started and the hooting stopped. In no time at all the car had been parked and we were in the nearest bar, my saviour to reward. There were no ignition or steering locks in those days, only a door key. The previous owner had inserted a concealed removable wiring plug, of which I was unaware. Suddenly after all my driving it had decided to fall out. Mr Summers just happened to be on the spot, to know the previous owner and so the car. He also just happened to know a lot of people I knew in England. It turned out that he was an ex-Rolls-Royce employee from Derby and was running his own engineering business in Johannesburg! We had plenty to talk about and I visited his Precision Engineering works several times. Small world!

Bond, the Marconi representative, was still around and had digs in Jo'burg although I saw little of him. Most of my new-found friends seemed to be scattering for Christmas so Bond and I, rather belatedly, decided to take the Riley down to Durban for a few days' holiday. For some reason I have forgotten, we couldn't get away until Christmas Eve. We must have been very optimistic, setting off in my not very young car to cover some 430 miles of atrocious dust and sometimes flooded roads in pouring rain and expecting to reach Durban in the day. In fact, we covered 400 miles and reached Pietermaritzburg before dark and got ourselves into a pub for the night. As I was the only driver, I was ready for bed after an evening meal and couldn't face the Christmas Eve party that went on most of the night, and had little sleep because of it. The weather had improved slightly the following morning and the road surface down to Durban grew better with every mile so we got settled into the Waverley Hotel with a drink with some others from Johannesburg before Christmas dinner. For once it was reasonably cool for this ritual, which in the Southern Hemisphere is normally much too hot for plum pudding. The sun wouldn't shine, so we drove and walked about the town for the next two days, had a look at a Blue Funnel liner in the harbour and a Short 'C' Class flying boat moored in the roadstead. Durban was very different from Johannesburg, more like an English town, and a pleasant change from the skyscrapers but I was disappointed not to be able to get another ride in a rickshaw powered by the fine figure of a Zulu with his colourful headgear. It was twelve years since the previous occasion when I had first visited Durban en route for England from Tasmania.

Suddenly the sun came out and it quickly became hot and humid. The world and his wife repaired to the beach to catch up with their sunbathing and we were not slow in following suit. After an hour or so I felt the sun was getting too hot, so put on a shirt, while Bond remained in his bathing trunks for much longer. By the time he covered himself, it was too late. That evening, feeling very sore and burnt, we went to a bioscope and saw Anna Neagle in *Sixty Glorious Years*. Next morning my legs were very red and painful and I had to turn up my shorts to make them even shorter to keep them away from the 'tideline' on my legs, but I managed to get about and appear for meals. For Bond, it was much more serious and he was in a bad way. I found him still in bed in a lot of pain and any question of food was out. I bought some soothing ointment from a local chemist who had a quantity ready made up for idiots like us, and in retrospect I suppose I should have called in a doctor. Bond appeared partially to have lost the use of his arms and legs and even after three days he couldn't move without my help, although he had by then found an appetite. In spite of Bond's discomfort, we decided it was high time we got back to Johannesburg. My legs were still a little sore but I could drive without much trouble, and having helped Bond with dressing and packing, I got him into the car and off we set. We took the same route back and after a short stop to enjoy the scenery looking across 'The Valley of a Thousand Hills', we reached Ladysmith by lunchtime. Bond was still in too much pain to move from the car, so I took some food out to him from the hotel where I had a proper meal. The remainder of the journey was rather hard going and I could have done with a co-driver. Darkness caught up with us some forty miles short of Johannesburg and near Heidelburg we ran into a cracker of a thunder storm. The lightning in the clear air at our altitude was quite disturbing and with each flash I could easily read the car's instruments. After delivering Bond to his rooms I was glad to get to my bed at the Manor. Poor Bond was in bed for a further week before he was able to walk normally again.

CHAPTER EIGHT

South African and Southern Rhodesian Air Forces

When I paid my first visit to Roberts Heights (now re-christened Voortrekkerhoogte) – the Aircraft and Artillery Depot, to give its official title – in 1937, I presented my Rolls-Royce letter of introduction to Captain Robert Preller, the Engineer Officer in charge of aircraft maintenance and production. He in turn introduced me to Colonel Daniels, the Commander of the Depot. This was apparently where new aircraft were assembled under licence and repairs carried out, and I saw no evidence for the 'Artillery' side of the title.

I had been in the country less than a fortnight and was confused by the differences between the Boers, the Dutch and the Afrikaners – if any, and what their relationship with the people of British descent was like. Most people I had met to date spoke English anyway, so when Bob Preller took me into the Mess for lunch it was surprising to find that Afrikaans was being used in about the same proportion as English. Bob was naturally talking to me in English, and I soon put my big foot in it – not for the last time – by saying *"So you can speak this language too",* after he had rattled off some Afrikaans to a fellow officer. The Prellers are an old established Dutch family. Ouch! Some time later Bob invited me to spend a weekend with him and his parents on their farm some miles from Pretoria, out on the veldt. I enjoyed the experience but things were a little strained at times. Bob's sister and brother-in-law spoke to me now and then – in English of course, but his father and mother said not a word, and they certainly resented this 'roynek' being in their house. At mealtimes Bob and I carried on a rather one-sided conversation.

It was very easy to be caught off guard with this nationality problem. One day a man turned up at the Aircraft Depot and asked for me by name, somehow knowing I was there and from Rolls-Royce. He had invented a new silent exhaust system for aircraft and would like me to interest the Company in his patent. I wasn't very impressed with his idea but I was with his accent, which was more English than mine, so agreed to visit his home in Pretoria for a demonstration of his idea. I was most surprised to find his home was not only very Dutch but his mother and sister chatted away in Afrikaans. If they could, they wouldn't, speak any English. The budding inventor had never been out of the country and had been educated at Cape Town University.

Bob Preller was so English in his speech, manner and outlook that I felt I need not look for an excuse for taking him for a South African of British descent, but I found one when I was in his rondaval (literally 'hut' in Afrikaans, but meaning 'room' in this context) at the Mess one day, looking at some of his photographs. One showed this Bristol Bulldog with RAF markings, sitting on its nose in the unmistakable setting of the sewage farm at the side of Brooklands aerodrome, Weybridge. This could only have been the same incident I had witnessed while running up a Hawker aircraft around 1933 when working between Vickers and Hawkers. Several of us had gone over to the luckless pilot who, in running out of aerodrome, said that from the air the whole of the area looked solid and anyway one normally would not expect to find a large 'bog' in such a place. The pilot was Bob, who was on a secondment course with the RAF at the time. We may even have spoken to each other, but neither of us could remember having done so.

The customs and traditions of the South African Air Force were naturally based on those of the RAF, or as the founder members were mostly South Africans who had served in the RFC in the Great War, it would probably be more true to say they were established on RFC procedure, which in turn had a British Army bias. They retained the old RFC (Army) ranks and khaki uniform, which was just as well, as being on such a small scale, the Army and Air Force had to share facilities and combine to form one Defence Force. The Officers' Mess at Roberts Heights was for instance shared by both services, and here the rules and etiquette were traditional as I found when I was made an honorary member. After the first guest night to which I was invited, I was quietly reminded to leave a visiting card on the Mess notice board. My dinner jacket blended with the navy blue mess kit worn by both Army and Air Force, which avoided jealousies with different uniforms and rank nomenclature.

It was the British Army which invented the Officers' Mess in around 1730 but I suppose it could be said that the RAF Mess of today is the result of the combination of the Army (Royal Flying Corps) Mess and Royal Navy (Royal Naval Air Service) Wardroom. However, the ranks of the officers and men are unique. Unlike South Africa, all the other members of the Commonwealth having an Air Force adopted these grades which, for the greater part, were contrived by the Royal Navy for their Royal Naval Service personnel. Warrant Officer, Flight Lieutenant and Wing Commander were originally Navy ranks and are now RAF, while Squadron Commander and Commodore are not far removed from the current RAF equivalent of Squadron Leader and Air Commodore. On the other hand, the lowest form of commissioned life in the RAF – Pilot Officers – must be thankful they do not have to answer to the old Navy equivalent of 'Probationary Flight Sub-Lieutenant'.

The badge of the South African Air Force (SAAF) was interesting, as while it roughly followed the style of that of the RAF – at least the same eagle and similar crown – I noted that the motto was slightly different. Instead of *"Per Ardua Ad Astra"* – the birth and Latin translation of which has always been in doubt – the South African version was *"Per Aspera Ad Astra"*, so I can only guess that reaching the stars in the Southern Hemisphere was considered to be rather more 'rough' than 'difficult'!

Squadron Leader P G Heming in his book, *Customs and Traditions of the Royal Air Force*, tells how *"Per Ardua Ad Astra"* was for many hundreds of years the motto of the Mulvany family. While two Royal Engineer subalterns on secondment to the Royal Flying Corps were walking across Laffans Plain, Farnborough, one suggested that this motto was most appropriate and seemed to be just what their CO, Major F Sykes, was looking for. When, on 15 March 1913, King George V approved the motto for the Royal Flying Corps, frantic efforts were made to establish an official translation, but this was found impossible. The best efforts ranged from *"Through Struggle to the Stars"* to *"Through Difficulties to the Skies"* and there was even a doubt whether 'astra' had anything to do with a star. This was strange indeed, as both the Greeks and Romans have words for it; there was even a choice. Selection of 'Astron' or 'Astrolis' or even 'Astrum' should have been enough to convince one that Astra was at least trying to be a star! Even if the purist cannot produce a true translation, the motto rolls off the tongue easily and for anyone who thought *The Way to the Stars* was a good film, then let that be his or her version.

The SAAF tie is – or was then – the same as the old RFC one, except the dark blue and red stripes ran diagonally in the opposite direction on the pale blue background. Round about the year 1921, when the British Government gave South Africa some hundred or so surplus aircraft left over from the Great War, the SAAF was formed with a couple of dozen local officers and men who had served in the RFC. The story is told that three years previously when the RFC and the RNAS amalgamated into the RAF, and the old RFC tie was offered to the Dominion and Commonwealth Air Forces, all except the SAAF turned the offer down. This did not go down at all well with the others as it was felt that the colours and tie should be allowed to pass into history with the old Service.

The aircraft establishment, as far as I could gather, was more or less spread equally over five aerodromes located round the Union – Zwartkop and Waterkloof (Transvaal), Durban (Natal), Bloemfontein (Orange Free State) and Cape Town (Cape Province). At first it was a little difficult to appreciate that this vast county – just over five times the area of the British Isles – could be adequately defended by such a small force. In England there might well be that number of RAF stations in one county alone, but then any enemy was bound to be nearer our doorstep. The types of aircraft were hardly suitable for long range work either – seven Hawker Furies with about

South African-assembled Hawker Hartbees in SAAF colours (orange replaced red in roundel) at Zwartkop.

the same number of Hawker Harts located at Zwartkop (Robert Heights), some one hundred Hartbees – twenty on each of the five stations, and twenty or more Avro Tutor trainers. The Hartbees (derivative of the Hartebeest, which sounded a more indigenous animal than a Hart), were Harts locally assembled at the Aircraft and Artillery Depot and test flown from Zwartkop.

The well equipped workshops were quite capable of erecting and repairing aircraft and the main fault with an otherwise well run engine repair section was that there was too much dust and sand about – something one tended to forget when it was so universal. The aerodromes were mostly dry and dusty and the first modification I 'sold' the authorities was air filters for the Kestrel engines.

I was aware of some resentment from time to time from some of the engineering staff. My services were free but at the same time they didn't exactly ask for my help, and they may have considered that were it not for the South African Airways job, I would not have been in the country at all. However, they were thankful for Rolls-Royce assistance on several occasions. A new engine test bed with test fan (propeller) was ready for operation but nobody really knew how to calibrate or run it correctly. Naturally the working life of an aero engine is in the air at different altitudes, and conditions are always at variance with those on the ground. So when testing an engine at ground level (or some given figure above sea level), various corrections have to be made to check its performance at different simulated altitudes. With the equipment provided this is quite simple – when you know how. The fact that ground level at the Depot was already 5000 feet or so above sea level seemed to cause problems for the test rig people. I even had a little booklet written in Afrikaans on another subject to help 'oil the wheels'.

I flew several times with Bob Preller in one of the Harts, ostensibly to find aircraft which had force-landed on training flights due invariably to fuel shortage, but it was a nice way of seeing the country. One day we looked at the Premier Diamond mine on the other side of Pretoria, which was a smaller version of the 'Big Hole' at Kimberley. Bob was an excellent pilot and was the first of many members of the SAAF to be awarded the DFC in the 1939-45 war.

I suppose by the outbreak of war the Hartbees contract had been completed and allowing for a few write-offs, there may have been sixty serviceable machines. Apart from these, the remainder of the aircraft making up the declared total strength of 98 of all types, could have been something of the order of 10 Ju52s and 12 Ju86s from South African Airways, possibly a couple of Blenheim bombers from England and the remainder a mixture of Harts (and variants thereof) and Tutors. Hardly adequate equipment with which to start a war. Things obviously improved later because by early 1941 SAAF No 1 Squadron had Hurricanes, as confirmed in F H M Lloyd's book *Hurricane*.

The Junkers aircraft – especially the Ju52 vintage – were most likely used for transporting supplies and equipment, while the Ju86 type were probably used on shipping and coastal defence. A few Fairey Battles were used to bomb Italian installations and by 1942 the South Africans were operating in

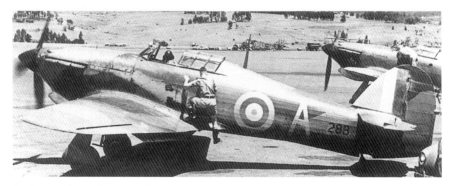

SAAF Hurricanes in East Africa during the Italian Campaign 1940/41.

Formation of SAAF Fairey Battles.

North Africa with Boston light bombers and Tomahawk fighters from America, as well as their trusty Hurricanes.

At the beginning of 1939 South Africa must have been counting on their friendship with Germany somehow to keep them out of the war. The Army consisted of one Infantry Battalion of around 1500 men, the Air Force perhaps had 100 men more than the Army, while the Navy was virtually non-existent, 17 men in total! The protection of the vast coastline was in the hands of the Royal Navy which for many years had Simonstown as its base and performed the dual role of looking after both English and South African interests. When South Africa did declare war on Germany on 6 September 1939, it was only on a very narrow majority in Parliament; something like 57% for and 43% against entering the conflict. Had Smuts been Prime Minister instead of Hertzog, the vote would not have been so narrow. For years, rather like England, South Africa did not want to face up to the fact that war was just around the corner. There were plenty of ostriches in that part of the world and an awful lot of sand in which to bury their heads. It was only when, in 1930, Pirow tried and succeeded in obtaining a small budget for the Armed Forces that any money was being spent at all, while being in any of the Services at that period was apparently considered to be a bit of a joke – playing at soldiers.

We may not have had much of an air force in England either, but – as was soon to be proved – we did have a small number of the best trained pilots in the world. We also had men with the foresight of an Ernest Hives (Merlin), a Sidney Camm (Hurricane), a Reginald Mitchell (Spitfire) and a Lord Rothermere (Blenheim). All these projects were classified 'PV' (Private Venture), which meant that the financial risks were wholly borne by the companies involved. The Government did not commit itself to any development or manufacture expenditure unless/until it was proved a success and they decided they needed it. Then, and only then, did the Air Ministry reach for its cheque book. Lord Rothermere ordered the Bristol 142 monoplane in 1935 at his own expense (or was it the *Daily Mail's*?) as a four-passenger, twin-engine, executive transport and called it *Britain First*. It had a top speed of 307 miles per hour – just one hundred miles per hour faster than the fleetest RAF fighter of the day. It was rapidly put into production as a light bomber – and indeed, subsequently as a fighter – and re-christened Blenheim.

Because of the limited opportunities offered by the small Air Forces in their own countries, many young men from the Dominions and Commonwealth came to England in the late thirties, often at their own expense, to join the RAF. Some of these, and especially those who found themselves in Fighter Command, were often in the news and became heroes. South Africa had her share and perhaps the best known was Group Captain A G ('Sailor') Malan, DSO and Bar, DFC and Bar, who served in the Royal Naval Reserve for two years before joining the RAF in 1936. He survived the war with 28 enemy aircraft to his credit, only to return home to South Africa and die of pneumonia. Sqn Ldr M T St J Pattle commanded No 33 Squadron RAF and was killed over Athens leading his Hurricanes during the ill-conceived Greek campaign. He was credited with the destruction of 58 enemy aircraft. A third South African, Wing Co P H Hugo, DSO, DFC was the best on his course at the Air-Firing School shortly before the war. This must have made this normally quiet and reserved man a formidable foe for the enemy to meet with his four gun Hurricane. Peter 'Dutch' Hugo was at various times CO of No 41 Squadron and Wing Co Flying at RAF Tangmere. Naturally, the main theatre of operations for the SAAF was in North Africa, a story in itself of which I know little. I do know that of the twenty-two South Africans who joined the RAF and took part in the Battle of Britain, nine were killed.

Soon after arriving in South Africa I had sent a report to Rolls-Royce outlining an article I had read on the poor service a batch of Hawker Harts was giving the Royal Australian Air Force, and that the Kestrel engines were not without trouble. No doubt Derby had heard all about this, but I had more than one motive for letting them know. When passing through Salisbury on the delivery flight of the Junkers aircraft to South Africa, I had heard that the Southern Rhodesian Government was in the process of establishing what they called an Air Service, which would be controlled by their Department of Defence. The aircraft would be second-hand Hawker Harts and they hoped eventually to build up a small separate Air Force. In view of the reported Australian experience, I thought it would be a good idea if I went up to Salisbury for a few days to offer any help I might be able to give. It would be well worth delaying my return to England if my visit could prevent the spread of any 'Antipodean Disease'. The second reason was that I wanted to have a look at Salisbury (Harare). My letter suggesting this prophylactic action to the Officer Commanding produced a reply from the Department of Defence, Southern Rhodesian Forces welcoming my proposed visit (provided it was free of charge) signed by Major Dirk Cloete, Staff Officer, Air Services. When I had passed through Salisbury on my first visit, he was Minister of Civil Aviation, so as in South Africa, senior officers had more than one hat to wear. Derby agreed to this visit, so I flew up to Bulawayo in a South African Airways Ju52 on 13 February 1938 and there changed planes to a de Havilland Rapide for the second leg of the journey to Salisbury. I had taken the precaution of pointing out to my boss – before there was any argument over expenses – that air travel was essential, as the journey would have taken four days by train and my return passage to the UK had already been booked – by sea.

It was nice to see the Union Flag ('Union Jack') again flying everywhere instead of the South African Tricolour, and yet this was the only place where I was not made welcome. It seemed that in those days everyone was *"terribly, terribly, county"* and you had to be introduced before anyone would speak to you. I was, however, met at the airport and taken to Meikel's Hotel and later to Defence HQ to meet Major Cloete and Flt Lts Powell and Maxwell, the two RAF officers seconded to Rhodesia as flying instructors for a period of three years.

The Air Service was not yet a year old and its equipment was very limited. Apart from a few 'ab initio' aeroplanes, its full complement was six second-hand Hawker Harts, two of which had been converted to dual control for instructional purposes. The Harts had been used by one of the London Auxiliary Air Force squadrons based at Hendon and had been shipped out in packing cases together with reconditioned Kestrel engines. Perhaps it was fortuitous for Rhodesia that Italy's annexation of Abyssinia necessitated the speeding up of the aircraft delivery but it also meant that they were not in very good condition. On my arrival only three had been made airworthy and some delay was caused by having to obtain spares from South Africa. I was taken to the new military aerodrome a few miles outside Salisbury, which had only recently been cleared from the bush and where there was precious

The RAF ground crew seconded to the 'Rhodesian Air Service'.

little else save the one solitary 'tin' or corrugated iron hangar. Here I met the RAF maintenance contingent consisting of a flight sergeant, two sergeants and two corporals, who between them appeared to have a good knowledge of the aircraft and engine type. It seemed the RAF lads thought they were on to a good thing; three years in a pleasant country with not very arduous duties, overseas pay and no parades. The war would have caught up with them before their three years was up, so perhaps they never got home! We worked well together and during the few days I was in the country we sorted out some engine details, identifying various spares and tools, engine equipment and modifications.

The Unit was run on Auxiliary Air Force lines, flying training being done at the weekend and early morning and evenings, whilst the pupils were chiefly members of the British South Africa Police and civilians. The soldiery were surprisingly conspicuous by their absence, as I had expected to find members of the Rhodesia Regiment were also learning to fly.

I casually mentioned to one of the pupil pilots – a sergeant in the police – that people seemed very stand-offish at the hotel, whereupon I was immediately invited into the Sergeant's Mess where I was made very welcome and spent a couple of enjoyable evenings there.

It is doubtful if any of the pupil pilots there at that time had heard of the lad of sixteen who had joined the ranks of the Rhodesia Regiment some twenty-five years earlier and had also become a pilot. He joined the RFC in 1914 and was a Major with the Air Force Cross by the end of the war. This boy had emigrated to Southern Rhodesia where he turned his hand to gold mining, driving coaches, farming, tobacco growing and then joining the army after having tried nearly everything else available to him. After that war he made the RAF his career, but always considering himself a Rhodesian, he returned there on retirement from the RAF at the end of World War II. By this time he had become Commander-in-Chief Bomber Command between 1942 and 1945 and had reached the highest rank in the Service, Marshal of the Royal Air Force, Sir Arthur Travers Harris – 'Bomber Harris' – died a rather embittered old man of over ninety, always maintaining that his 'bomber boys' who he had driven so hard did not receive the recognition they so richly deserved.

A fair mount of ground had been covered, considering I had only three clear days in Salisbury but I did get an extra night in Bulawayo. A Rapide again transported me to the latter town and I was surprised that there was no direct link between Salisbury and Johannesburg. No doubt Imperial Airways had a monopoly on that route. I joined my half dozen fellow passengers bound for Jo'burg at Bulawayo airport and we eventually boarded a South African Airways Ju86 powered by the opposition – two Pratt & Whitney Hornet engines. We were all ready to go, but alas, one of the engines failed to start. After a delay of half an hour or so we were allowed out of the aircraft and I took the opportunity to casually do a little eavesdropping which told me that the trouble was an electrical fault exactly like that I had experienced at Dessau with the Kestrel installation. This was none of my business, so I was content to join the others in having a pleasant night at The Grand Hotel where the manager, Mr A Schierhout, entertained us – at the expense of South African Airways of course! When we arrived at the aerodrome the following morning, we found that a relief aeroplane was on its way to pick us up. We eventually got away that afternoon and I was allowed up on the flight deck for a while during the trip. I observed that ......*"the power output at cruising speed must be much lower than that of the Kestrel XVI engines, as the speed was only 164 mph using automatic mixture control....."* which in those far off days seemed to be worth a mention in a report I sent to Derby. Arriving back in Jo'burg after the four-hour flight, there was just under a week remaining in the country to get rid of my car, pay last visits – and bills – pack, and say my goodbyes and be on board the *Balmoral Castle* docked in Cape Town by 25 February.

After a not too promising start, my nine months stay in Africa had been interesting and immensely enjoyable – once I had made a few friends. While I think I was wise not to remain in the country for good, my otherwise sorrowful departure was animated by the thought that I might well be returning one day and in any case, there would surely be a wider and better future for me with Rolls-Royce, should I not return.

For some time I had seen nothing of the South African Airways people who had flown with me from Dessau – Michael Gaze, Bond, Barton and the German staff, so I went over to Germiston to say goodbye to as many as I could find. My Manor House friends were not keen on having a farewell party, just a few drinks in my room on the remaining evenings – except the last – when I intended to have an early night. This was not to be. I had a phone call alerting me that some of the Air Force lads were on their way over from Pretoria to have a drink with me at the Manor. We all had more than one and the party went on into the small hours – all night in fact. Few in the Manor could have had much sleep that night but complaints there were none. We called it a day – or night – as dawn was breaking, but just before my guests departed my tie was cut in two in the traditional manner, and I was presented with a SAAF tie together with a document giving me permission to wear it. And to wear it I had, as all my bags were packed and had gone on ahead. This was to cause a spot of bother.

Before my taxi arrived one or two sleepyheads appeared in night attire to wish me well; the lack of sleep and an over-sufficiency of booze made the occasion somewhat emotional. At the airport I found that some of the Air Force boys had shown up to 'ease' me into the Cape Town bound Ju52 – a rather hazy scene! Even before take-off I was confronted by a fellow passenger – an Englishman – who recognised my tie and insisted that I was much too young ever to have been in the RFC and my 'opposite handed stripes' story fell on deaf ears. Soon after we had reached our cruising height and I had settled down to catch up with some lost sleep, I was roused by the chatter of the other passengers who seemed to be attracted by something outside our aeroplane. There on either side were two Furies formatting on us and getting a little too close, I thought, and every now and then a wave from the pilots. The four Furies escorted us for ten minutes or so before waggling their wings, breaking off and returning to Zwartkop. What our pilot or the other passengers thought of the incident I never knew.

The Hotel Assembly in Cape Town provided a bed for the night, and by mid-morning on the following day I had found my cabin aboard the *Balmoral Castle* – her last run before being broken up. We were not due to sail until early next morning so I thought it would be nice to have a look at the top of Table Mountain. A bus took me to where the ground started to rise fairly steeply and where the cable car station was situated. I was surprised to find that travel on this type of conveyance was not particularly enjoyable. There seemed to be an awful lot of space beneath us; our machine was 'flying' much too slowly for the angle of climb – and it had no wings. There was the feeling that we would stall at any moment, a sensation I have only had in an aeroplane when it was done on purpose.

The top of the mountain is just as flat as it appears from sea level but a little too rough for easy walking and it seemed to stretch for miles, a vast, uninhabited and useless area with a magnificent view of crowded Cape Town and Table Bay. A quick run was taken out to Sandy Bay and Camps Bay and then to the ship, only to find to my alarm that there was no full laundry on board – and I only had a couple of dress shirts. A dash into town relieved this situation somewhat with what little South African money I had left. And so home to England. Tot Siens Suid Afrika – Goodbye South Africa.

CHAPTER NINE

'Trusting in thy defence'

The MacRobertson Air Race to Australia was staged in October 1934. Hawkers thought it a good idea to use the occasion for a sales promotion exercise and to demonstrate their Harts and Furies in Melbourne at the end of the race when a large aviation audience would be present. Imagine my joy when I was selected to look after the Kestrel engines, and the thought of being able to look up old friends in Tasmania was too good to be true. This would be my first overseas job. But it was not to be. Somebody else coveted the job, and strings were pulled in high places. I was told that on second thoughts I was unsuitable. Among other rather ridiculous accusations I was *"too young"* Eric Platford, my boss, told me, looking hard at his desk with obvious embarrassment. In the event the Hawker project was cancelled and my replacement was sent to India on other work where he contracted some strange disease which baffled the doctors at the Derbyshire Royal Infirmary on his return to UK. I suppose EP thought the best and most convenient sweetener would be to post me to the area vacated by my colleague, which was in the south of the country and covered a number of RAF stations. I was given a rise in salary, my car was 'put on the driving list' which gave me a mileage allowance instead of booking the equivalent rail fare for a car journey on Company business. Compensations like these, plus some words of good advice from a respected old boss, persuaded me not to take my complaints any further.

I set up shop in Andover, as being central for the shires of Oxon, Berks, Hants and Wilts, which counties played host to eight or so RAF stations on which were Kestrel-powered aircraft. Three-quarters of these were well established camps which had been created during the First World War – even before the birth of the RAF. The histories of Upavon and Neatheravon are interesting. Their location between Avebury and Stonehenge, where once lived a people even older than the Ancient Britons, seems incongruous enough, but then was not Brooklands, the nursery of British aviation, once the site of an Ancient Britons' settlement?

In 1934 Upavon was still the Central Flying School and had been built for the newly formed Royal Flying Corps, being opened in June 1912 (I can claim to be older than the RFC – by one day!). One of the school's COs was a Major Trenchard, but in my time the establishment rated a higher ranking officer; Group Captain J M Robb DSO, DFC, was the 'station master'. We can be sure Major Trenchard had not been the first flying instructor at the unit: he had to have a short 'crash' (!) course at Brooklands in order to be able to transfer from the Army to the RFC and was tutored by a certain T O M Sopwith. The appointment of Squadron Leader D'Arcy Greig as Chief Flying Instructor seemed appropriate enough as he had been a member of the RAF High Speed Flight at Calshot, and had come third in the 1929 Schneider Trophy race in the Supermarine S5. It was said that if you could fly one of those seaplanes you could fly anything!

The neighbouring station situated in the vastness of Salisbury Plain, had its own little bit of history. It was at Neatheravon with its magnificent custom-built officers mess (the dining room was more like a ballroom), that in June 1914 the whole of the RFC was assembled – with their Farman, Bleriot, BE2, FE8 and Avro aeroplanes – to plan and organise before going over to France. One gathers that strict security was maintained and all ranks were confined to camp; at least the nice name it earned of 'The Concentration Camp' would suggest this. Two months later four Squadrons with sixty-three aeroplanes – about one-third of the total air force strength – flew to France to join the British Expeditionary Force. The remaining aircraft were left at home under the command of the now promoted CO from Upavon, Lt Col Trenchard.

That was all long ago, and my job was to advise the RAF technical and maintenance people on the operation of their Rolls-Royce product, not to have history lessons, however interesting. The Kestrels were installed mostly in Hawker aircraft, variants of the Hart in training rôles, as a light bomber or in the Army's Audax co-op Squadrons. With some of these establishments equipped for overhauling engines in the station workshops, as well as general engine maintenance, my life was busy and the work interesting. At the age of twenty-two I had my own area and a free hand to go round my 'constituency' as I felt fit. A breath of sea air was a welcome change when I made the occasional visit to Supermarines at Southampton where the Southampton Mk IV or Scapa, flying boats (two Kestrels) were being built, or to an engine test on Fairey's S9/30 (Kestrel) single-float seaplane at Eastleigh. The Gloster TSR38 aircraft built to the same specification was carrying out deck landing trials on *HMS Courageous* at this time with a Kestrel engine (later on a Goshawk was installed). However, so much time was spent on its development that by 1934 the specification had been brought up to date and reissued as S15/33. Fairey meanwhile had gone ahead with an alternative design to their contribution, and this won the competition and was manufactured in vast numbers. It was named Swordfish, but later became better known as the Stringbag. It is incidental that the Gloster aeroplane happened to look like a Hawker design, and was 12 mph faster than Fairey's Swordfish.

I suppose it was at this period that I began to recognise the RAF as a fighting force rather than a collection of interesting aeroplanes and 'the best flying club in the world where you are even paid for being a member'. This prompted me to question the efficiency of the equipment – in particular the aircraft. Were they not becoming obsolescent and outdated? I naturally believed that as a nation we had the best aero engines in the world and that Rolls-Royce had established itself as leader in the field right from the 12-cylinder Eagle of the First World War which was designed by Royce itself. This was the engine which was installed in airships and aeroplanes, from single-engined fighters to four-engined bombers, and even in a five-engined flying boat. It had a total production run of 4696 and was followed by two others of different sizes, providing the backbone of the RFC in the latter part of the war.

The Hawk was a small six-cylinder 75hp engine used in training aircraft such as the Avro 504F and Sage III. A small number were installed in BE2Es and the majority were used to power small dirigibles such as the SS Zero Blimp (Submarine Scouts), for which over 200 engines were built. The third engine of this period was the Falcon; similar to, but slightly smaller than, the Eagle. This was installed in the Bristol Fighter and, after the war, the twin-engined Blackburn Kangaroo. It also went into probably the first purpose-built passenger aeroplane, the Westland Limousine. Over 2000 Falcon engines were delivered. In the mid thirties the Kestrel was establishing itself in the true tradition and various Marks were eventually installed in at least twenty-five different types of aeroplanes, with a total production run of 4750 engines. For peacetime this is quite impressive considering that the applications were mostly for military aircraft.

Furies of No 25 Squadron from Hawkinge at the 1933 Hendon air display ready to perform their 'tied together' formation flying. My first solo job with the RAF.

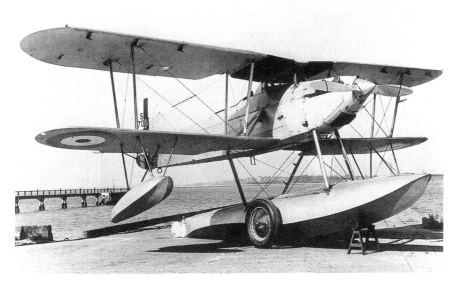

The Fairey S9/30 single float seaplane with Kestrel II MS.

Of the 76 Submarine Scout 'Blimps' (75 hp Hawk) built, only one was lost to enemy action.

A Blimp's car with its Hawk engine aft and 'heavy armament' in the bow. The crew could have included two young midshipmen, Ralph Cochrane and Victor Goddard, who became RAF Air Marshals in later life.

So where were our modern aeroplanes to match these modern engines? It was no secret that Germany was well advanced with the design and manufacture of monoplanes such as Heinkels, Dorniers, Messerschmitts and Junkers, but they were lacking modern engines. It so happened that the other Kestrel-engined aircraft in my area was the RAF's latest bomber, the Handley Page Heyford (Type HP 50), twin-engined 'heavy' bomber. It was a biplane, of course, and designated 'heavy' as I suppose it was the largest aircraft we possessed at the time. Handley Page had made a heavy or two back in 1918; the V/1500 for instance, powered by four Eagles, and I wondered whether twenty-six years later the Heyford was considered an example of our progress in aircraft design. I wondered what had happened to the two four-engined prototypes I had seen flying, each with four Kestrels; the Vickers Type 163, merely called the 'Four Engined Bomber' at Brooklands, and at Hendon in 1932 – the Gloster C16/28 bomber/transport? In fact, both aircraft did a considerable amount of test flying – the former doing 40 hours. However, both had their troubles – the latter a persistent rudder flutter, and were broken up in 1934. The story behind these was as follows.

The Gloster C16/28 (T33) bomber/transport (4 Kestrels).

In 1927 the Air Ministry (AM) had invited Vickers, Handley Page and Fairey to tender for a twin-engined bomber (with Kestrels), to Spec B19/27. HP and Fairey were each given an order for one aeroplane; surprisingly the Fairey machine was to be a monoplane and it – the Hendon – was ready for trials by 1932, and was handed over to the RAF's proving ground at Martlesham Heath. The Heyford was already there and half way through its handling trials and met the AM's specification and was liked and accepted by all who flew it. However, it was soon realised that the Hendon was by far the better of the two. Flight tests proved that it was faster, had a greater load carrying capacity, had an acceptable landing speed, and handled as well as its rival. When Vickers entered this competition they knew that this new aeroplane was to replace their 'Virginia' aircraft which had served the RAF for many years, and were confident that they could produce another winner. The front fuselage of the 'Vanox' was in fact that of a modified Virginia and with the FXIV (early Kestrel) engines, it flew late in 1929. After many modifications, changing engines to Kestrel IIIs and then to Bristol Pegasus, work on it ceased, as by this time the Hendon and Heyford were well advanced and had commenced acceptance trials. Vickers, however, felt that the experience gained was encouraging and so designed a private venture bomber of larger size. The aeroplane was basically a scaled up Vanox and when C16/28 was issued, with minor alterations, the specification was met. Thus the Type 163 four-engined bomber was born.

Returning to the B19/27 twin-engined bomber, once Vickers were virtually out of the running, Fairey thought they were in with a chance of a production contract but found that the AM had already awarded the prize to Handley Page – who eventually made 125 Heyfords. Did the AM get cold feet when they saw the large wing span of the Hendon, with visions of money to be spent on larger hangars, or were they merely in a panic to bolster up our bomber force as quickly as possible? For whatever reason, it seems the wrong aeroplane was chosen. While all this was taking place Fairey had not been idle and had produced designs for a proposed aeroplane which they called the Stage 6 Hendon. It was to be an all-metal stressed skin four-engined (Kestrels) monoplane bomber with guns in the nose, mid-upper and tail positions, and a retractable undercarriage. The 'powers that be' predictably turned the project down. Two years into the Second World War, or EIGHT years later, when engines had become more powerful and protective fire power had increased – thanks to the advent of the Frazer-Nash and Boulton Paul gun turrets – we had arrived at precisely the conception of the machine Fairey had had in mind. In other words, there had been the makings of a Short Stirling, a Handley Page Halifax or an Avro Lancaster. What a bomber force this country might have had if the Stage Six had been given a development contract; a Lancaster look-alike in, say, 1936/37.

What of the fighter aircraft of the day? As early as 1919 Saunders-Roe built their A10, a neat Kestrel-engined biplane and Westlands had produced a parasol monoplane with a Kestrel engine which they named the Wizard with a performance of 188 mph at 10,000 feet, but in the eyes of the Air Ministry no magic was produced. Being at Brooklands during 1933/34 I had some idea of Hawkers contribution; how the Kestrel engine had turned the Hawker Hornet into the Fury – *the* RAF fighter of its day. In 1931, and not before time, the AM had launched a new specification (F7/30) on the industry for a high performance day and night fighter to be ready by mid-1930. Such a lucrative prize for the winner attracted a baker's dozen of designs from seven or eight different manufacturers. If the number of prototype aircraft powered by Rolls-Royce engines alone was anything to go by, surely a modern machine would evolve.

Although not a flight engine, an experimental sleeve valve Kestrel was built about this period from which valuable experience was gained for later engines. By this time the name Kestrel was getting a little monotonous, so it was as well that the new engine Rolls-Royce produced in 1932 was not another mark of Kestrel – then five years old – and was given a new name. The Goshawk was practically the same size but required less water in its evaporative cooling system, hence incurring less installation weight.

When the High Speed Fury No K3586 had its Kestrel VI replaced by a Goshawk with the complementary replacement of a radiator by wing leading edge condensers, it might well have been considered as an F7/30 contender with its speed of 260 mph. Instead, Hawkers made a Fury-looking machine, the I-PV3, with a neatly installed Goshawk – but the AM were still not impressed. They did not think that the general arrangement drawing of the Goshawk-powered Monoplane Fury (which eventually turned into the Hurricane) which Camm presented in December 1933 had any future either! Bristol offered no less than five projects for the F7/30 contract, two with Rolls-Royce Goshawk engines, the Type 123, a biplane which flew in 1934 but suffered from severe stability problems, while the Type 127 never left the drawing board. It was a pity Westlands' PV4 could not have been a monoplane as originally planned, but a biplane it had to be to conform with the restricted landing speed laid down by the F7/30 Spec and this made it too slow. With its Goshawk mounted amidships behind the pilot, it was a forerunner by five years of the Bell Aerocobra. The other innovation from Yeovil was the Goshawk engined Pterodactyl V (F7/32); an unusual tailless sesquiplane with a rear gunner and two forward facing guns. Blackburn's contribution to F7/30 had a stressed-skin fuselage for its biplane with fabric covered wings mounted in a similar way to the Heyford. The upper wing of this F3 was located on the centre line of the fuselage, the lower being some distance below, between which was placed the radiator (condenser). While I was at Brough, looking after the Goshawk, this F3 did a lot of taxiing, but I never saw it fly.

The name Saunders Roe is synonymous with flying boats but in 1929 they built the Saro A10 fighter powered by a Rolls-Royce 'F' (Kestrel) engine.

103

The Westland Wizard parasol monoplane fighter Mk II (Kestrel).

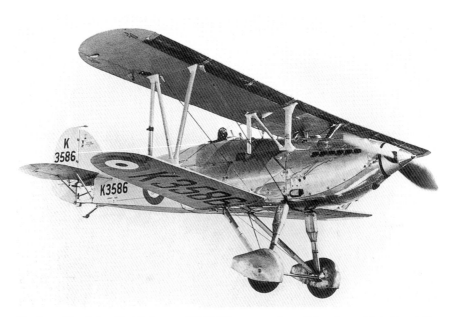

Hawker offered the Air Ministry a PV F7/30 spec version of the above High Speed Fury which they rejected as they did the proposed Fury monoplane (Goshawk). The latter was enlarged to take the Rolls-Royce PV12 (Merlin) so creating the Hurricane.

The Bristol Type 123 fighter (F7/30) with Goshawk engine.

The Westland PV4 (Goshawk), F7/30 fighter.

The Westland Goshawk-engined F7/32 Pterodactyl V two-place fighter.

The Blackburn contribution to the F7/30 competition was the F3 powered by a Goshawk.

By March 1933 it appeared that Supermarines were likely to win the prize with their Type 224 Goshawk-powered gull-winged monoplane with stressed-skin construction and incorporating ideas from the S5 and S6B seaplanes including leading edge condensers similar to those of Hawker's High Speed Fury. But the wing loading had to be decreased to reduce landing speed and the aeroplane was too heavy and top speed was only 228 mph. R J Mitchell was disappointed, he did not like the proposed name of Spitfire and had already started on a new design. Time was now running out. It was mid 1934 and no suitable aeroplane was emerging. Realising the situation J P Folland got to work on the Gloster SS19B (Gauntlet) and in short, cleaned it up, increased its speed and with its new name, Gladiator (SS37), won the F7/30 contract. By 1935 he had secured an order for 200 aeroplanes. So, after four years of effort, this was the best the nation could produce. We were still where we had started, with a biplane for a front-line fighter. It was not until seven year after Spec F7/30 that the modern fighter arrived – thanks to Messrs Hives, Mitchell and Camm, each of whom had elected to go their own private venture ways.

When I got back from South Africa in the Spring of 1938 the Company considered that my leisurely return by sea covered my holiday entitlement for that year, a point with which I could hardly argue, so after three days at home in Somerset, I returned to Derby to catch up with developments that had taken place while I was out of the country. Several new engines were in various stages of design, development and production. This was indeed an exciting period; the middle of the golden age of Rolls-Royce reciprocating aero engines – or was it the beginning of the end? The war clouds were gathering and it was now urgent to get new engines into production. The promising test results with sleeve valves, evaporative cooling, pressure air cooling, or employing the two-stroke cycle, fuel injection etc, would have to wait.

Three engines of basic design were planned for numerous aeroplanes, one of which was already in production; they ranged from 860 to 1800 hp, which would seem to cover the requirements of any size of new aeroplane. The smallest engine – the Peregrine (the ultimate Kestrel), used the same cylinder blocks as the 'top of the range' 24-cylinder X-shaped Vulture. The former was planned for three twin- engined fighters; the Supermarine F18/37 which was never made, the Gloster F9/37 only one of which flew, while only two squadrons of the Westland F37/35 Whirlwind reached the RAF.

At least seven aeroplane makers had plans for the Vulture. Apart from bomber designs there was the Hawker Tornado, Boulton Paul F37/35 and the Blackburn B20 flying boat. As recounted earlier, the last of these aircraft had a sad ending when Ivan Waller, the Rolls-Royce service engineer had to return to earth by parachute. Of the three medium bombers expecting Vultures only the Avro Manchester went into service with the RAF. Even then, only 202 machines were made and a quarter of these were written off in crashes. Sadly the Vulture was not a happy engine, its con-rod/big end design was its Achilles Heel, and derating did little to improve reliability.

The engine in the middle of the range of three, on which I was now concentrating, was quite a different story and had been in production for two years. Whether the name Merlin was used to conjure up thoughts of the Court of King Arthur or a bird of prey, half a century later it is still remembered as the greatest aero engine of all time. This was the engine that saved the Avro Manchester when it turned into a four-engined Lancaster and the Handley Page HP56 by never having its two Vultures installed, so allowing it to metamorphose into the Halifax with four Merlins instead. It also saved this country by winning the Battle of Britain when installed in Hurricanes and Spitfires. But the Vickers B1/35 Warwick was not so lucky. Its two Vultures held up its trials and with changes from Bristol to Pratt & Whitney, then back to Bristol engines, its final role was as a general reconnaissance aeroplane.

In addition to the three twin-engined (Vulture) medium bombers, the Air Ministry invited three manufacturers to tender for a four-engined bomber to Spec B12/36, as a result of which Shorts and Supermarines each received contracts for two aircraft; the Supermarine Type 317, using Kestrels or

By 1933 it appeared that Supermarine's type 224 with a Goshawk engine would win the F7/30 contract.

108

Only one of the two Gloster F9/37 fighters, L8002 flew with Peregines, while a development aeroplane named Reaper with two Merlins was turned down by the Air Ministry.

Merlins among the alternative engines. Both Supermarine fuselages were destroyed by bombing and were never replaced. It appeared that Shorts had a lead by anticipating requirements. I remember seeing the fuselage of the prototype Stirling before I left Rochester in mid 1936 and was told that the bomber was designed around the wings of the existing "C" class Imperial Airways flying boats to speed production. The Stirling was the first four-engined bomber to enter the RAF but not before its performance had been jeopardised by the AM insisting that the wing span be reduced to comply strictly with the B12/36 Spec to enable the aeroplane to fit into the existing RAF hangars. Shades of the Fairey Hendon! This reduced the Stirling's wing area by over 200 sq ft and its ceiling to 17,000 feet, compared with the Lancaster/Halifax figure of around 25,000 feet. So, instead of two or so twin-engined medium bombers, the AM found they had two four-engined heavies (Lancaster and Halifax), and from their four-engined heavy Spec (B12/36) they had one (Stirling).

By this time I had been 'Merlinised' by going on a course and could have been sent to cover Fighter or Bomber stations almost anywhere in the British Isles, as by then there were at least a few Hurricane, Spitfire and Battle Squadrons with this new engine installed. To my surprise, I was posted to my old stamping ground of 1934/35 which was good news: I could see my parents occasionally. On two new stations, Benson and Harwell (the latter now on atomic research) and on some of the old Heyford camps were some ten squadrons of Fairey Battles with Merlin I engines. A number of teething troubles were being experienced in which I found myself involved immediately. What became known as 'Merlinitis' was a disease which took a little sorting out. The first demonstration I had was at Andover with No 12 and No 143 Squadron's Battles, where Flt/Lt 'Jimmy' Riddell took me up to demonstrate how every now and then the engine would cut out and then come to life again when it felt like it! The cure was a fairly simple modification (the introduction of flame traps) and teams of fitters were sent out from the factory to the squadrons and aircraft constructors to rectify all Merlins in Hurricanes, Spitfires, Defiants, Whitleys and Battles, some types of which had not yet reached squadrons.

During the next eighteen months or so I naturally got to know the Merlin like the back of my hand and also became well acquainted with the Battle. According to the press of the day this aeroplane was a high performance light bomber; the fastest in service with the RAF and compared with the Hawker Hart which it replaced, this may have been a fair description. It was certainly well made; right up-to-the-minute with all metal stressed-skin construction. It handled well and had no vices but with a crew of three plus its bomb load, it was just about twice the all-up weight of a Hurricane and yet, like the Hurricane, it had only a single Merlin. In August 1932 the AM had invited several firms to submit design studies for an all metal two-seat light day bomber to specification P27/32 and Fairey – or designer Marcel Labelle – visualised a small single engined monoplane. However, with the AM's revised requirements for extra equipment plus a third crew member, the size of the proposed aeroplane grew until it became obvious to Fairey that either a much larger engine was required, or better still, it should now have two engines, or return to being a lighter aircraft. The Air Ministry would not agree to either plan but with the promise of a development contract, Fairey was persuaded to go ahead with an airframe to the AM's specification. Fairey was still convinced that an aeroplane with two engines or one of greater power would be the final answer, so cleverly built all alternatives possible into a single design which could be switched from one to the other with the minimum of cost and time. He then presented a further project to the AM for a five cannon fighter powered by two Merlins which was promptly turned down. It has been said that the aircraft that was finally built to Spec P23/35 was christened the 'Battle' by Fairey because of the battles he had with the Ministry to get anything finalised at all!

The Battle, however sturdy, could hardly ever have been a successful bomber but, if nothing else, it was superb as a flight-test vehicle for many an engine of the day including Fairey's own Prince and Double Prince, the Vulture, Merlin and the larger Rolls-Royce engines like the air-cooled 24-cylinder sleeve-valve Exe which came later. The Napier Sabre and Dagger, as well as Bristol's Hercules and Taurus engines were also tested in Battles, as were various types of propeller. It must not be forgotten that it was the Battle that launched the Merlin into the RAF.

Two years before the Gladiator won the F7/30 contract, Sydney Camm, the Hawker chief designer, had turned his attention to what he called the Fury Monoplane (F5/34) to be powered by a Goshawk, but then decided to give the Goshawk a miss and in its place used the new PV Merlin engine from Rolls-Royce. The design of the aeroplane was modernised and among other modifications, it was given a retractable undercarriage. Now looking not at all like a Fury, the 'paper' aircraft was known as the 'Interceptor Monoplane' and the AM agreed to purchase one prototype only, for which a new specification (F36/34) was drawn up. The first aeroplane now borrowed the name of an earlier Hawker machine and was christened Hurricane. It flew in the hands of 'George' Bulman for the first time in November 1935, the year in which Glosters started making Gladiator biplanes.

After the failure of Supermarine's Type 224 to come up to scratch, Mitchell and his design team concentrated on their Type 300 (Spitfire), on which work had already commenced and this was designed from the start to take the Merlin. Perhaps the 224 cost Supermarine six months in the competition with Hawker, yet maybe that experience resulted in a lighter, smaller, better Spitfire with its superior performance. Before the Hurricane and Spitfire proved more than adequate to meet the challenges of 1939/40, numerous specifications were drawn up to produce more effective fighters armed with cannon. The F7/30 fiasco of the past decade seemed determined to repeat itself and it was as well that the Hurricane and Spitfire could be developed beyond all expectations. The Tornado, the Hurricane replacement, was not a success in its intended role but did good service as a tank-buster once the initial service problems of the Napier Sabre were overcome. The versatile Spitfire, with a little help from the ever increasing power output of the Merlin – and then the Griffon, became a legend in its time, a time extending to more than twelve years of a continuously expanding role, surely the most famous fighter of all time. The Type 371 Spiteful (F1/43) failed to emulate its predecessor in spite of its ultimate Griffon giving it some 480 mph at altitude, though its 'slimline' (laminar flow) wings were ready-made for the E10/44 Attacker (RR Nene), Supermarine's first 'jet'.

Sadly, the first operational cannon fighter, the F37/35 Westland Whirlwind, was too sophisticated for its time and too small for its Peregrine engines to be replaced by Merlins for improved altitude performance, though two Squadrons went into the RAF. The suggestion of installing air-cooled Exe engines was not taken too seriously. Early in 1938 when the Battle had been in service for about a year the AM realised the shortcomings of the Whirlwind and in a panic asked Fairey to give design details and costs for a twin-engined version of the Battle. Hasty plans were drawn up on an update of the original twin-engined (Merlin) fighter Battle project – only to be cancelled just as quickly! The AM thought they had found a quick (and cheaper?) answer by converting the Beaufort torpedo-bomber into the Bristol Type 156 Beaufighter, but it was hardly surprising that it did not fulfil the role of a Whirlwind replacement, being under-powered and nearly twice the weight of the latter. Merlin XXs were installed to improve performance for five squadrons in service and a pair of Griffons was installed in one aircraft for trials while the Hercules engines were searching for more power.

Perhaps by 1938 it was getting a little too late to consider all the 'paper' aeroplanes that were on offer. These included Supermarine's F18/37 (two Peregines) and their updated Type 327 (two Merlins) six cannon fighter, along with others from Bristol and Boulton Paul using Griffon and Vulture engines. It is a great pity the opportunity was not taken to give Gloster the chance to modify the proven F9/37 to the F29/40 spec with two Merlins, which they renamed Reaper. Had the Martin-Baker MB 5 (F6/42) been given more encouragement from the AM, this six cannon single-engine fighter with its Griffon 83 (contra-prop) might well have become a world beater. Suffice it to say that the Hurricane soldiered on until the end of 1945, and the Spitfire to early 1952, so contriving to pull the dithering Ministry's chestnuts out of the fire until jet fighters became established.

The Avro Manchester with two Vultures had a short production run before being converted to the Lancaster.

The Vickers B1/35 Warwick started life with two Vultures.

The Fairey Battle launched the Merlin into the RAF.

The Supermarine Seafang F Mk 32 was the naval version of the RAF Spiteful with a Griffon 87 (contra-prop).

Two squadrons of the Westland Whirlwind (2 Peregrine) went into service with the RAF. This aircraft is the prototype with 'handed' engines i.e. they turned in opposite ways.

The Martin-Baker MB 5 (F18/39) with contra-prop Griffon might well have become the best wartime fighter.

CHAPTER TEN

War is declared

With the imminence of war being so plain, I was anxious to get in a weekend at home with my parents who had by this time moved to Winscombe. This worked in well with a planned visit to Boscombe Down on Saturday 2 September 1939. To say the Boscombe visit was routine would be an exaggeration, as that Sunday was the crucial day and it was rumoured that Boscombe's Battle Squadrons, 88 and 218, were off to France that very day. There was certainly plenty of activity with last-minute spares and equipment being loaded frantically into the aircraft, and the fitting of a crude form of armour plating – a belated gesture to give the crews some moral support, not that they needed any at that moment. They were confident in their aircraft and in their own ability to do whatever job they were called upon to carry out. During the past eighteen months I had got to know the 'Battle Boys' pretty well and was now getting involved in the excitement of the moment. There was nothing much more I could do on the engine side; all the Merlins were up to date with all the latest modifications and were 'healthy', so I just hung about while they were run up and checked. I forget which Squadron took off first, and after forming up, flew over the aerodrome for the last time. All this reminded me that a few miles down the road lay Neatheravon, where in June 1914 the RFC had foregathered before moving over to France; history was repeating itself. Little did I know that within ten days I would also be on my way to join the Advanced Air Striking Force (AASF) over there.

The sun was shining that weekend at home, even if the outlook was grim, and somehow it was comforting to be with one's parents on such a fateful day when a decision would be made one way or the other. I didn't get home often enough, but when I was there on a Sunday we often attended the 11 o'clock service in the parish church. At 11 o'clock on this Sunday we heard a different message: *"This morning the British Ambassador in Berlin handed the German Government a final note … unless we heard from them by 11 o'clock … a state of war would exist between us …"* After the initial shock and mother had dried her tears, I began to wonder what part I was going to play. Uncertainty did not last long: just as we were finishing lunch the phone rang and it was my boss instructing me to proceed immediately to Biggin Hill – probably the most important Fighter Station in the defence of London. Why only one station to look after – why the sudden switch to Hurricanes with which I had had no experience, I was not told – just to get there. At least it was something definite to do, which is always so much better than waiting. Right then there was plenty to do preparing for a hasty departure. Just before I left, cousin John Bisdee called and informed us that he had been given a fortnight's leave, as apparently in the panic of everything the Air Ministry didn't quite know what to do with the Volunteer Reserve (VR) boys. At that time, John was a Sergeant Pilot and flew Spitfires. He did some very good work in 609 Squadron and ended the war as a Group Captain OBE, DFC.

That night I got as far as Croydon just as it was getting dark and found it almost impossible to get a bed for the night but eventually found digs of sorts. The landlady had a husband who spent the night at his ARP post, a daughter who worked in a factory and one lodger. I slept soundly in the attic until just after midnight, when I was awakened by that now familiar sound of the wailing air raid sirens. It was very unnerving hearing them for the first time, as thousands of people who were living in London that night will agree. Nobody knew what air raids on towns were going to be like. I jumped out of bed, grabbed my little cardboard box (gas mask), and rushed downstairs to the basement kitchen which was empty. The rest of the inmates had apparently slept through everything, so I proceeded to wake everyone up. We all sat in the kitchen where the landlady told me my fortune, reading my hand in a very professional way. It turned out that she had been a fortune-teller in a circus at one time. I remember she told me that I would be taking a trip overseas before the year was out but this didn't impress me much at the time. There seemed to be a lot of aeroplanes overhead but no bombs had dropped, so we concluded they were ours. Getting tired of waiting, I went back to bed but No 3 Squadron (Hurricanes) kept me awake long after the all-clear went. They seemed to take a long time getting back to Croydon aerodrome and landing. They certainly had a nice moonlit night for their first operational, but false, 'scramble'.

Arriving at Biggin Hill I met the CO, Wing Commander Grice, DFC, and the Engineer Officer whom I knew well, Flying Officer (F/O) Jackson. These were the only two officers I knew, having only once been there before and that was many moons previously. There were two Hurricane Squadrons – No 32 and No 79 on the station, plus No 601 (City of London – Auxiliary Air Force) Squadron (Blenheims), and I really couldn't see how I was going to occupy my time just looking after two (Merlin) Squadrons or 24 aircraft when I was used to watching over at least fourteen. As there was no room in the Mess, I found a room down the road at the famous White Hart Hotel, Brasted. A few nights later my boss rang and asked whether I would like to stay at Biggin or go to France with a Hurricane wing. It was no contest and I chose the latter without hesitation. Orders were to proceed the following day to Tangmere, the home of No 1 Squadron (Hurricanes) who had been ordered to France, and I was to go with them. Very thrilled, I rushed over to

Tangmere and found that the CO, Squadron Leader Halahan, had already flown over in a Miles Magister Maggie to sort things out before the Squadron arrived. The first person I met on arrival was F/O P P Hanks ('Ducks'), who gave me a beer in the mess but was quite firm about seeing my passes etc. Nobody was expecting me but F/O M H Brown ('Hilly'), the adjutant at the time, remembered something about a Rolls-Royce man joining them. I had never met anyone in No 1 or 43, the second famous Fighter Squadron living at Tangmere, and so at first I felt a little out of place. First thing was to book a room at The Dolphin in Chichester where Pat Bate, the Rolls-Royce representative from whom I was taking over, was also staying. Later that evening a few No 1 boys came in for a drink – perhaps their last in England. I did not know more than one or two by sight then, but as far as I remember, the party consisted of Ducks, 'Johnny' (F/Lt P R Walker), Hilly, 'Leak' (F/Lt C G H Crusoe), Leslie (F/O Clisby) and 'Boy' (P/O P Mould). What a gathering of flying talent to find in one small pub, would be realised in the coming months! As I was staying in the hotel I fixed it for them to have a drink with me after hours, or rather I thought I had. After a few cross words with the waiter and the manageress, we got no drinks, and the boys went back to camp, leaving me feeling and looking a bit flat.

The following day the boys hung around the Mess anteroom waiting for the word to go. It was a lovely morning and the atmosphere was full of suppressed excitement. The pilots wandered about and tried to look calm. Some picked up papers and pretended to read, while others tried to show that everything was quite normal by sprawling in sofas or armchairs and closing their eyes but not one of them had any intention of falling asleep just then. At last the Squadron was called to readiness and a few minutes later an unforgettable scene took place. No 1 Squadron was off to France, and to let off a bit of steam, there followed a gentle spot of 'beating up' the aerodrome. We wished them luck whilst the Station CO was trying to get the numbers of the low flying aeroplanes in true 'red tape' style. He knew some of those boys were beating up their home station for the last time and would never see England again but it is a serious offence to low fly over an aerodrome, and offenders have to be punished, so he felt it was his duty. However, a few members of 43 who were watching 'helped' him by getting the numbers muddled up. Just as No 1 had taken to the air, 73, 85 and 87 Squadrons appeared on the scene, as they were to land at Tangmere to refuel before flying over the Channel. The sky seemed full of Hurricanes and there were aircraft taking off and landing all over the aerodrome. Eventually things died down and, led by Johnny, No 1 landed at Le Havre – the first Fighter Squadron to land in France.

Leak was left behind to bring the rear party out, consisting of the ground

" .... As No 1 took off for France ... watched by No. 43, the other Tangmere ... Hurricane Squadron". Painting by Sqn Ldr Chris Golds.

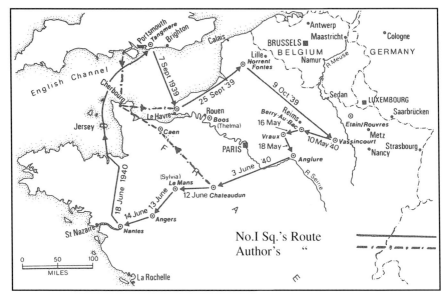

The routes through France.

crew, the Squadron Warrant Officer (W/O) Wortley and F/O Chambers ('Jimmy Champers') and I was to go along with them. We were not to leave until the following Friday, so I paid a visit to Derby and had a night at home before returning to Tangmere. Father came down with me so that he could take the car home for safe keeping. I hated saying goodbye to him. This was a different farewell from all the many others I had had to make. That afternoon, Friday 14th, I went to the Medical Officer (M/O) to have both arms filled with lots of anti-this and anti-that, which was intended to stop me catching all the bad things one is supposed to get in France. I just about 'passed out' that evening in the Mess and was told I looked awful, so fell into bed about 8 o'clock. I didn't get much sleep, especially as we were awakened at 5.00am the following morning, me feeling ill and stiff. We grabbed a hasty breakfast, our kit was thrown out of a window into a lorry, and by 6.00am all were present and correct on the tarmac. After roll-call the whole party climbed into three double-decker buses and off we set for Chichester station. We had a wait of about half an hour for the train and after a short run we arrived at Southampton Docks feeling ready for another breakfast. Following numerous roll-calls, checking of numbers and equipment, the ground crews were marched aboard the channel steamer which was to transport us to France. Leak, Jimmy and I found the Marine

120

Café, which was full to overflowing but was the only place on the docks we could get a bite to eat. I sent a wire home, and we were on board by 2.00pm to find that our cabins had to be given up to some nurses who had suddenly turned up. These ladies of mercy were quick to discover that their cabin doors would lock from the inside! The troops lay about the decks and down below, while we tried to make ourselves comfortable in the smoking room. Here I met John Martin, the other Rolls-Royce representative who was going to France to look after Nos 85 and 87, the two Hurricane Squadrons attached to the British Expeditionary Force, the Army regiments attached to the French Army.

It was good to see John, as I had not known anyone else was going out from Rolls-Royce and we stuck together as we rather felt out of place being, as I thought, the only civilians aboard. Later, when it was found that the nurses didn't want all the cabins, John and I shared one. The ship sailed late in the afternoon but we anchored inside the boom until midnight, when our convoy of six troop ships proceeded on its zigzag course across the Channel. We awoke in the morning to find ourselves in Cherbourg harbour, which seemed full of troop ships, filled mostly with soldiers. We docked at 8.00am and boarded the train waiting for us on the quayside and were given tea, which looked like coffee, but it was wet and hot which was all that mattered. Leak, Jimmy and I shared a compartment and for the first part of the journey we occupied ourselves by converting English money into francs which I worked out with great accuracy with my pocket 'guessing stick' (slide rule). At the first stop we paid the men in francs, and some of them thought they were getting a year's pay by the amount of paper money we gave them but they were not slow in learning the value of the franc.

The train was slow and we seemed to be stopping constantly. At every station French nurses and girls gave us free coffee and rolls, while passing through orchards the peasants threw us apples. They were all pleased to see us. Having skirted Rouen, we got onto a line which took us to Le Havre, where we arrived at 2.30am on 17 September, having left Tangmere early on 15 September, and by now we were all full of bully beef and biscuits. Someone managed to muster the men in the dark and the CO, Sqn Ldr 'Bull' Halahan, and Donald Hills (Equipment Officer) came to the station to meet us. Leak introduced me to The Bull but he couldn't see me and I couldn't see him, so we were just polite to each other. The French didn't seem to bother much about the blackout, but it was pitch dark so we couldn't see that the building we were being taken to was a convent, which was to be our Mess for three weeks. All the boys were asleep but Leak had them awake fairly soon, and there were shouts and yells coming from all over the building. The rooms were pretty small, and not enough of them, so for the remainder of that night Hilly Brown invited me to put my camp bed in his room. There was not really enough space for one bed, let alone two, but at least we had a roof over our heads. And so we were now in France and the first fortnight of the war was over and nothing had happened. Perhaps I should have mentioned that someone had taken the precaution of evacuating all the nuns before the arrival of the RAF!

I understand from my 'Oxford Concise' of current English, that knackers are folk who buy worn-out horses for slaughter, and can find no other formal meaning for the word. I have never been a horse dealer in any sense of the word, so my RAF nickname can only refer to a derivation of my surname. About the first morning after our arrival Johnny Walker asked Leak what my name was, and when he replied *"Henniker"* Johnny suggested shortening it and calling me "Knackers" – and it stuck. I've noticed that when my name is called 'across a crowded room' at a party or such like, there is a hiccup in the babble of conversation and a few heads turn! Can't think why: it has been published in Paul Richey's *Fighter Pilot* and Michael Shaw's *No 1 Squadron* after all!

No 73 had also arrived and were sharing the Mess and the aerodrome with us. Apparently things hadn't gone too well at a recent guest night and there had been a couple of scraps through some misunderstanding, so feelings between the two Squadrons were rather strained. This was a thousand pities as No 1 and 73 were now sister Squadrons and were to work together throughout the French campaign. The result was that it was some time before they got on friendly terms again. However, they spent three very pleasant weeks at Le Havre although Leak and I had only a fortnight there having arrived a week after the rest. I had got to know Leak pretty well by now and though I hardly knew any of the others at the time, that was soon to be rectified. So far it was a grand war. Flying consisted chiefly of practice, firing guns into the sea and keeping an eye on the shipping in the event of attacks from the Germans who never showed up. No 1 made a trip to Cherbourg and the boys spent the night there sleeping in a large hangar, which I understand was not fun, while 'Pussy' Palmer smoked his foul French cigarettes most of the night and didn't help matters. Personally I didn't enjoy Le Havre very much and I think it was for two reasons. I was still a civilian and so felt rather out of place; whenever I went into the town with the boys people were looking at me and asking who in the hell I was and was I a fifth columnist? The other reason was that I hadn't yet got to know the others and so did not go out in the evenings often and, of course, an evening spent in an empty convent was as dull as ditch water. Although I did not get around as much as the others, on odd afternoons a couple or so of us might get a lift into town and have a bath at the Hotel Nomandie, do some shopping or have a drink at one of the cafés. In the evening a drink at the Guillaume Tell, followed by a terrific meal at the Grosse Tonne, where

No 73 Squadron's Hurricanes by the monastery at Le Havre.

the food and cooking could not be beaten anywhere, was a typical programme. The Grosse Tonne was in a street where one would least expect to find it – or was it? Right next door was La Lune, an establishment where the young ladies were not there just to have a glass of champagne with you. Madame Gladys wasn't always best pleased with us as we used to sit around drinking beer, and if the girls didn't like drinking beer with us instead of the usual champagne, well, they just had to look around for other customers. Madame sang to us one night, and while the girls giggled we tried to keep straight faces, as it was all very serious. Poor girls – what a life they had.

Some of the boys had made friends with the locals and others made several trips out to Etretat, where a hotel had been taken over by the American Hospital in Paris. (Leak does not talk much about the very pleasant fortnight he spent there later after he crashed in his Hurricane!). I was told that the nurses were good sorts and those who went there had fun, but thankfully I never had to go there to verify this. There was also a golf course and one or two produced clubs and played a round or two. Stanley Baldy, in particular, was a very keen player. On those evenings we stayed in the Mess, our bar came into operation, which incidentally ran at a heavy loss and as a lot of the French drinks were new to us the results were amusing. One night – a champagne night – Ducks and I got very whistled but we were happy. I think Pernod was met for the first time by most of us, and four or five of those produced disastrous results. In these early days it was still a good war. After the first week, the Sergeant Pilots who had been sleeping in the attic of the convent were turned out to make room for the late arrivals of the two Squadrons. This was when I found myself with a real bed, in the attic with about nine others. It was pretty foul as there was hardly any light or ventilation and we all washed in one basin, which caused a bit of a shambles in the mornings. One invariably got awakened every night as there was sure to be at least one member of the 'dormitory' who returned late, and kicked things over as he tried to find his bed, but it did have its lighter moments.

One night Jimmy 'Champers' Chambers came in late with Dicky Martin of 73, (who was later to become the Prisoner of Luxembourg), both a little 'under the weather' and having a terrific argument. It seemed that Dicky had had a row with George Plinston that evening and, stimulated by a few drinks, those two had decided to settle things with pistols the following morning. (By the light of day, of course, the whole thing would have been forgotten). Jimmy, being the Armament Officer to No 1, had decided he should step in and see what was happening. So, as I woke up, the scene was opened for me by Dicky and Jimmy – also a bit whistled – coming through the door of the attic waving their guns about. Jimmy was saying that Dicky was too young to have a gun anyway and what was more Jimmy would take it from him. In fact, he would put Dicky and George back-to-back and finish them both off with one bullet! Now I don't know how serious they were about all this, but the fact remained that there was a lot of shouting and waving of guns going on. Worse, my bed was in a direct line with Dicky and Jimmy so the whole thing seemed like bad news to me. However, after a lot more talking, I think

Home mail arrives at Le Havre from Tangmere, in a conscripted DH89 Dragon Rapide.

Jimmy and Dicky finished up by just about kissing each other before falling asleep and they both forgot about George and the duel.

Then there was always the body of Pussy Palmer, horizontal on his bed with a foul French cigarette in his mouth, and Liepman, our – fifth columnist, we thought – interpreter, who generally went to bed with his uniform on and only shaved when he felt like it. The weather was still good and when not around the aircraft, we dug trenches, read letters from home or heated water in an old boiler for a bath in the garden. Boy and I were having a bath one afternoon when the de Havilland Dragon arrived from Tangmere with our mail. Somebody threw me a letter which went straight into the water and it took an hour to decipher when it dried out. Of the original convent furniture – beds, tables, chairs, kitchen utensils etc – there was none, but I still have a cushion I found laying about which I 'borrowed' for a pillow and used it as such for the nine months I was in France. It had a crest worked into the centre on one side with the motto *Pro Deo et Patria*. The same God I thought, but a different country – and now the same enemy!

I introduced myself to the CO of 73 soon after arrival and got what seemed a rather cold reception. Their engines were not giving any trouble and they did not want any help. As I had travelled to France with No 1, I suppose he looked upon me as a member of No 1 and so was not exactly welcoming. This was all altered later on and when I was posted to 73 for a while, I got on very well with all the boys. There was now plenty of time to take stock of my position. Rolls-Royce had asked me to come to France and I had agreed without hesitation; beyond that it seemed I was more or less on my own. There was never any question about kitting me out with anything, I bought my own camp-kit as I knew I would require one and took what clothes seemed appropriate. I had no passport or identity card and from that day to this nobody at Rolls-Royce was the least concerned from whence I could get any cash while in France. I treated all these factors as normal and was expected, and indeed used to, making my own arrangements. I had signed a new two-year contract with the Company – not that I had much option – in which, among the ten clauses detailing what I could, should and must not do, was one which stated that after three months of illness or accident … *"we are to be at liberty forthwith to determine the employment"*. So what was there to worry about? Just the ticket to go to war on, where accidents seldom happen and never any illness! Before departing from England, Tangmere had given me a tin hat, gas mask and cape and I had had as many inoculations as both arms could decently hold in one go! But what was I doing here exactly? Indeed, what were we all doing here? The war was three weeks old and fighting had not yet started and what were the only two fighter squadrons with the Advanced Air Striking Force (AASF) doing in this particular spot – a job which could have been done from England? Why were we not up close to the Battles which our Hurricanes were supposed to protect? Again, why did two Hurricane Squadrons require my services while the ten or so Battle Squadrons (which I knew well) called for no help at all? And finally, what was starting to concern me more than a little was that here I was a foreigner, in France, in civilian clothes and a war was on. We thought even the spies were in uniform! Under these conditions I was not in a position to ask too many questions, just keep my eyes and ears open. I did not know that just before leaving for France the Air Officer Commanding (AOC) Fighter Command, had reviewed No 1 Squadron and told them that their job was to protect the British Army and Bomber Force from the Luftwaffe. That sooner or later the Germans would launch a tremendous attack (we had to wait until 10 May), violating Belgium and possibly Luxembourg and little help would be forthcoming from the French.

I was also not to know that the British Government had promised the French that the whole of the RAF's bombing force would be used to resist an invasion of her country, and would operate under the direction of the French High Command – including not only the AASF, short range (Battles and two Blenheim) Squadrons, but also home-based long-range bombers. That France had virtually no Air Force to speak of, and that Goering had a tremendous one. All this became too tragically apparent later on, but for the moment I was quite pleased to leave Le Havre, in total ignorance of the facts.

The boys had made lots of friends in Le Havre and when we left on 28 September and the Squadron 'beat up' the town with some close formation flying the folk were thrilled but sorry to see us go. I went to our new base in advance of the Squadron with Billy Stratton in the Squadron Maggie and a cold trip it was too. We met a French flying-boat of old design patrolling the coast, and so we formatted it and after doing a bit of waving in an 'Entente Cordiale' fashion we left it to carry on its work. Actually we overtook the poor old thing – in a Maggie. Doc Cross and Sqn Ldr Pemberton ('Pembers' was the Operations Officer for both Squadrons, but until No 67 Wing was formed, he lived with No 1) had gone on ahead by road to our new aerodrome at Norrent Fontes and the only thing they found in the way of buildings of any sort was a nearby café which was proud to be called The Green Dragon. The actual village was on the far side of the aerodrome where it had been decided that 73 should dig itself in. After landing we had a typical French lunch in a private room at The Dragon (it only had three rooms) with a French doctor and two French Army officers. After lunch Billy took Doc back to Le Havre and I was left with Pembers to organise the camp. My extra-mural duties had started! The aerodrome was of a large 'L' shape with quite a good surface, but there was very little cover around and a winter there under canvas would only be appreciated by Boy Scouts. At this period, Pembers took rather a dim view of me, quite seriously thought I should be made a Corporal and was rather stand-offish, as I was still, of course, in 'civvies'. Naturally the Doc and Bill Stratton took this news back to the Squadron at Le Havre and it was considered a good joke all round. When the Squadron arrived the following day I was dubbed 'Acting Corporal' for quite a time. Some joker labelled one of the seats in the latrines 'For Acting Corporals only' just to rub it in! Soon after this when the Bull instructed me to put on a uniform, poor old Pember's face dropped a mile when he saw me appear one day as a Flight Lieutenant!

Pembers and I had chosen a site to pitch the tents in two small fields at the edge of the aerodrome where it was at least surrounded by hedges. We chose the corner near the St. Omer road, which was straight and bordered with tall poplar trees evenly spaced on either side. This reminded one of the pictures of our troops in France in the last war, which was sobering. On a clear day one could see Vimy Ridge from the aerodrome, and on the other side of the road we dug up an old German tin helmet near the coal mine which had sheltered the wounded of a Scottish Regiment a quarter of a century before. It was hard to realise that the war had started again and after a month everything still seemed quiet and peaceful.

The Squadron arrived the next day and I understand they had a bit of a party at Le Havre the night before as several white faces climbed unsteadily out of the Hurricanes and Paul immediately went to sleep on the floor boards of one of the tents. We eventually got settled in and pinched a large French

'Boy' Mould and Paul Richey relaxing at Norrent Fontes, Pas de Calais.

tent for the Mess. Pembers spent a lot of the Mess funds in buying pansy chairs, which we thought unnecessary and not in keeping with the trestle dining table. Our tents were lined up along one hedge and once we were settled in and had made a certain amount of 'furniture' out of petrol tin cases, we got down to digging trenches, which provided us with exercise. The manufacture of tent furniture out of petrol tin boxes reminded me so much of my native Tasmania, where boxes holding two four-gallon tins of kerosene were used for all sorts of jobs, while the tins made anything from a flower pot to the roof of a house. As a lad I had made a very successful raft once out of six kerosene tins and four boxes which provided many hours of amusement.

As already mentioned, soon after arriving, The Bull told me I would have to wear a uniform and until my Commission came through I must borrow one. As is usual with a crowd of types in the RAF, everyone seems to be wearing other people's belongings and so before the evening was out I found I had borrowed Johnny's tunic, Duck's trousers and Pussy's hat, while the remainder of the outfit was my own. Jimmy Chambers took umbrage straight away. He, the old so-and-so, had been in the Service for twenty-five years or more and was still a Flying Officer, and here was I, not in the Service at all, prancing about as a Flight Lieutenant, and with wings up too. It was all too much for him and he started talking about being captured, authority, the King's Regulations, and twenty-five years ago…. Later I went to Paris in one of Shepherd's uniforms, and Lewis' greatcoat. A Pilot Officer's uniform was thought to be a little nearer reality than a Flight Lieutenant's. One day John Martin – the second Company man in France – came over to our camp, though not to see me. Apparently he had been put in charge of scrounging some plumbing (he was looking after Nos 85 and 87 – the two other Hurricane Squadrons in France), for a shower for the Mess he was living in and thought our spot would be a likely place to find the odd pipe or two. I felt very proud when he gazed upon my uniform, as he was still in civvies, and as we strolled about together talking things over I almost convinced myself that I had been in the Service for at least four years. Later John, still in civilian clothes, got locked up by the French a couple of times and had to be bailed out by the CO of the Squadron he was with.

There was a certain amount of flying most days but the Germans never came and everyone was beginning to wonder whether there was really a war on at all. We experienced little trouble with the Hurricanes or Merlins and the couple of times I went over to 73, all their aircraft were serviceable but I only saw the NCOs and didn't look up any of the Officers. Billy Drake took me up in the Maggie one afternoon with a view of doing a bit of dual, but my first attempt at a landing shook him so much that before I knew where I was he was shaking me by doing slow rolls over the camp and then did three turns of a spin, which nearly made me lose interest in flying altogether.

George Plinston was a champion scrounger and was always getting up to his old tricks. Every now and then he would 'find' a stray hen or duck which was just asking to be caught, and good eating they were too! He also had a pleasant habit of finding corn on the cob growing at the side of the road, or so he said, and we didn't ask questions! Boiled in a petrol tin of water and spread with butter they were excellent, and when I closed my eyes and let my mind wander, I was back sitting next to Bob Preller (later Major, DFC) at the Garrison Officer's Mess at Roberts Heights, Pretoria. But there, the heat of the Transvaal melted your butter before you got it onto your corn cob. I might mention that Bob Preller and I had become great friends while I was in South Africa and there is a very interesting account in *South Africa Fights* of how he won his DFC – the first member of the South African Air Force to receive this decoration. He was certainly a good pilot and I have a photograph I took from the back of a Hawker Hartebeest while he was flying me in the Premier open-cast diamond mine outside Pretoria. Well, if it wasn't actually *in* the mine, the photograph shows that the sides of the mine were just about level with the aircraft!

It is strange looking back and realising that we were only eleven days at Norrent Fontes, but we saw so much of each other, and waited so long for something to happen, that it seemed like a month at least. The day we left was quite eventful. The weather was not good and threatened to get worse later, and it was getting cold. The Bull, therefore, decided to leave directly it was light, so the whole camp was aroused at 5.00am and after a hasty breakfast Billy Stratton and I climbed into the Maggie feeling cold and dirty. No fires or water were obtainable as most of the camp had been packed up the night before. The Squadron took off soon after us and after ten minutes flying the boys had overhauled and passed us in their Hurricanes. We decided to take a slightly different compass course from the Squadron as we had ideas of calling in at Mourmelon and having a decent breakfast with the 'Battle' boys (No 88 Squadron – my old friends from Boscombe Down). Billy was flying at about 1000 feet and the Squadron were two miles off, on our port bow in open formation, when I saw what seemed in the grey light of dawn four red balls of fire leaping up from the ground into the midst of their Hurricanes. For a second I thought it must be a Very signal of some sort, but when the Squadron immediately broke formation, I realised that they were being fired upon. I tapped Billy on the shoulder and we both had a good laugh – but only for a second – as soon I, at any rate, was laughing on the other side of my face. Those four shells – there may have been more – acted as an unofficial signal to more gentlemen down below with itchy trigger fingers. The next thing I knew the little Maggie gave a nasty lurch as a dirty great puff of smoke appeared much too near our port wing tip, and it was obviously something big. Maybe I should have gone by road after all, and at least I would be warm down there and I wouldn't have that horrid dry throat one gets when one is scared stiff! We were still at a thousand feet and of course still over French territory, but the fact remained that we were being fired at, so I bent down and put my hand on the release pin of my Sutton Harness (seat belts), I didn't see how they could miss us at that height and, as there was not much air between us and the ground, I was going to see to it that I wasted no time in bailing out if necessary. I looked behind and now a smaller gun had started firing at us and was sending up tracer shells in batches of four in quick succession. They appeared to come up straight at us and then, for no reason at all – except Billy's skill, they seemed to disappear. Billy was taking lots of avoiding action by now and our inoffensive little Magister was twisting and turning all over the sky. We were certainly not over Germany and if those shooting at us could not see our colours at a thousand feet they didn't deserve to be in anybody's army. Eventually the shooting stopped and I sighed a large sigh of relief when our wheels touched Mother Earth again.

Billy and I touched down at Mourmelon without further incident but the anti-aircraft practice was not yet over. Our ground crews were to be brought on later by four Air France passenger aircraft which the French loaned us for the occasion and Paul Richey was in charge of the party. These aeroplanes, admittedly similar to the German Junkers 52, were not as lucky as we had been and at least two were hit. One had to turn back and the other got a shell through its fuselage and tail plane, and another shell through a wing. However, there were no casualties though we thought there would be a row about the incident. Things were hushed up a bit, however, and we didn't hear much about it. The story as we heard it was that a British Territorial Unit were the culprits and before coming over to France had never fired the new Bofors guns, neither had they any idea what the difference was between British, French and German aeroplanes. They said they had not been warned of our movements and so directly they saw any aircraft at all they just had to start shooting. (I seem to remember hearing of similar incidents occurring in the 1914 war). They certainly wanted practice, but why pick on No 1 Squadron and a poor little Maggie for their targets? No 73 moved later in the day and got lost for a while when the weather closed in, but they did not have the same experience, so maybe they flew on a different course. Charles Gardner in his book, *AASF*, says *"About this time there was a lot of grumbling about the French AA gunners – who were apt to take a crack at anything within range. … Several 'Battles' complained at being shot at – and so did one Hurricane and, of all things – a poor inoffensive little Miles Magister"*.

I had met the CO of No 88 Squadron on several occasions at Boscombe

British and a few French aircraft were shot at by anti-aircraft guns over French territory. Billy Stratton and the author had this experience in "...of all things, a poor inoffensive little Magister" (Charles Gardner).

Down before the war, so when we landed at Mourmelon we went straight to the village where the Squadron HQ was established. It was a good thing the CO remembered me, as both Billy and I must have made a sorry picture, looking more like tramps than anything else. I had no hat, a polo sweater under my tunic, while an old raincoat and a pair of gumboots completed my dress. We were both unshaven and in need of a good haircut. The CO was very kind to us and offered us baths and breakfast, for which we were taken to the Mess. No 88 were lucky in having a real live house for a Mess and, as there was little for the bombers to do at that period, the anteroom was full of clean faces, uniforms with all their buttons done up and even regulation shirts and shoes. Yes, they certainly took a poor view of these scruffy Fighter boys turning up as we did. However, after a very pleasant breakfast, we bade them farewell without waiting for a bath. I felt very guilty in my Flight Lieutenant's uniform and of course I had to do all the talking as I was the (pseudo) senior officer and it made it even more embarrassing, the CO knowing me. However, he asked no questions!

We, or rather Billy, located Vasincourt Aerodrome without being used as a target again and found that the whole Squadron had landed safely. Arriving at our new aerodrome, the outlook was not rosy as it was cold and raining and when we eventually got into the village of Neuville-sur-Marne, which was to be our home for many weeks, we were rather depressed. The Army Signals had taken over the large room of the village Mairie and we suspected this supported the only fire in the whole village. Doc Cross had been in the village for a few days to get things organised and if he had not made the best of the place, he had certainly found the right spot in Bar-le-Duc, our nearest town. This spot was the Hotel de Metz et Commerce and Madame Jean will never be forgotten by anyone who served in No 1 Squadron. It was at The Metz where the boys were now having the best meal they had had since Le Havre, while we shivered in Neuville. Somehow, Leak was left in the village too, so while the rest of the boys were making merry, Billy, Leak and I caught up with our toilette. This involved getting mugs of water heated on the fire and scraping our faces with a borrowed razor in the room in which we were later to spend long winter evenings and days while it snowed and rained incessantly. In this same room combat reports and letters to home were written, a German prisoner, an ENSA concert party and Sir Cyril Newall were entertained. It was also the room in which Lord Londonderry, Billy Cotton and others ate with us, and where we sometimes got a little whistled. If walls have ears, and those four could talk, they would have an interesting tale to tell.

CHAPTER ELEVEN

The village of Neuville

For the first few days at Neuville we had our meal in the one and only café in the village – chiefly consisting of eggs and anything the local inhabitants could supply direct from the land. In the evenings we got a good meal at The Metz Hotel, and this programme lasted for about three days until we could move into the farm building we had taken over as a Mess. When we were settled, it was here we had all our meals and only went to Bar-le-Duc for a night out. Neuville itself was a small village of only a few hundred inhabitants and it was quite amazing how it managed to absorb the whole Squadron as it did. The choice of building for a Mess was unfortunate but there was nothing else available at the time.

It comprised two rooms of a farmhouse and a kitchen situated across a passage, which was the access to the farm buildings behind. One room was used as an ante-room and the second, leading off it, was our dining room. Both were too small and smelled of horse manure, though with the change of wind direction we were treated to the alternative pigsty atmosphere! In the evenings the wind whistled under the door and through the broken window and even with a fire in each room the place was miserable. As the kitchen range would not work, all our cooking had to be done on oil stoves in the passage, and when a meal was ready it was generally cold by the time it had been dished up and brought in to us. The building was also in a dirty part of the village and most of us had to walk quite a way to get there from our billets – generally through mud and snow. Whatever the deficiencies, we made the best of it and there were plenty of times when we had fun there. Later on The Bull suggested that the top room of the Mairie would make a good Mess; few opposed the idea and Pembers, who had been using it as an 'ops' room, had to clear out. But the old Mess holds memories for me and there are several incidents to recall before moving to our new quarters. It was here we organised our first concerts and had rehearsals across the road in Secundus Palmer's billet; and when Boy Mould brought down the Squadron's first enemy aircraft, the trophies were hung proudly on the oak panelled walls of the ante-room. The old Mess was the venue for the village mayor to air his grievances. He was against us coming to his parish in the first place, as it would attract the attention of the German bombers, and he did his best to encourage us to move on. As time went on and no bombs were dropped, and money started to flow from the visitors' pockets into those of the villagers, the old boy realised that anyone who did anything worthy of being called a trade, made more money in those seven months than they had

Some members of No 1 Squadron outside the Mess at Neuville: Drake, Clisby, Lorimer, Hanks, Mould, Halahan (CO), Demozay, Walker, Brown, Richey, Kilmartin, Stratton, Palmer.

ever made before or were likely to make in years.

What started 'Black Sunday' nobody will ever know. It was just one of those things which have a habit of developing from time to time. It was a foul day and there had been no flying in the morning, so midday found several of us in the ante-room when somebody opened a bottle of champagne. A few more were opened and before very long things began to look as though a lunch time session was developing. Even the smell of the horse manure had changed to that of violets and from the noise that had now developed as more of the boys came into the Mess, a passer-by might have thought that a party was underway and that a lot of people were happy and enjoying themselves. We were, and nobody cared a hoot whether The Bull stayed in bed an extra few days with his bout of 'flu, or whether he joined the party. Now we thought this a little unfair, but just as we had lined the champagne bottles up on the table and Hilly was starting another row who should walk in but the Air Officer Commanding (AOC) plus the usual retinue of Staff Officers. We must have looked very sheepish, having visions of Air Vice Marshal Playfair taking drastic measures to stop the 'Young

Blood of England' from drowning themselves in drink. He spoke to some of us but nobody could remember what any of us said in reply, though all were certain that a pretty large 'black' had been put up. One of our more sober members conducted the visiting party round the village and we later heard a rumour that the AOC considered the whole village smelled like a stable and that it was enough to drive anyone to drink! The village wasn't quite as bad as that, but the fact remained that there were no repercussions from the AOC's visit: indeed he had lived up to his name!

I don't really think any of us could have faced lunch that day, and in the early afternoon I remember finding myself and Billy Stratton conducting Ducks along the main street towards his billet, as this was where he was determined to go and he obviously had little chance of making it by himself. When we got to his house, Billy pushed off and left Ducks in my tender care and he proved a bit of a handful. No sooner had we got up stairs when he expressed a desire to visit the mayor; not the kind of thing one did for fun under normal conditions. However, Ducks was quite adamant and so it wasn't long before Monsieur le Mayor was inviting us into his house, having heard our rather unsteady and noisy approach. The mayor was in his Sunday best, and his sitting room was full of his housekeeper (his wife must have died a decade before), his nephew and three other men folk who had come in from far and wide to have not-very-important-looking papers signed. It was certainly the occasion to produce a bottle of home brewed Kirsch and before we had been inside the house for more than a few minutes, sure enough – out it came. Ducks was supplying the entertainment for the gathering, while I was going easy on the Kirsch, as I had a horrid feeling I would have to get both of us home later on. As my normal slender command of the French language increased, so my understanding of the general conversation diminished, but I got the impression that the company present were getting rather a kick out of seeing one of the brave young Englishmen who normally diced with death with a clear head on a clear day, was now in a thick haze similar to the day's weather. If I remember correctly, the first bottle was half full when it was put on the table, and by the time the third was coming up, Ducks had quite faded into the background, while our French friends had come into their own and were making a great deal of noise and the old Mayor was shouting through his large grey moustache something which sounded like 'Encore de Kirsch'. Then one of the members of the party decided that he and Monsieur le Mayor should make (unsteady) tracks towards a house which they had promised to visit that afternoon. The mayor was eighty if he was a day and booze was now having a little more effect on him that it used to, so when he eventually got to his feet his old pins started playing tricks. The last we saw of him that day he was being escorted down the street between the two largest of his visitors. We heard later that we had nearly done for the poor old boy and he had remained unconscious all the following day.

By tea time the AOC and party had departed but not before visiting The Bull, sick with 'flu. Instead of the expected raspberry, the former was full of praise for the Squadron. I had long since lost Ducks but it wasn't long before we in the dining room became aware of his approach, and none of us could reach him in time to warn him that quite out of the blue an RAF padre had turned up for tea and intended to hold a church service that evening. Directly Ducks came into the Mess and caught sight of the padre he started giving him his views on the practice of wearing collars the wrong way round. The incident was rather embarrassing and Ducks had to be taken into the ante-room. Actually the padre took it all in good part, but when we had a visit from another cleric later on, he arrived full of the stories of the wild Fighter Boys and how he would have his hands full trying to keep them sober. The Bull must have realised from his sickbed that something was afoot that fateful day and he made the unexpected church parade compulsory for all Officers, but as his orders came a little late, only Birch, Secundus and I turned up on time. A few more staggered in late and leaned against each other for support at the back of the airmen's dining hall where we held all our gatherings. Jimmy Champers put up a marvellous show. Hearing that there was a church parade on, he vaguely thought 'church' so reeled round to the village Catholic church. Once inside he found the place in darkness which he thought strange, so proceeded to find his way about by striking matches. After a vain search for a service in progress, and having used up all his matches, he gave up, collapsed into a pew and passed out. Daylight was breaking and he was very cold and stiff when he woke up. So, with other minor incidents, Black Sunday came to a close – a longer day than normal.

By now the airmen were mixing with the villagers, learning their language and passing their free time by a family fireside, making up a little for what they had left behind in England. There weren't any attractive daughters around, which was perhaps just as well – with the exception perhaps of Collette who was generally very well chaperoned. Most of the young folk found work out of the village in nearby Bar-le-Duc. The old mayor had by now become friendly, and later when we moved into the new Mess he used to visit us occasionally to look at his maps of the district etc, but he was always a little uneasy as we wouldn't let him leave before he had a drink with us, and then 'the other half' was followed by 'one for the stairs' and on occasion one more 'in case of fire'. When we eventually left Neuville the folk were genuinely sorry to see us go, and when I returned on a visit a few weeks later, they wanted to know when we were returning as they found us preferable to the French Squadron which had taken our place.

Our billets varied somewhat, but on the whole they were not too bad and certainly better than living under canvas. It was natural that The Bull and the other two members of his Flight – Hilly Brown and Leslie Clisby – should have the best the village could offer. This was, in fact, the only decent house for miles around and belonged to a well-to-do timber merchant who could afford a wife, two servants, two cars and a gardener; why he chose to live in Neuville was a mystery. The house even supported a bath (surely the only one in the village), central heating and H&C in each bedroom, though all these comforts were kept as a tight secret from the rest of us, as I found when I stayed there for a night later on. In fact, most of the rooms were locked up and the water was always cold. 'The Pink House' was the dwelling of Johnny and Leak, who shared one room with Ducks and Pussy in the second. Between these two rooms was a tiny one where Stanley Baldy (and later, when his place in the Squadron was taken, by Killy) who found room for a mattress on the floor. The big asset here was that the two larger rooms had fireplaces which were lit every evening. The drawback was that not a stick of furniture was supplied. This meant camp kits had to be used to the full and nails in the walls sufficed for wardrobes. Just to have a heated bedroom during the coldest winter that Europe had known this century was a luxury beyond compare and I spent many an evening with Johnny and Leak reading and writing letters before retiring into my own ice box for the night. Most of the other billets were dirty and damp; the living rooms, kitchens, etc either being occupied or locked up. The owners were paid by the RAF at rates varying with the accommodation supplied: whether furnished or bare rooms and whether the owner kept the room clean and generally 'did' for you.

A mobile Squadron did not carry a bevy of batmen with it. Sqn Ldr Pemberton had grabbed a billet for himself which was central and right opposite the new Mess, but when we arrived in the village with the whole Squadron, The Bull had other ideas. Any billet that was fit for a Squadron Leader was also good enough for a Pilot Officer (or Acting Corporal), so Pembers was kicked out and the billet was mine for the remainder of the time we were at Neuville. It was certainly one of the cleanest houses in the village and my landlady looked after me very well. The chief snag was that to get to my bedroom – the only room to which I was entitled – I had to go through the kitchen, the tiled floor of which was always spotlessly clean. The form was that my slippers had to be kept outside the back door with the two pairs of clogs of the household, and no outside footwear was allowed in the house. Secondly, the room had no fireplace or heating arrangements and it was bitterly cold. With the window and wooden shutters closed all night, the water in my wash basin jug had a considerable layer of ice on it most mornings, and my shaving brush had to be thawed out. A bottle of Vichy water remained frozen solid until Donald Hills supplied me with an oil stove to take the chill off the place. My landlord was the village carpenter and he had made practically every bit of furniture in the house including my very comfortable double bed, the large carved wardrobe (not for my use) and wash-stand to match – even down to the wooden door locks and hinges. The community was very poor and led a hard life, having to do without many basic modern comforts: there was no main drainage system and few houses had running water. There was one surprising exception: everybody had electric light – no power, or perhaps pockets deep enough to afford any appliances, but every house had light in each room.

Madame's heart was nearly broken on one occasion when I was smitten with the dreaded form of 'flu that many contracted that winter, and with which I had to retire to my bed for a week. The Doc (it was still Doc Cross who was to be replaced by Doc Brown at a later date), with his orderly, paid me two visits per day. My batman brought me my meals when I could eat and several of the boys came to visit me in their gumboots (or 'wellies' as one now has to call them) or flying boots. I am glad I never saw her cherished kitchen floor during this time, as it must have been in an awful heart-breaking mess for Madame. She tried to keep pace with the mud that was brought in but in the end gave it up as a bad job and just let it collect. Towards the end of the week, I noticed that she seemed to be taking more interest in my welfare and kept on enquiring when I would be well again. On

Lewis, a young Canadian, and George Plinston. George survived the war.

Left to right: Hanks, Brown, the author (the only survivor), and Crusoe. Hilly Brown joined No 1 from Canada in 1937 as a P/O and made it to CO in 1940. He was killed leading a Spitfire Wing over Sicily. The Luftwaffe dropped a wreath over Malta saying he had been buried with full honours.

the day I announced I was leaving my bed, she was full of joy and I heard great activity going on downstairs – the rattling of buckets and a lot of water being pumped. Then I knew the answer: every now and then a splash beneath my window told me that another bucket had collected a portion of mud off the kitchen floor and this was being returned to the street from whence it came!

Compared with the lofts and barns the airman had to live in, our billets were palaces (and we often wondered how the British Army troops were living at that time). Their quarters were cold and damp and a lot of the men went down with 'flu and bad colds. One contracted pneumonia and it surprised me that more did not go down with it. I am sure it was only their spirits that kept them going and that they all felt they had to pull their weight in the Squadron and those Hurricanes had to be kept in the air. There was also the little extra 'something for England' outlook, which comes to all when serving in a foreign land, which I am sure would not have been present in any Squadron operating from its home base. I remember taking a pay parade for Donald Hills when he went on leave on one occasion and the sights I saw shook me a bit. Normally this exercise took most of one day to get through; the morning being taken up by first paying the men whose work kept them in the village and then covering those on the aerodrome. The afternoon was spent in paying anyone who missed the morning parade and those who were sick, which entailed going round the various billets. On this particular occasion it took me and a corporal all one Friday and part of Saturday morning getting round to all the men who were ill. One loft we came to held about a dozen men and all except one were in their home-made beds, laid low with 'flu. They had lost their voices and were too weak to sign their names in the receipt book, so the one man who was well enough had to tell us the name of each man and sign for him, while his pay was put under his pillow. It was almost like identifying corpses: nearly fifty percent of the ground staff must have been sick that week. When I questioned Doc Cross he didn't seem at all concerned and sure enough it was only a matter of days before they were all up and about again, doing their work on the freezing aerodrome.

The aerodrome was situated about two miles from the village and was actually on the outskirts of Vasincourt, where we would have lived initially had it not been occupied by part of a French Squadron. They soon left but

The aerodrome at Vasincourt was a sea of mud most of the winter. All maintenance and engine changes were done in the open.

rather than have another move we stayed in Neuville, although Vasincourt was a higher and more healthy place in which to live. When there was no panic on, walking to the aerodrome gave us a little exercise and there was generally something to see which, however dull, was a change from the perpetual sameness of our everyday lives during the worst of the winter. Firstly one crossed the River Meuse which was in flood for quite a time and threatened the village, and after it had returned to normal, it was said to have held a fish or two, and a few enthusiastic members of the Squadron sat on its banks and let large ones get away. Continuing towards the aerodrome, the Paris-Metz railway line was crossed by a perfectly good stone bridge which was unusual as the very secondary road only led to the village of Vasincourt yet even the main roads in France at that time had to be content with level crossings. One day two French soldiers were posted on the bridge armed with very WW1 looking machine guns *"to protect your King when he travels on this line when he comes to France"*, we were told! They were probably Fifth Columnists. After crossing the Bar-le-Duc canal which even in winter seemed busy with barge traffic of all shapes and sizes, the road wound up a small hill at the top of which was the aerodrome.

This aerodrome was really just a large field, having no natural cover and of course no buildings of any kind. Most of the winter it was a sea of mud – or snow; at least the perimeter where the Hurricanes were dispersed was such and was hardly ideal for aircraft and engine servicing. It was all too easy to execute a ground loop if an undercarriage wheel dropped into one of the ruts. Later when the better weather came, we were supplied with Nissen huts to replace two small tents for 'A' and 'B' flights and two larger ones for Maintenance: everything seemed to arrive too late. It was a great credit to the ground crews carrying on in the bitter cold, doing their routine inspections, warming up engines every morning before daylight; refuelling and re-arming with no protection from the elements. They did magnificent work for which they received little praise, though none was expected. I never saw the same keenness in England. There was a small 'pub' near the canal bridge on the way to the aerodrome which we never frequented for no good reason that I can remember, but one day when the weather was foul, several of us had walked up to the aerodrome for something to do and on the way back George Plinston (who was later replaced), Billy Stratton and I decided to try the very weak tasting beer. On the way back to the village for tea we became tired of walking, so hailed a farm cart making in our direction. The old farmer was quite pleased to give us a lift but there was no room to sit down, so one-by-one we mounted the horse and arrived in the village rather like the Grey Mare of Widecombe Fair, while the noise we made brought folk out to watch our arrival. Perhaps the beer had more about it than we had realised.

A No 73 Squadron Hurricane after nosing over onto its back.

Re-arming a 73 Squadron Hurricane at Rouvres, 1940.

It was from this aerodrome that the boys took off to have their first scraps with the enemy. At first an odd reconnaissance aircraft and then small dog-fights with Me109s, and later Me110s (or to give them their full title – Messerschmitt Bf109 and Bf110). In this way they gradually gained the fighting experience which was to stand them in such good stead when 10 May came. Then they needed everything they had learned to be able to face the tremendous odds which they encountered. But what nobody could learn was how to keep flying and fighting with insufficient sleep: it appeared that a handful of Hurricanes were taking on the whole of the Luftwaffe. Several French fighter Escadrilles could be seen on the ground but were seldom in the air. When the fun started other fighter squadrons came over from England; some for the day and one – No 501 from Filton, Bristol – stayed until the evacuation, but the odds were too great. New pilots were rushed into battle with only text-book experience and when they found themselves surrounded by superior numbers of the enemy their training of carrying out No 1, No 2 or No 3 attacks had to be modified on the spur of the moment to meet the unrehearsed situation. The boys in No 1 and 73 had learned the new tricks of the trade gradually and were able to survive to fight for many 'another day'.

The first Squadron success was on 30 October 1939, just short of two months since the outbreak of war, and Boy Mould was the one who got his sights on that Do17. He had just done a patrol and his aircraft was being refuelled when the Dornier came over the aerodrome pretty high up. Boy immediately took off and gave chase and, after going full throttle for some time, he caught it up, gave it a few short bursts and the Dornier, to his surprise, burst into flames almost immediately. This was in the days before we got Rotol variable pitch props, and Boy's Hurricane had an early Merlin II engine with a fixed pitch wooden propeller, so it was a long chase. This victory cheered things up a lot and from then on everyone was as keen as mustard. I was away at the time with The Bull and his Section, so we missed the celebrations which followed. This was the first fighter victory in France during the 1939/45 war and it seemed to herald the slow beginning of more frequent triumphs, although December and January were bad months weatherwise and flying suffered badly. No 73 were not out of the picture; in fact they seemed to see more of the enemy than No 1. On 8 November, they got a Dornier 17 (I think 'Cobber' Kain accounted for it) and this was the day that Dicky Martin – also of 73 – force-landed in the wrong country and became 'The Prisoner of Luxembourg'. Still in November, on 23rd, there was considerable activity in both Squadrons. Pussy, Killy Kilmartin and Sergeant Soper got a Do17 between them, The Bull and Hilly a second Do17 and Sergeant Clowes a third one. No 73 accounted for four more Do17s, so this was really the first big day and a total of 7 victories for the two

Squadrons was big stuff for 1939.

The following day, 24 November, was even more active and a few more Dorniers failed to reach Das Vaterland, but the day was made unique by an incident which reached the British national Press and prompted Grimes of *The Star* to come out to sketch our Mess. Pussy Palmer had assisted in bringing down a Do17 but before the crippled aeroplane crashed, Pussy thought he would fly up alongside the Dornier and have a good look at it. The gunners had been killed and as Pussy drew level, he saw the pilot sprawled over his controls. I am not sure whether Pussy then went on ahead or if the German pilot throttled back on his one surviving but failing engine. Before Pussy knew what was happening a stream of bullets went whistling past him, hitting his Hurricane and causing him to force-land. This was a pretty good effort for a 'dead' pilot and The Bull thought he must be a bit of a sportsman. Rather in the spirit of 1914 and 'The Dawn Patrol', when gentlemen fought as gentlemen, The Bull thought it would be a good idea to be British and entertain this enterprising member of the Luftwaffe to dinner in our Mess. After a lot of arguing with the French, who by now had taken the German prisoner, it was agreed that it would be in order if we had him for an hour or so while on his way to the prison at Verdun. So the following evening Billy Drake, who could speak a little German, and two others collected the prisoner and with a French Gendarme entered the Mess. Our guest looked scared stiff and things went slowly at first, but with the aid of champagne and the warm welcome he was receiving, by supper time he was in quite a relaxed frame of mind. Everyone by now had got used to the presence of our unusual visitor and we just carried on with our meal in the normal manner. To us our food was reasonable – nothing to write home about – and our victuals that evening were in no way exceptional, but either the German considered our meal a magnificent spread or he hadn't eaten for some time; whatever the reason, he got down to it in typical Teutonic style and tucked in with 'both feet in the trough'. We were laughing and joking as usual and I think because

The German who came to dinner – Unteroffizer Arno Frankenburger.

145

of this he thought we were making fun of him, as he had no idea what we were talking about. Suddenly he completely broke down and started sobbing, whereupon The Bull and Billy Drake took him out of the room onto the landing at the head of the stairs. While we continued with our meal the German explained everything to Billy.

He was a Corporal pilot, just over thirty years old, and before Hitler came to power had always thought the English were good people and that the Great War had been a big mistake. But now he was a Nazi, his ideas had altered and he had learned to look upon all Englishmen as swine, and had been firmly convinced that we had taken him away from his French captors in order to shoot him. When he found that we were kind, giving him good food and drink, and seeing all the laughing faces in the Mess, it was too much for him. We made him feel at home – in fact, he would have felt better than being at home were it not for the wife and children he had left in Germany. Before the war he had been a glider instructor and liked flying – but not in war time: in fact many of his comrades were secretly against war. Not very well educated, he was a typical example of one of the sheep that had followed the New Order and had been made to believe all the lies that the Nazi propaganda merchants had fed him. He knew the *Ark Royal* had been sunk (which it hadn't), because it had been given out on the German wireless, and what was more he had a friend who had a friend who was in the 'U' boat that did the sinking! Now he was confused and bewildered; the futility of war seemed more real and all he had believed in had suddenly crumbled to nothing. All this seemed pretty genuine and we were convinced he was not putting it on, or even capable of putting on such an act. The German continued his meal and afterwards we had some more champagne and all became quite merry. When the time came for him to go, we could not get rid of him; he hated the French and wanted to stay with us as our prisoner (no wonder). He shook us all warmly by the hand and nearly kissed Pussy and gave most of his belongings – including his glider pilot's licence – to the Mess. We gave him some cigarettes and French money and, after more farewells on the doorstep, we eventually sent him on his way with his escort of gendarmes.

By the time my Commission came through on 15 November 1939 I had a fair idea of why I was in France and what my duties were, but had not realised with what degree of flexibility the 'Administration and Special Duties Branch of the Royal Air Force Volunteer Reserve' could be interpreted – at least in my case. By now, besides my own official job, I had one or two others to occupy my spare time. For the first few months of the war the Fighter Squadrons in France did not have a full time Intelligence Officer, but as time went on and things became a little more lively, this was found necessary, so until one was posted to the Squadron – in the form of

F/O Harris, a 1914 war pilot – The Bull gave me the job. This entailed seeing that all the pilots saw the latest reports of enemy movements, where their anti-aircraft guns were situated, types of enemy aircraft, what armament they had and what part of the aircraft it was best to attack. Our patrol lines had to be marked up on maps along with the position of allied aerodromes and anti-aircraft guns. The worst part of the job was making sure that all the pilots read the latest intelligence reports. This entailed chasing them round their billets, the aerodrome, the Officers' Mess, the Sergeants' Mess, the Orderly Room and anywhere between all those places. Another job was that of Messing Officer for a time, and in this capacity I was ably assisted by Sergeant Stone, who did most of the organising of the rations and the 'extras' which were generally bought in Bar-le-Duc. He also looked after the batmen and the cooks and thanks to him our food was really pretty good. It must have been through Sergeant Stone that I discovered that one of the MT drivers had been a chef in peacetime and it was not too difficult to have him re-mustered as a cook for our Mess, whereupon our meals improved rapidly. It was a revelation to discover the number of ways bully beef can be disguised. Once or twice when visitors turned up unannounced and the meal was not up to scratch I got a dirty look from The Bull, but he couldn't say much – I might have resigned! Considering our kitchen was normally a small storeroom in which we placed one twin burner oil stove, supplying hot meals for anything up to twenty at one sitting was quite a feat. When Sir Cyril Newall visited us we even ran to tablecloths borrowed from Madame Jean.

One day it was announced that the AOC in Chief, British Air Forces in France, Air Marshal Sir Arthur Barratt, along with the AOC/AASF, Air Vice Marshal Sir Patrick Playfair, were to visit No 1 (as, no doubt they did No 73). The whole Squadron was to be all present and correct up on the aerodrome, though no special preparations were to be made. I was detailed by The Bull to meet the party at the edge of the aerodrome when they arrived by road and escort them across to the Flights and introduce the CO to them. By this time I had my own uniform, so there would be no embarrassing questions about why there was a supernumerary Flt/Lt in the squadron. With my greatcoat on, there was nothing to show that I was not a pilot (nothing to show that I was not a regular Air Force Officer either – merely a Rolls-Royce representative!) The party duly arrived and I flung the C-in-C one of my very smartest salutes, and on the way over to the Nissen huts he asked questions about the Squadron – which I was able to answer – but thank goodness none about myself.

The weather on Christmas Day 1939 was fine and there was a fair amount of flying and patrol work, so the Officers could not have had Christmas dinner then, even if it had been planned that way. Actually it is an RAF

The AOC in C British Forces in France, Air Marshall Sir Arthur Barratt and Air Vice Marshall Sir Patrick Playfair AOC, AASF visited No 1 Squadron – I was detailed to meet the pary.

custom – and probably the same in the other two Services – to give the airmen a good 'blow out' on Christmas Day – generally in the evening. The Officers then have their celebration on Boxing Day. It is also the custom for the Officers to serve the men their dinner and to wait on them at table. So at about 6.00pm we went round to the Airmen's Mess and started the good work. It was a great success, the meal was excellent with enough turkey for two helpings if required, and finished up with plum pudding, all washed down with quantities of wine. Naturally each Officer looked after the men for whom he was responsible in the work of the Squadron. Each pilot saw to it that the crew which looked after his aircraft had plenty of food, while for my part, I saw to it that some of the Maintenance personnel had everything they required. It was amusing to see the Officers queuing up with empty plates and then charging back with a choice piece of bird for his Airman. If you returned with a leg or wing instead of a nice juicy piece of breast, you were letting the side down! After all had dined and wined well, Johnny made a speech (The Bull was away) and then the Officers had to swallow a pint of beer without taking a breath. There was so much food left over after the men had gone that a lot of us had a very good meal from the leftovers. We then invited some of the NCOs round to our Mess where we wished them a Merry Christmas in champagne. Of course a gang of the bright lads had formed a carol singing party and went round the village making awful noises and when they arrived at our Mess we invited them in and we had quite an amusing sing-song.

We had our own meal on the evening of Boxing Day and by then The Bull had returned, bringing a few French Officers to join us. I had managed to get hold of six good turkeys in the village but they would not go into our small oven, so we had to get the local baker organised and he certainly cooked them beautifully in his bread ovens. The meal seemed to go down very well and I was congratulated, although again the faithful Stone had really done all the work. After dinner The Bull decided it was time for games so after clearing the Mess we played rugger and various other strenuous games which, on top of a large meal, didn't do us or our uniforms any good at all. We went to bed that night exhausted. On New Year's Eve we went round to the room the Maintenance Section had fixed up as a café-cum-pub for themselves, where we had a sing-song led by Sergeant Pilot Soper with his accordion. A good time was had by all, but I remember going outside for a breath of fresh air and finding Boy Mould sitting down in the snow feeling rather sorry for himself: we both felt a very long way from home at that moment and wondered what fate the New Year held for us and our country.

The weather was foul well into the New Year and aerial activity was at its minimum. At the beginning of March the clouds lifted occasionally and the odd Heinkel or Dornier came over to collect more and more pictures: many never returned home. On 2 March, Mitchell – a newcomer to No 1 – and Sgt Soper chased a Do17 and Soper shot it down but Mitchell was killed while having to make a forced landing. The next day, 3 March, Hilly Brown and Sgt Soper got a Heinkel III, but Hilly had to force land at Nancy, as his wooden propeller was hit and had disintegrated. Nine days later Bishop, another new boy, dived straight in from 20,000 feet. The only explanation was lack of oxygen. One tended to try and forget the losses – only to record the 26 successes chalked up before the massive German onslaught, after which life, especially for the pilots, became so hectic that statistics had to go by the board.

Being confined together for so many months in our little Squadron-world,

149

we couldn't fail to get to know each other intimately very quickly, and stories could be written ad infinitum about the different characters. Nicknames had been established before I joined No 1, so I have no idea why F/O Charles Gordon Huthwait Crusoe, was called 'Leak' rather than 'Robinson', why F/O Peter Prossor Hanks was named 'Ducks', and many others; but Flt/Lt Peter Walker answering to 'Johnny' was as natural as 'Timber' and 'Chalky' is to Wood and White. The Outposts of Empire were well represented; three – or was it four – New Zealanders between the two Squadrons. When I joined the first leave party to Paris (wearing the uniform of Shephard, a Canadian) and becoming the fourth member of The Bulls' Section, it was Marjorie Dunton (of whom more anon – herself a Canadian), who pointed out something that nobody seemed to have thought of before – that we were a truly cosmopolitan lot. The Bull was Irish, Hilly Brown a Canadian, Leslie Clisby an Australian, and to round it off I had to be a Tasmanian. But one more character must be mentioned and, like me, he wasn't really a member of No 1. Our second interpreter, Pierre Garnier, seemed to disappear before the end of 1939, and we coped very well without one until 'Moses' arrived, which must have been early in January 1940, and he stayed to the bitter end. I suppose I knew him better than anyone else in No 1 as we travelled many miles together, shared a triple berth tent and some cold nights under the stars. He was a bit of a mystery and, although later on in the war he joined the Free French in England as Captain J E F Morlaix, I was sure that was not his real name. (See Appendix). He had been a commercial pilot until 1935, and what happened in the next five years I know not, but for whatever reason he had not been able to get into l'Armee de l'Air, which caused him to carry a permanent chip on his shoulder. Moses' English was not of the best, which enhanced his character, and later in England some of the non-drawing room language he had picked up from us turned a few heads, but his later exploits showed him to be a remarkable individual and I am proud to have known him.

These were early days and nobody could foretell what the future held for any one of us. The days dragged on with little change from one to the next: we knew it was Sunday when Paul Richey would wander off looking smart in his Best Blue and flat hat on his way to Mass. There were no daily papers or news bulletins and the calendar on which you crossed off each day was one you had made yourself. The Esquire lovelies had been invented, but the Pirelli calendar curves had not. Later on the names of some good young men had to be crossed off the roster board too.

CHAPTER TWELVE

Entertainment and leave

With the approach of winter in October 1939, it wasn't long before we realised that we would have to organise some sort of show for our own entertainment – especially the airmen. Spending the long winter evenings in a small French village with no interests other than books, darts, cards and beer, might lead to a little too much indulgence in the latter, and in any case after a few weeks of this way of life, boredom is likely to be followed by standards and morale slipping. We decided to start our entertainments with a smoking-concert just to see how things would go, and Secundus Palmer was naturally the man to get things underway. Before joining the RAF, Secundus had had a shot at film acting and had played small parts here and there, so he knew something about the business. Why I don't know, but I was chosen as one of the unlucky victims to take part in the few little sketches the Officers would be putting on between sing-songs. Secundus wrote the scripts, we had a few rehearsals in his billet and really got quite a lot of fun out of the idea. To describe the first concert, extracts from a letter I wrote home dated 23 October will give a fair idea of the evenings happenings.

… *"The biggest event that has happened here of late is the concert we held in the village hall, or Airmen's Mess. We only decided to hold it last Friday evening, so we didn't have much time to prepare. All we had was a bare hall with nothing in it except a few electric light fittings, four white walls and a few chairs. However, the Squadron joiner made a stage out of scrap wood and rigged up some footlights…Some artists among the airmen scrounged some red and blue paint and made a very effective RAF Bull's Eye with a large "No 1" underneath on the wall at the back of the stage. The whole Squadron turned up for the show of course, and the hall was filled to overflowing. The programme consisted of sing-songs, piano (borrowed from the Mayor), and piano-accordion solos; four sketches by the Officers and a few quite clean jokes to fill in with. I took part in three of the sketches and naturally they went down well: troops always enjoy Officers making fools of themselves! The first was very short. I walked on in a very small P/O's uniform wearing a tiny cap and did a smart salute to my CO who was sitting at his desk. He ticked me off for being late and talked a lot of nonsense about me forgetting to do something for him, and I excused myself by replying that I had forgotten to remember to remind myself. So it went on until my CO (Secundus) told me to follow him as he was going to take me to the Group Captain. As soon as the CO got up to go out, it was seen by all that he had forgotten to put his trousers on. Hardly an original but you must appreciate that we were ready to laugh at anything at that time.*

For the next sketch Secundus and myself dressed up as old farmers and, with a Somerset accent, had a short conversation all about nothing and then went into the old tale of how my horse had become ill and I am recommended to give it turpentine as this was what George had given his horse when it was ill. A little later when George enquires after my horse I have to declare him dead, whereupon George announces that his died too! The third little episode – again with the two stars – was longer and original; written by one of the boys. I took the part of Hitler, wearing khaki shirt and breeches borrowed from an Army signals officer and finished off with his Sam Browne and a pair of flying boots, not forgetting the moustache I made out of a tassel from a curtain in the Mess. My main prop was a large book with MINE GAMPF written across the cover in large letters, while the outstanding feature of Stalin (Secundus) was a magnificent hat made out of two rabbit skins and artificial snow on his flying boots. In short we argued over Poland for some time with a quite clever script and finally I exchanged half of Poland for a pat of 'Best Bradford Buttervich' in order to make some more guns. I then bought a Daily Mirror to learn the truth about the progress of the war, and found that No 1 Squadron was knocking down too many Messerschmitts (actually in the script the word was 'Messershits' which brought the house down), so we both decided to go to Iceland and conquer the penguins instead. I got a lot of boos from the audience and of course there was a lot of saluting and "Heil Hitler-ing" (I had had plenty of the real thing), and the scene went on for fifteen minutes or so. Peter Matthews, with Secundus at the piano, gave a good impression of the Western Brothers and the show came to a close with The Bull (our genuine CO) giving us a vote of thanks. All today the troops have been giving me a slightly different salute to the official one!"

Soon after this we had a second concert which was really a repeat of the first with a few items added, for those who had missed the first. We read in the English papers that concert parties were going around the country giving shows at home and we knew that the theatres and cinemas were still open, while we had nothing. Later on the NAAFI gave us an occasional picture show which was a great thrill. Some of the films were not of the best, but the good ones I remember were *The Lion has Wings*, *Jamaica Inn* and *Rose of Washington Square*. One amusing incident, which went down well, occurred when two films got slightly mixed. We were all breathless watching James Cagney rushing into a room with a revolver in his hand being chased by 'G' men, when suddenly Alice Fay and Tyrone Power appeared on the screen whispering tender words of love to each other. The sudden change was quite dramatic. Later, various stars came out and did shows for the AASF, but unfortunately they only got as far as Rheims. Thus the Opera House was full of Headquarters people and boys from a few Battle Squadrons who were lucky enough to be stationed near the City. I suppose Gracie Fields, Josephine Baker, Sir Seymour Hicks and Maurice Chevalier could not be expected to leave the comforts to be found at the Lion d'Or to come out to entertain the Squadrons who could not get into Rheims, or maybe nobody thought to tell them about us. When I was at 73 we did, in fact, go to Rheims for a show but it meant setting off in the Squadron bus one afternoon and returning in the small hours of the morning. It just wasn't worth it.

During this period, Secundus re-wrote *Robinson Crusoe*, giving it a Squadron atmosphere and we started rehearsals and intended putting it on for Christmas, but various things cropped up to hinder progress. Finally, when it seemed we were getting regular picture shows and the prospect of ENSA concert parties in the near future, the panto was shelved, never to see the light of day. News of our home-produced concert had somehow reached the ears of the BBC and they wanted to record the repeat for broadcasting in England, but it was realised that apart from some of the jokes not being fit for general consumption, they were mostly about our Squadron life and personnel, so listeners at home would not understand them. However, we did put on a third concert and that seemed to achieve the objective.

On one occasion we took over a small cinema in Bar-le-Duc for our NAAFI picture show which was fortuitous. Suddenly, out of the blue we were told that a concert party had arrived in Rheims especially to entertain the outlying Squadrons: this was before ENSA had been formed. Donald Hills and I were detailed to collect the first party from Rheims, so we set out in the Squadron coach and picked them up at the Lion d'Or. There were about twelve girls in all plus a manager and on the journey back I memorised each girl's name so that when we arrived at the Mess for tea, I was able to introduce them to all the boys. By the time they had to make tracks for Bar-le-Duc for the evening show, everyone knew everyone else. The show went with a swing and as the company knew something about the Officers by then, they were able to crack topical jokes about certain individuals, which of course the airmen loved. After the show we foregathered at The Metz, except for the airmen, who had to go back to camp. There we had an excellent dinner provided by Madame Jean. As the weather was bad and there would be no flying on the following morning, it was decided to take the party back to our Mess before returning them to Rheims. Here we had a few wallops of champagne and, as it was our turn to do the entertaining, led by Leslie we all sang until we could hardly speak. Donald and I took them back to the Lion d'Or and had a coffee with them before returning to Neuville where we arrived at 5.30am. In all, we must have had five or so similar shows – perhaps more, and the Fol-de-Rols, *The Ten of Us, The Piccadilly Revellers, Ralph Reader's Gang Show* are well remembered, but the best was Billy Cotton's Band.

There was snow on the ground when Billy came and it was cold enough to freeze anything off a brass monkey. We met them at Bar-le-Duc railway station and had tea with them in The Metz where they stayed the night. After the excellent show, which the airmen seemed to appreciate more than any of the other concerts, we had the usual dinner at The Metz. Afterwards, being an all-male party, we listened to Alan Breeze singing some of his endless supply of songs which have never been heard over the air and these kept us in fits of laughter into the small hours. We sang our Squadron song and later on in England the same tunes were used for *The Quartermaster's Stores*, and *Boo Hurray* in Cotton's band, but I don't suppose the tunes were original. No 73 had roughly the same shows as No 1 and I saw two of them when at Rouvres (73's home village) but somehow they didn't go down so well; the atmosphere was different. The last concert was on 23 March, as soon after this things started hotting up and we made a move to Pontavert. By this time there was too much daylight and the priority was to get enough sleep rather than while away the long dark evenings.

In the early days at Le Havre, Doc Cross once said jokingly that it would be a good idea if we could have a spot of leave in Paris as it looked as though we would never get any home leave. He said he would put the idea up to The Bull. A nice suggestion but none of us took it seriously and it was not foremost in our minds at that stage of the war. In our innocence we reckoned Paris would be too far away from Berlin, where we would be when we were ready for wine, women and song. We thought that once Berlin was reorganised the Rio Rita, Femina and Haus Farterland clubs would provide enough fun. However, Hitler had other ideas, and didn't start the shooting war just then, so we were to see Paris before Berlin. One night late in October I walked into the old Mess at Neuville and found The Bull, Leslie, Hilly and Pierre Garnier, our interpreter (at the time we called them interrupters), in high spirits, sitting around the fire. Paris weekend leave had just been granted for personnel of the AASF and three could go at a time from each Squadron. The Bull had decided that his Section should be the first to go, just to see if Paris was a safe place for the others. Pierre was going to help with the language question (actually he had a flat in Paris which only The Bull saw), and catching sight of me The Bull shouted *"Let's take Knackers",* and I don't remember having said 'no'. So it was decided that the five of us would catch the morning train the very next day, 29 October, much to the envy of all the others, though they knew their turn would come soon.

We caught the train at Bar-le-Duc and shared a compartment with a middle-aged French Army Captain, who was a wine merchant in civilian life. He was now returning to Paris, having been cashiered for putting up a number of 'blacks'. Apparently he had been caught with his batman one night staggering around arm in arm, having had more than enough to drink, and when brought before his Colonel, had told the latter in no uncertain manner what he thought of the Army and what he could do with it. This did not bother him; his present worry was that he had gone to war with quite a large amount of money, but finding things rather too good away from his wife, had spent the lot and didn't know how to face his better half. He invited us to his home in Paris to give him moral support but we declined his kind offer. However, he kept us amused for the rest of the journey and he certainly knew his wines. When the train stopped at Chalons and Vitry he replenished our 'cellar' with the best that was available.

I got talking to a Foreign Legion Sergeant who was most interesting. He had come to France with his regiment a week previously and was stationed somewhere near the south end of the Maginot Line. He told me a little of the life they led in the Legion and said that most of the stuff which one read and saw in books and films was quite untrue. But they were tough all right. His regiment had come straight over from a comparatively warm Africa into one of the coldest winters France had known, wearing exactly the same clothes and uniform as they wore in the desert, and they did not feel the cold. This was just another change of location for them and at the moment a rest, as they spent most of their lives fighting somewhere. France being at war didn't make much difference to them and they rather welcomed the change of theatre. Perhaps he was pulling my leg! I believed him when he told me there were few Englishmen in the Legion as they were generally caught before they could join up. Also, the language question didn't encourage them as they had to be fluent in German as well as French. My travelling companion could speak five languages and certainly his command of English was perfect. Many of the German nationals in the Legion were longing to have a crack at Hitler – the remainder would fight anyone they were ordered so to do. I took him along to our compartment and introduced him to The Bull and the others, and he translated the leaflets we had collected from the 'Whitley Boys' – some they hadn't dropped on Germany. By this time our ex-Army Officer wine merchant hadn't a care in the world. Feeling very jubilant, he was entertaining us with his antics, and even Pierre couldn't understand what he was talking about half the time. According to him, the only way to find whether a bottle was empty or not was to hold the neck of the bottle up to your eye and look up it telescope fashion.

Arriving at the Gare de l'Ouest, Pierre thought it would be a good idea if we stayed at the Hotel Terminus St Lazare as he knew Felix the doorman would look after us – and he did in more ways than one. We had an excellent meal at a nearby cafe, which I slept off on my bed in the hotel. Hilly rang me late in the afternoon and announced that The Bull and Pierre had gone off somewhere, so would I meet him and Leslie in the bar in half an hour's time. Having made friends with George the barman we decided to discover Paris and after a short walk found ourselves in another bar which was deserted except for a middle-aged woman reading a newspaper. Hilly started our conversation by saying in his loud Canadian accent, *"Don't these French dames wear large hats",* whereupon the 'French dame' dropped her paper and said, *"Say, I'm an American citizen and I ree-zent that ree-mark".* It took a few drinks to laugh that one off, but eventually we introduced ourselves to Miss Maxwell of Associated Press, and having made friends 'Maxie' decided that she should show us Paris. The word 'gay' used to be synonymous with Paris but now its meaning has been debased and a word such as 'vivacious' has to be substituted; either way, the city was pretty dead when we arrived, with only a few clubs and restaurants open and all the theatres were closed. However, under Maxie's guidance we soon found ourselves at the Boeuf-sur-le-Toit, which was closed except for one small room. We created a bit of a stir when we entered, as apparently nobody had seen RAF uniforms before, and several people came up and bought us champagne. The hostess was all over us, and the pianist – an Englishman living in Paris – started playing English and American tunes, and a little Mexican girl, Rita Ray, sang *Down Mexico Way* very sweetly. We were introduced to Rita and some more champagne, and after a while Hilly had fallen for Rita, and Maxie had fallen asleep. Before Leslie and I left with Maxie, Rita had told us of a Canadian friend she would like us to meet and if we returned to the club the following evening (more trade for the club) she would introduce us. This friend was Marjorie Dunton, a charming lady of about thirty-five, who afterwards kept open house for any member of No 1 and was always looked up whenever any of the Squadron was in town.

Maxie took Leslie and me along to another small café but it was very crowded, so we went to her flat for coffee and a snack. Directly we got there Leslie fell asleep, which was a pity as I received all the glory bestowed upon the RAF – how fine we looked in our uniforms, etc – which I didn't deserve and Leslie did. Anyway, Maxie was going to tell them 'back home' exactly how she felt. Taxis were few and far between but Maxie's persistent 'phoning eventually produced one into which I assisted Leslie. But the night was not over yet, and having got him to his hotel room, I was about to undress when a loud noise came from our corridor. I rushed out to find Leslie, now fully awake but a little under the weather, very busy rolling up the carpet which ran the whole length of the corridor. Having settled that little episode, Leslie then informed me that he had shut his bedroom door and left the key inside, but on second thoughts, he then remembered taking a dislike to the key and throwing it out of his bedroom window. Down we went again into the street and with the aid of Felix who used his torch with great skill, we carried out a fruitless search. When we eventually got inside Leslie's room with a pass key, there on the table was the missing object.

In the morning Leslie was very late in rising. Hilly was also a late riser, so The Bull and I were shown Paris by Pierre, and very impressed I was. We picked Hilly and Leslie up for lunch, which we had in a small restaurant known to Pierre in Montmartre. That evening we went to the Boeuf in force where we met Marjorie Dunton and some of her friends. A pleasant evening was marred when the time came to pay the bill and leave. Whether we looked simple or rich – or both – I don't know, but the proprietor thought this was the moment to make some easy cash and had charged us double for what we had, or had not had. If we had been by ourselves we would have soon sorted the place out, but under the circumstances we couldn't create a scene so after a little argument we paid up. The 'Ox on the Roof' had thus killed the Goose that laid the Golden Egg. Perhaps a few of the boys returned, but we never went near the place again. The cocktail party Marjorie laid on for us the following evening was a great success – that was after we had found her flat, which took about an hour. The taxi driver didn't seem to know the address, Pierre wasn't sure and eventually we decided to find it ourselves on foot. It all seemed rather strange as the flat was only just off the Place de la Concorde, and while our excuses for being late were well founded, it dawned on us that the taxi driver had made a small fortune driving us around in circles. He must have been related to Pierre. This party was the start of a great friendship, and Marjorie became the Squadron's 'Mother' in Paris. We met her husband and some girls she produced from somewhere, including Bertie who was a charming young French girl with whom I did rather a heavy line. Rita Ray was there, chaperoned by 'Momma', who never let Rita out of her sight, and the latter played and sang for us, and we joined in *I Get Along Without You Very Well*. The party went on into the small hours, and then I took Bertie home and we sang *Parlez moi d'Amour* in the taxi on the way to her flat. The Bull took great umbrage at this and when I arrived back at the party I received a few dirty looks. All too soon our weekend came to a close and we all tumbled into the train bound for Metz at the terribly early hour of 10.00am the following morning. Turner, The Bulls' driver, met us at Bar-le-Duc station and gave us the grand news about Boy getting the first Dornier shot down by any of the Squadrons in France.

The remainder of the boys took turns in visiting Paris and came back with different stories of where they had been and the people they had seen, but none failed to pay Marjorie a visit, and she pushed the boat out for them every time. After one trip a Paris Gendarme's helmet appeared on the wall of the Mess to add to our other trophies. When my turn came around again for Paris leave I went up with Leak and Billy Stratton. On his first trip Billy had met a French dentist (in 1939 it seemed that all doctors and dentists were called up, put into uniform and attached to the French Army, but as time went on they were allowed to return to their practices – still in uniform). This chap took him to a lovely little café tucked away in the St Cyr district, the name of which will only be remembered by the three of us and all the friends we made there. No more Boeuf for us! After paying our respects to Marjorie we went round to the café, met Billy's friend – Jean R Khun, Chirurgien Dentiste, DFMP – and it wasn't long before a party had developed at Jean's flat. We had a right royal time to say the least of it, and half way through the party Jean took me into his surgery – the most elaborately equipped I have ever seen – and proceeded to pull the nerve out of a tooth that had rotted on me. He said that in my condition I wouldn't feel anything: he was right – I went to sleep, and I considered him very efficient at repairing 'maladies de la bouche et des dents'. That weekend we got to know most of the regular customers of the café and we always found a lot to talk about: there was never a dull moment. We of course spent our money, and naturally the café and the friends we made got the benefit of it, but we were having a good time and making the best of our break from the humdrum life we were accustomed to at Neuville. The business world in Paris at that time was at a pretty low ebb and things were deteriorating, and I am sure that some of the folk who joined us were having their first decent meal that week. I hope our little café is still going strong though it is too much to hope that any of the old customers still frequent it, but it is just possible that on the wall behind the bar there hangs a caricature of Gallo. Gallo was the little dog that belonged to the café. It wasn't good – I drew it, and his collar was made up of RAF buttons, which were no doubt removed during the Occupation.

The next visit to Paris was to collect my uniform from an English tailor I had found on a previous visit, and I was hoping for numerous fittings, but no such luck. I was alone on this trip which wasn't so much fun but by now I had plenty of friends to see. My final visit – also on my own – was to collect my little Renault from the Rolls-Royce Paris Depot. It was on the cards that the balloon was about to go up, so I only stayed one night, but managed to click for a very enjoyable cocktail party and I'm sure none of the guests gave war a single thought that night. I felt that this was probably the last time I would see Paris – and it was.

Today one hears a lot about a thing called 'R and R' from our armed forces serving abroad, and I gather it means something like 'Rest and Recuperation', or perhaps Relaxation; maybe Recreation or even Rehabilitation, but as far as I remember in 1939/40, all this was summed up in the word 'leave' – or if you were about to be married – compassionate (or was it passionate?) leave. I am certain the only R and R I was conscious of in those days was Rolls and Royce. Home leave started early in the New Year as far as I can remember, and my turn came on 6 February. Leak was the second Officer from No 1 making the party of only two with myself. After travelling all one day by bus, train, boat and more train, we found that we had been organised into the Charing Cross Hotel. We signed the visitor's (military) book at 6.30pm and by 7.00pm we were both in hot baths soaking the layers of dirt off. I rang my parents, had a meal and, leaving Leak to soak, decided I wanted to 'do' London. A taxi was hailed as the blackout was so effective (compared with Paris) that I felt I would soon be lost in the darkness. *"Take me somewhere",* I demanded of the driver, who was not encouraging and said that all the clubs were closed and all the shows were full, but he would take me to the Palladium – I think it was. A review called *Black Velvet* was on; the only dim light visible guided me to the box office where a man wearing a dinner jacket was very sorry but the house was full. As I turned to walk away he called me back and suggested I wait a minute before going. Less than five minutes later a man came out of the theatre and as he passed he wished me luck before he was lost in the darkness of the street. While I was wondering what this man meant the dinner jacket reappeared and said, *"Will you please follow me?".* Before I quite grasped what was happening, I was being shown to a 'found' seat and people were already standing up to let me pass. Realising what I thought had taken place, I shrank into my seat in H M Bateman style, getting hotter and hotter, still with my greatcoat on and nursing my cap, bulky gas mask and tin hat. At the interval – surely there were not two – I got out of my coat, trying hard not to look at anybody or start a conversation. Goodness knows what the manager had said to touch the heart of the kind man who gave up his seat, but Corporal Steve Race might have remembered.

This sounds strange, so let me explain. Many years later, on the TV programme *My Music*, Steve mentioned one February night when he went to see *Black Velvet*, the house was full and a civilian in front of him gave up his seat for a RAF Officer. I wrote to Steve and we established that it was in fact the self-same incident. As it happened, I did not enjoy the show, nor do I remember any of it, except for a vague recollection of a young girl with a beautiful voice. That voice was to become famous in later years, but in 1940 nobody had heard of *My Fair Lady* or *The Sound of Music* let alone Julie Andrews!

The next day, 8 February, happened to be a Thursday, so Leak and I decided to do a little shopping before travelling to our respective homes for the weekend. This would give us a clear week at home, except I had to spoil at least two days by visiting Derby. It was a lovely sunny morning and I had arranged to meet Leak at his tailors somewhere round Victoria, so decided the walk would do me good. It was around mid-morning and there were not many people about, which struck me as unusual for London on such a lovely day. While most males in Paris seemed to be in uniform, here I was vaguely conscious of there being only a few soldiers about. I then realised I was having to return quite a few salutes from Privates and NCOs and this made me feel slightly self-conscious; then two Army Officers approached. From a distance they seemed to have enough pips a-shining to make them Captains (later confirmed), so I got all ready for a 'longest up, shortest down' when to my surprise they both beat me to it, so I hastily changed gear to a slightly casual and not too superior reply! Before I could collect my thoughts, and while still enjoying a private chuckle at the Army's expense, another 'Brown Job' appeared from somewhere, who as far as I could see from the single 'pip' was at least the same rank as myself, so no problem was anticipated, but as he drew near I saw – yes, you've guessed it – his pip was a crown: he was a Major, and he flung me such a snappy salute that his hand quivered at the peak of his cap and vibrated like a bow string! This charade had to stop: how far now to Leak's outfitters? Not far, but not before a Naval Lieutenant Commander passed who gave me nothing but a quick glance: I in return gave him nothing. Leak roared with laughter when I told him this story and we both decided that it was fit and proper for any rank of either of the two senior services to respect the RAF – especially an Honorary Pilot Officer from Rolls-Royce. We could only assume that so early on in the war RAF uniforms were a rare sight in London at least, so few understood the different ranks. Needless to say, we returned to our hotel by taxi to avoid further embarrassment.

Hilly was away when I arrived back at Neuville and as my own billet was temporarily occupied, I borrowed his bed, while Leslie, Hilly's room mate, graciously stuck to his camp bed. I remember poor old Leslie – sometimes called 'Clissers' – was very down in the mouth as he was as keen as mustard and yet he had never had the enemy in his sights. Most of the others had at least had a quick squirt at one, and by now the Squadron had the odd Dornier, Heinkel, Me109 and Me110 to its credit. I tried to reassure him by telling him his time would come – which of course it did – and when he got going he really knocked them out of the sky. Perhaps he was too keen, and when he and 'Lorry' Lorimer were lost on the same patrol, it was thought that they must have attacked a whole bunch of Germans instead of leaving them alone, to live to fight another day with more reasonable odds.

The next time home leave came up for me, all the other Officers from No 1 had had their second UK leave, so although I was with No 73 at the time, it was suggested by Wing HQ that I should take the next No 1 leave party and so have my own second leave at the same time. It was arranged that I should take a party of seventeen airmen consisting of Warrant Officer Lee (who did all the work), a couple of Sergeants and five Corporals, the remainder being aircraftmen of varying lower ranks. On the train was Peter Walker from 73 (from whence I had just come) and he was also taking a party home, so I had a kindred spirit in London with me and we met up again after our ten day's leave. To my great relief, Mr Lee and I found all our airmen present and correct on Waterloo station, so enabling me to relax and savour, like the others, a fond farewell from my girlfriend. This time we crossed on the Dover-Boulogne route which was much quicker and our mine sweepers had been at work, so night crossings were comparatively relaxed. We arrived back at Rheims on my twenty-eight birthday, still with all the men present. Of course, I realised that I had been given the job as the only Officer who Wing felt they could easily spare. Had anything gone wrong I suppose I would have been held responsible – even if I had pleaded that I was merely the Rolls-Royce representative. No doubt the situation was well covered by *"...to have, hold and enjoy your said Honorary Rank accordingly..."* to quote from my Commission, which I am sure could be interpreted into meaning almost anything.

While we had been away both the Squadrons had moved, 73 to Rheims Champagne aerodrome, and No 1 to Berry-au-Bac, which until then had been used only by No 142 Squadron (Battles). The No 1 boys had moved into a chateau to share with No 12 Squadron (Battles) and our wing HQ was established at Guineacourt.

It was soon after this leave that my car was ready for collection from the Rolls-Royce Depot in Paris, so up I went on what was to be my last trip, although I didn't know it at that time. I didn't stay the night, but called at Marjorie's flat to give her a couple of what were by now rare bottles of booze as a small present from the Squadron. As she was out I left a note with them. I had been back with the Squadron for some ten days when I was surprised to receive a letter from Paris which read as follows:

Marjorie Dunton

Tony,
I adored your note – it was beautifully presented! To whom am I indebted for a stirring bottle of whisky and gin? You can well imagine the results were all that could be expected!

Stan and Bill (bless the Colonials), Peter and Ian have been so nice – we all had nostalgia however for our four mousquetairs! We had drinks and some dinner together last night, later going up to the Boeuf for a nightcap and coming back here for another. We hope soon to be better organised to receive you. We are all meeting again tonight to finish the last night in Paris until next time. Bertie was thrilled to be remembered by you. I heard some talk of her sending you a record of "Parlez-moi d'amour", so it would seem that first impressions are lasting!

We are looking forward impatiently for your next leave; George joins me in sending best regards – I feel that you all belong to me – the Commander included, so I shall send you my love.

Thank you again for everything – take care of yourselves please and know that No 1 Squadron is very dear to the friends you have made at No 3 Fb St Honoré.

Saturday night.
(Signed) Marjorie Dunton

By now all home and local leave had come to an abrupt halt, and while it was sad not to see Paris again, I think we all understood that these little excursions would have to stop sooner or later, and the pressure of coming events left no time for regrets.

CHAPTER THIRTEEN

Sojourn in 73 Squadron

To go back to the days 'before car': while 73 Squadron had been at Le Havre and Norrent Fontes I could easily keep my eye on both as we shared the same aerodrome, but on 2 March 1940 No 1 had moved to Neuville while 73 was despatched to Rouvres, some seventy miles away. As I was living with No 1, 73 then saw little of me. Both Squadrons were short of transport, especially light vans, and this was a sore point as Rheims seemed to be full of cars, while we were using three-ton lorries to take a few pilots backwards and forwards to the aerodrome. Early in the New Year during one of our coldest spells, it was imperative that I should make a visit to 73 as they were experiencing bad starting with their engines and, if anything, their aerodrome was even colder than ours. All winter the Hurricanes stood out in the open with no protection or covering, much less any heating arrangements such as the French aircraft enjoyed. Under normal conditions the engines would start reliably with just a few turns of the electric starter, or hand-starting which was accomplished by two men turning handles fitted through the cowling on either side of the engine. Snow was still on the ground and with the east wind blowing across the open aerodrome it was bitterly cold, but each engine had to be started and warmed up ready for flight by daybreak whatever the weather. The men were getting to the aerodrome an hour or more before dawn. Even using tricks like removing the twelve exhaust-side (or outer) sparking plugs to pre-heat them and melt the condensation frozen across their points, and operating the starting handles and the electric starters together, they could only get a few of the aircraft serviceable. Frozen electrical relays, carburettors – and fingers – added to their troubles. Panther, the code name for AASF HQ would not tolerate the poor serviceability returns morning after morning. So Panther, (as the ground crews reminded everyone, living in their hotels with central heating and offices in the Château Polignac with its fires), wanted to know why and signalled that P/O Henniker was to proceed there immediately to investigate.

As already indicated, this was before I got my own car, so I scrounged a lift to Rouvres on a three-ton Crossley ration lorry, which took the whole day and despite snow chains on the wheels, there were some hectic moments. Now, I had a suspicion that the CO of 73 didn't really want me there at all; if he really wanted me quickly he could have sent his Maggie over, whereas No 1 naturally didn't see why they should fly me there. It was dark when I arrived and when I found the Mairie, which doubled for the Officers Mess, the whole place seemed cold and uninviting. I went inside and nobody stirred. The silence was broken now and then by Doc Outfin and Graham Paul playing 'Battleships' over the bar which was at one end of the dimly lit room. About five other Officers were huddled over the small fire which held the concentrated attention of three of them while the other two were reading. This human fire screen was quite enough to keep the temperature of the room little above zero and I had no difficulty in picking out the largest member of the quintet to whom I now reported. Squadron Leader Knox stretched himself, and then in a loud voice asked me to have a drink. Ian Scoular then left the fireside and, by way of conversation, challenged me to a game of darts, and showed me the Squadron Diary which had been started in 1914 by a Major Hubbard, the Squadron's first CO. Ian was a flight commander and, if nothing else, he was very much in charge of this interesting record of the Squadron and it was his job to keep it up to date. In 1938 when 73 was re-formed, the Squadron's old CO presented them with the diary on which was the crest they had made up during the 1914 war. This depicted a dog with its front paws on the empty shelves of a cupboard: today the official Squadron Crest contains the head and shoulders of a begging dog. The most interesting thing about the diary was that the early entries could have been written in 1939/40 instead of 1914/16, with the exception that the aircraft type had changed. If Ian was away for any reason 'Henry' Hall, the Squadron adjutant, kept the daily entry going. When I was officially posted to the Squadron later on, I was greatly honoured to have my photograph put in the diary with some explanation for my presence and when I left – so I was told, for I never saw it – a few suitable wisecracks were added!

Eventually supper time came round and that meal was to be the first of many I was to have with the 73 boys. It was a bad start; I think they were even more disgusted with the food than I was, and although all agreed it was awful, apparently nobody had the energy to do anything about it. At this time we were having excellent victuals in No 1 as we were supplementing our normal rations with extras, for which we each paid ten francs per day, and France knew no food rationing or shortages until after the German occupation. I was glad when this meal was over as uninteresting food does not help to engender interesting conversation and the spirits of the 73 boys seemed to be at pretty low ebb. Perhaps it was just the contrast with the atmosphere of No 1, where in spite of everything – the cold, the conditions, the inactivity – everyone was in fine form. There, we had fun amongst ourselves, pulling each other's legs, knowing each other's character and perhaps where a foible could be played upon in not too unkind a way. In No 1 we kept reasonable Mess rules and the evening meal was made fairly formal. We would foregather in the Mess roughly half an hour before feeding and have a few drinks round the bar. Even if we were sick of seeing the same faces day after day, we always found something to talk about. When our messing Corporal informed me that the meal was ready to serve I would inform The Bull (I was Messing Officer at the time). He would tell me to have it brought in straight away, or hold for ten minutes or so depending how things were going. We always sat down together and if anyone was late he informally apologised to The Bull. It was only later on when the Spring Offensive began that one had to feed as and when one had the opportunity.

Now being in 73, I was told I could sleep in E J Kain's billet on this my first night at Rouvres, as the owner was away on leave. Corporal Softly, his batman, was detailed to take me to his room. Softly looked after me very well and took great pride in showing me photographs of the two Dorniers 'EJ' had shot down, which for that time was a record. The room was warm, the bed comfortable and I switched on Kain's little radio and heard Judy Garland sing *It never rains but what it pours*. Although it meant nothing to me then, I was sleeping in the famous Cobber Kain's bed but at that time he was just 'EJ', to distinguish him from the other Kain in the Squadron, who not only also came from New Zealand, but even from the same home town, though neither had heard of the other until they both joined 73 before the war. I spent two days at Rouvres and was able to help them a little with their starting troubles. We had to get some heat from somewhere and the only supply appeared to be low powered oil lamps designed to keep the damp out of the aircraft wireless sets. My partners in crime were the Squadron Engineer Officer, W/O, 'Jumbo' Neil and two Flight Sergeants, and we found that these lamps just fitted inside the cowling of the engines so – with the connivance of Bill Williams, the Equipment Officer – we raided his store and rounded up all the lamps and as many spare blankets as we could lay our hands on. With one lamp per engine burning all night and with two grey 'blankets, airmen-for-the-use-of' wrapped around the outside of each engine cowling, the aeroplanes could be warmed up ready and serviceable by dawn. Four months later proper heating lamps arrived on the Squadron – presumably in time for the following winter!

After a couple of days with 73, I was glad to get back to No 1 and smiling faces and good food. To be fair, when I was posted to Rouvres later on, things were very different and I made many friends in what seemed a completely changed Squadron. In the meantime, though the roads were clear of snow, I could still never get transport when needed. Things came to a head when Mr 'Bill' Lappin came out from the Company's London office to pay a visit to each of the Squadrons with W/Co Tighe, the then Senior Repair and Maintenance Officer at Panther. It was decided that the only thing to do was to provide me with my own transport. This would take some time to arrange and until then I was to be posted to 73 for a period as I was obviously favouring No 1. Whenever I did make a trip to 73 the CO never seemed keen to see me so he really had little idea of my movements while there.

Towards the end of February I said goodbye to No 1 and arrived at Rouvres with all my kit. The differences I met this time were striking. The sun was shining, which always helps, but the main improvement was the new Mess which was a private house which had previously been occupied by a French Army unit. Everyone seemed cheery and I received quite a welcome, even from Sqn Ldr Knox. It didn't seem long before I felt like a member – if only temporary – of the Squadron, and after all I wasn't exactly a stranger. In looking back now I find it much more natural to use the first person plural (being made to feel one of 'them') when describing life in 73 Squadron made me feel I was a member, it just took a little longer with 73. My first meal – tea – was even better than we generally had in No 1 and the whole atmosphere was more lively and friendly. Doc Outfin had now taken the food situation in hand and each member of the Mess paid five francs per day for 'extras', which helped the normal rations out, and nobody had any grounds for complaint. Tea rather reminded me of my school days as the usual bread, butter and jam supplied by normal rations was augmented from one's tuck box, and now by 'Private Guz' or tit-bits sent from home. As at school, cakes and food from home saved officialdom from spending adequate amounts on enough grub to do more than just keep body and soul together. Here, Private Guz was not private at all as everything that arrived in the Mess was given to Corporal Softly who rationed the goods, and if anyone felt he wasn't supplying his share to the pool, he bought something from the NAAFI which was conveniently situated opposite. If one spoke nicely to the cook, for the price of one franc, a boiled egg would be produced.

We had always been on top of each other in the Mairie at Neuville as it had only one large room for everything, while here at 73, we had a dining room and an anteroom downstairs plus, of course, a kitchen. Upstairs were two rooms; one was used as a cloakroom and the other – perhaps the most frequented one in the house – was the Bar. The big attraction in this room was naturally the bar itself; completely redesigned when brought over from the old Mess, it now had an imposing array of very French-looking bottles along a shelf on the wall behind it. Beneath the bar counter were two other shelves for the 'cheap' drinks, such as champagne, beer and minerals, and one helped one's self and signed for whatever one had – no cheating. The top step of the stairs was decorated by an embedded bullet from a Mauser automatic pistol Cobber had captured from one of his victims and had fired off one night just to keep everyone awake. Perched on a stool behind the bar was a favourite spot for letter writing – especially as the necessities of life and inspiration were close to hand. The only snag was that you were always being interrupted to get someone a drink and there was always someone ready to add an inappropriate note to the bottom of your letter. On one occasion 'Tubbs' Perry pretended to pour some whisky over a letter I was writing to a girlfriend, when someone jolted his elbow and my letter was soaked. While I cursed him, he dried it off on the coal stove (one of which Bill Williams provided for each room) and having written so much I would not repeat the effort, so sent it off with an explanation. The reply from the current loved one was that I was to kick Tubbs in the pants. I wish I could have done. He was killed the next day.

The wife of the other Kane, Bill, had embroidered some cushion covers with appropriate suggestions for dealing with Hitler, but they were much too good for the cushions, which we didn't have anyway, so they enlivened and brightened the walls of the bar, alternating with the young lovelies from *Esquire*. Where the radiogram – (record player, for those who don't go back that far) – appeared from, history did not relate, but it certainly worked overtime and there was a large variety of records to suit all tastes, which steadily accumulated as the boys returned from leave. The most popular ones were naturally what were called 'dance' records in those days and if I ever hear *F D R Jones*, *Scatterbrain* or the selection from *Gulliver's Travels* again, I am sure I will be taken back to Rouvres. 'Henry' Hall on the other hand liked classical music and he would sneak into the bar when nobody was looking and put on Wagner, Mahler or Bruckner. We used to stick it for a while, then one perfectly good Squadron Adjutant would find himself sailing down the stairs. After all, there was a war on and we thought it would have been more appropriate if he had chosen Rachmaninoff or Tchaikovsky. How things in 73 had changed!. It wasn't long before I realised that I was just as happy in Rouvres as in Neuville – providing the CO made himself scarce, which he normally did. Knox was an awkward character and took a delight in trying to make fools of people. During the winter there was plenty of time for letter writing and, of course, all mail had to be censored. There was a vast amount to get through from the whole Squadron, so all Officers mucked in about three evenings per week. One evening he roared into the dining room and in a loud voice asked me what I thought I was doing censoring letters when I wasn't a member of the Squadron. I said nothing – just got up and poured myself a drink at the bar, and two of the other boys came and joined me and we just looked at each other and laughed.

From the two windows of the bar one got a commanding view of the blank wall of the house next door on one side, while from the second window one looked out upon the back garden that had once been, and the countryside beyond. In this garden a 'convenient' site was found for our home made 'loo' which of course had no water but it was a friendly two seat, dual-control job. It was strongly built, with a stout weatherproof corrugated iron roof and it even had electric light laid on from the house. There was just one snag – and it was a major one – it was in full view of the bar. Just when one was sitting in solitary state and quiet meditation, some kind of collective telepathy or urge would possess the occupants of the bar, and they knew as one man that the time for action had arrived. In a flash empty beer and champagne bottles would find themselves hurled through the air with superb accuracy to converge on one spot – the corrugated iron roof. The lads were obviously as good bomber pilots as fighters. It depended largely where you happened to be to appreciate this action to the full. If you were in the bar it was funny; if you were under the tin roof it nearly scared you off the throne and out of your wits. Syrup of Figs and Epsom Salts were completely redundant!

Billets were at a premium when I returned to Rouvres and the best Bill Williams could find me was, to put it mildly, grim. The house was certainly near the aerodrome, but this was its only asset. To get to it involved a walk through a sea of mud – the remains of the winter snows – until a stable was reached. The latter, until the end of the winter, seemed permanently full of steaming horses, cattle and pigs and it was above these friendly creatures that my bedroom was situated. The first few nights in a large damp bed in a room completely devoid of furniture – excepting units of my camp kit – were anything but pleasant and, in spite of the window and door being open all night, I could not sleep for the sheer stink. It seemed I might as well join the 'others' down below where I would at least be moderately warm. However, after a week or so I lost my sense of smell and slept soundly. My batman for the time being was a good sort from Yorkshire possessed with some odd ideas. I was awakened every morning by a scraping noise in my room. This would be Binley removing the mud from my boots onto the bare boards of the floor, after which he would laboriously sweep it all up and throw it out of the window. My repeated suggestion that he scrape the mud off the boots directly out of the window fell on deaf ears; or better still, why not wait until after I had walked through the mud to the Mess for breakfast and clean my boots there? I soon moved, however, to a much better billet and back under the care of Corporal Softly. Softly was not only an excellent batman, but ran the Mess catering under Doc Outfin most successfully. Softly gave me one of his letters to censor one day and it was addressed to his married sister – a Mrs Golightly – nice family I thought. I now had one of the two rooms rented to us in the Vicarage – or should it be Presbytery? – Doc Outfin having the other one. My room had become vacant when Claudy Wright had a nasty crash and was taken to Metz hospital for a long stay. This billet was dry, warm and clean and only lacked bathing facilities, which was standard practice. Here I remained for the rest of my time with the Squadron.

Metz was no distance away and was paid visits by several of the boys, but I only went there once and that was with Sqn Ldr Knox (no doubt in one of his better moods) to see Claudy Wright in hospital. He, poor chap, was in a bad way and had sustained nasty head injuries. Again I was glad to get out of a hospital full of the wounded. We had tea in the place and a quick look round and it appeared to me to resemble an old German town rather than French, while half the population seemed to be of German descent. What a hot bed for 'Fifth Columnists'.

Verdun was our nearest town of any size and although getting over the fifteen odd miles was a problem, we always managed to scrounge transport of some sort – generally an ambulance and driver from the Doc to do a spot of shopping and have a haircut and a bath. It was much larger than Bar-le-Duc, with better shops, cafés and hotels, and in this and their village, 73 certainly did better than No 1. The Hotel Coq Hardi had AA and RAC signs outside and advertised the fact that The Duke of Windsor, when Prince of Wales, had stayed there. The management didn't exactly make us welcome, though Fanny Orton, Dicky Martin and I had baths there a couple of times for which we paid through the nose, and they refused to serve tea until 5.30pm. When the ENSA shows started coming through, the Coq was used for the cast's accommodation until one night after The Fol-de-Rols had performed, and it had been arranged that we should all meet there for a meal, we were informed that nothing had been prepared – even for the cast who were staying there. This was just not good enough but the situation was saved when we found the Veaubon and Marcel.

Even at the midnight hour Marcel took no persuading to provide for the lot of us, including the whole concert party, a five-course dinner, all in no time at all. This was very cheering, but the high spot of the evening was when Sqn Ldr Knox announced that the King had just awarded the DFC to Cobber. This was marvellous news and everyone went mad with excitement as this was a unique event at that period of the war, and if it was not the first, it was most certainly one of the first, awards in the RAF. The date was 15 March 1940, two months before any fighter Squadron had fired a shot at an enemy flying over England. Soon Cobber became the first RAF hero of the war and it wasn't long before his name was on the lips of people the world over. On this night as we went into the dining room, he was a hero to us, and I think it worried him a little as he felt he was being put on a pedestal above his comrades and that was the last thing he wanted. Now he could not face the girls of The Fol-de-Rols who were eagerly waiting inside the dining room, each to give him a kiss. They all asked which one was Cobber and he made matters worse for himself by hiding in the passage but they soon found him. By the time they dragged him into the room, his rosy complexion was not entirely due to his blushes! After the excellent meal, the toast was *"Cobber"*, drunk in champagne – lots of it.

From that moment The Veaubon became the Squadron's favourite hotel. It was more lively and we always had a welcome from Marcel and his wife. It was an old building but had been modernised and was in many ways a larger version of The Metz at Bar-le-Duc. Marcel could produce a meal, a bath or a drink whenever any of us turned up. He was no fool and probably made a small fortune out of us, but he gave good value for money. It was in his champagne cellars that Marcel let us loose on one occasion with all the champagne we could drink 'on the house'. As far as I was able to remember at the time, the results were quite amusing. Having consumed wine much faster than we normally would, were we footing the bill ourselves, we found our way up from the cellar and having thanked Marcel as best we were able under the circumstances, launched ourselves into the night. Parked in front of the hotel was a small Peugeot motorcar, which wasn't particularly unusual, but for some strange reason, presumably that particular vintage champagne, we felt sorry for the poor little thing, there all on its own in the cold. Imagine the amazement of the owner (a French Army Doctor), when he came out of the hotel next morning to find his little car sitting on its roof with its four wheels in the air, rather like a beetle cast on its back! It was not long before the local Gendarmes suspected who the culprits were and several kept appearing in Rouvres demanding to see the CO, but strange to say he always seemed to be flying when they called and nobody else could understand what they were talking about. After a while they tired of coming out on their fruitless journeys and eventually the whole thing fizzled out.

Verdun was still struggling to rebuild itself from the damage it had received in the 1914 war, and was a city of the old and the new. A few fine old buildings stood with the modern ones and there were many gaps around the town which had been cleared for the buildings which never materialised. France had the appearance of a poor country; their extravagance must have been the Maginot Line which certainly cost a pretty penny – and the country its freedom. A chap named de Gaulle wanted to spend the defence budget on tanks and wrote on his theories, which the Germans took note of but his own country did not. The graveyards of the Great War just outside Verdun were awful and yet in a way magnificent – there were so many we had to remember, and now, just twenty years later, we were adding to their numbers by having another *"war to end wars"*. It seemed that thousands of white stones massed in groups all over the north-east of France were not enough to impress upon nations the futility of war. Every time you took off from Rouvres aerodrome and flew near Verdun the graveyards stood out as landmarks and must have been an inspiration to the boys of 73. One concert party was shown round in the morning and it upset them so much that they

On a visit to No 73 at Rouvres I take Ducks Hanks and Leslie Clisby. Ian Scoular (73) mysteriously parks my car in the back of a Crossley lorry. Top row – Author, Marchant (73), Leslie Clisby (1), Fanny Orton (73), Prosser Hanks (1). Bottom row – Kain (73), Bill Williams (73), Graham Paul (73), Peter Ayerst (73), Scott (73).

were reluctant to perform that evening.

Later on when I had returned to No 1 Squadron and had got my own transport, I went over to 73 quite often and always took a couple of No 1 boys with me, and I think this helped in a small way for the members of the two sister Squadrons to get better acquainted. On one occasion I took Ducks and Leslie and the visit nearly had disastrous results, or at least we put up a pretty good 'black' between us. By the time we reached 73 the weather had deteriorated, and after lunch I went round to check the grounded aeroplanes. On returning to the Mess I found the boys still round the bar and it looked as though a pretty good session was developing. Nobody noticed Ian Scoular disappear for fifteen minutes or so, but when he returned he had a naughty twinkle in his eye. Suspecting something was afoot I went downstairs to find that my car had disappeared. About an hour later somebody came running upstairs with a large grin on his face saying my car had turned up. We all trooped down to find a three-ton Crossley lorry parked outside with my poor little car inside it! The question was how did it get there, and how was I going to get it out? Ian, of course, had told the lorry driver to 'get lost' and only return when sent for by him. What had happened was that Ian, in league with the MT driver, had driven my car to the top of a sand pit about three miles away, the lip of which happened to be level with the tail-board of the lorry when the latter was backed into the pit. All Ian then had to do was drive straight into the lorry – which was how I eventually got it out. During that afternoon, Ducks came across a British Army motorcycle belonging to an anti-aircraft battery, which had recently arrived. He grabbed it and started to ride it about the village. Then some of the other boys thought they would like to join in so the wretched machine was made to carry Ducks, Leslie, Graham Paul and Fanny Orton up the village street. Ducks was the pilot and all went well until they rounded the church and were on their way back – slightly down hill. By this time many of the locals had turned out to watch the fun. On the homeward journey a drain in the road had to be negotiated and the bump threw one of the boys heavily onto Duck's arm causing him to open the throttle. The bike started to gather speed, while four very scared aviators clung on like grim death, and it looked as through the fun and games had got a little too serious. However, another bump in the road brought the incident to a happy and amusing ending, although by now Ducks had completely lost control and was heading for disaster. As luck would have it, the four went straight over the handlebars into a large heap of manure, much to the delight of the onlookers. Hank More had now taken over 73 Squadron and he took rather a poor view of the proceedings, so made Ducks take the motorcycle back and apologise to the Army. After supper we left Rouvres under a bit of a cloud. However, by the next time I visited 73, Hank had decided it had been a good show and told us to come over again soon. Hank was a vast improvement on 'Red' Knox and was liked by the whole Squadron, but I hardly had time to get to know him well before I found myself on the move again with No 1.

CHAPTER FOURTEEN

The war begins in earnest

It was early in the morning of 13 April 1940 when our leave party climbed off the train at Rheims and by the time I reached the château it was still well before breakfast and all the boys were in bed. I wandered round the various rooms and found Leak and Johnny 'fast off' in one, while Boy and Ducks were out to the world in another. We could have done ourselves proud here with the numerous bathrooms and H&C in most bedrooms, though there was no furniture, but we were only staying for three nights.

While we had been in England the Squadrons had been hurriedly moved because Allied intelligence had predicted – as it turned out, a month too early – a German advance on all fronts and Rheims must be protected. No 1 found themselves on an aerodrome at Berry-au-Bec and as a temporary measure were sharing No 12 Squadron's (Battles) Mess, which they had well established in the adjacent château. I found I knew many of the No 12 boys from their Bicester and Andover days before the war and they made us very welcome. I suppose officially I was still posted to 73, but No 1 were not nearly so well off, so having delivered the No 1 leave party back, I stayed with them for the remainder of the campaign. I shared an attic bedroom with Billy Stratton and Peter Matthews, which we reached by climbing four flights of stairs, but this comfortable existence was short-lived.

After three or four days Moses and I found ourselves going round the village of Pontavert with the mayor to arrange new billets. For several reasons it was not a good thing to share the château indefinitely with a bomber Squadron. By the end of the day we felt we had walked miles, but the village was modern and clean, having been rebuilt after the 1914-18 war, and we felt our efforts had been rewarded. For the Officer's Mess we took over a wooden bungalow belonging to a champagne merchant from Rheims, normally his summer retreat. This provided enough room for six living-in Officers – ground personnel such as Robbie, our new Adj, Doc Brown, Donald Hills, Moses and myself – as well as a dining room and ante-room, kitchen and a bathroom, but no water at all. Frost had damaged the electric water pump, but I managed to get that working again.

The bulk of my kit had been left at Rouvres when I had taken my second home leave and all I had were a few necessities in a small suitcase. However, Bill Williams, 73's Equipment Officer, turned up trumps and when they left Rouvres he packed up all my gear and took it along with them to Rheims-Champagne. So on my first visit there I was able to collect it and call on Sqn Ldr Hank More, their new CO. The boys were certainly not very

At the height of the Battle of France, 13 May 1940. Of the eight pilots of No 1 relaxing outside our Mess at Pontavert two survived the War. Left to right: Boot, Brown, Sgt Soper, Clisby (behind Palmer), Lorimer, Walker, Kilmartin.

comfortable there and I heard stories about rats running about the filthy sleeping quarters, which had been a French Sergeant's Mess before 73 moved in.

Yes, I had been wise to stick to No 1 with their shared château and later the comfortable bungalow! We had only been in this bungalow two days when I received the signal that my car was ready for collection in Paris. I drove the little 8hp Juvaquatre Renault back slowly the following day, finding my way to Panther via Soissons – religiously running the new car in – and was nearing Pontavert, our village, when I met 'Sally' Salmon and 'Dopey' Shaw (two new arrivals in the Squadron). They calmly told me that the Squadron had just moved, lock stock and barrel, back to our old home of Neuville as the flap had now died down. Sally and Dopey had been left to settle accounts and bring up the rear party. It seemed that every time I left the Squadron for a day or two they moved off somewhere else. Was someone trying to tell me something? It was getting late, so I stayed the night in Rheims and went over to Neuville in the morning, proudly driving my little car up the village street.

So we were back to normal in the village we called 'home' except the weather was now improving slightly, which meant more flying and, for my part, life with a car was very different. I could get over to 73 – who had returned to Rouvres, or go in the opposite direction to see the Engineering Staff at Panther and do some useful scrounging for the Squadrons. A few replacement Hurricanes were coming through with de Havilland (DH) and Rotol – Ro(lls–Bris)tol – constant speed propellers, instead of the old single pitch 'lump of wood' or variable pitch, two-position jobs, but as so often happens no tools were supplied for changing or maintaining them. This meant scavenging around any RAF stores depots I could find, and most help came from the RAF Maintenance Depot at Mourlemon where I even found facilities for making those tools we were short of; for engine as well as propeller maintenance.

We were now in the month of May and the general feeling was that as soon as the weather was settled, something big was bound to happen. Here is a page from my small diary for that month:

2nd May   Hilly Brown flew the Me109* from Orléans to Amiens before flying it to England for evaluation.

3rd May   A few of the boys went up to Amiens to see the Me109, and Ducks had a scrap with it in his Hurricane – Hilly flying the 109. The show was impressive, and although the 109 had a better climb, the Hurricane was more useful in a dog fight

My little 8hp Renault Petit Juvaquatre supplied by Rolls-Royce Paris. Hanks, Clisby and Mould.

4th May	*I set out with Killy early in the morning in the Maggie for Amiens to see the 109, but after several attempts to get through cloud right down on the deck, decided to give up and return to Rheims Champagne for a second breakfast.*
5th May	*W/O Lee gets his Commission and is returning to England.*
6th May	*Mel of the 'Tatler' came over to Neuville and sketched a selected few.*
7th May	*Leak leaves for England to do an 'Air Fighter Tactics' course.*
9th May	*Something seems in the air today and rumour has it that the balloon is half out of its hangar and ready to go up any minute now. The complete lack of activity in the air today heralds something.*

*The Me109 had force-landed in France and was the first of its type anyone had seen or had been able to fly. Orléans was the French equivalent of our Martlesham Heath, or present day Boscombe Down and Farnborough rolled into one.

On the following day the balloon really did go up and, although we did not realise it at the time, this was the first day of the real war. From then on life suddenly changed. There was no time for parties or entertainment of any kind – Paris was forgotten and it was just hard work and little sleep. Perhaps 10 May 1940 will never mean quite as much to people in England as it did to those living in France, Belgium and even Luxembourg.

There was a battery of four 1914/18 guns (3.5s I should think), situated between us at Neuville and Bar-le-Duc, and the French gunners used to do some rather pathetic shooting at odd Germans coming over in the daytime, but at night they generally went to sleep – except of course on the night they had a crack at a damaged Battle returning from a raid. Just as dawn was breaking on this morning in May, I was awakened by gunfire from the battery and by the unusually large number of aircraft overhead. There was no question of turning over and going to sleep again. By the time I had dressed, gone over to the Mess to see what was happening, snatched a quick breakfast and reached the aerodrome, the first patrol had returned, having been in the air since 4.15am. 'A' Flight were the first to put up a show, and already Ducks had accounted for a Do17, Lewis a second Do17, while Boy and Billy Stratton had downed a He111, but Boy's aircraft was shot up beyond repair. He got it back to the aerodrome and miraculously he was untouched. Johnny Walker had to land at Rouvres with a slightly bent Hurricane, Lorry had to bail out of his as it was well alight, and Leslie was missing. A hectic morning so far and it wasn't our normal breakfast time yet! This was the longest or possibly the first of many long days that anyone living in this part of the world had ever experienced – nor were they likely to forget. We seemed to lose track of time completely and it wasn't long before we had a meal of eggs and bacon brought up to us on the aerodrome, and it gave one the strange feeling that the day had started all over again. At about 11.00am a Hurricane was seen approaching the aerodrome and there was no mistaking the 'Z' on its fuselage. It was Leslie, and how glad we were to see him back. He had got lost after shooting down an Me110 and had landed at an aerodrome south of Paris which had just been bombed. Everyone was still taking cover and it was some time before anyone would come out to tell him where he was, then he couldn't let the Squadron know as all the telephone lines were down. So the score was five for the loss of none which was a good start for the day – although we did lose three aeroplanes.

At midday we received word that we were to move back to Berry-au-Bec, so I returned to the village to help pack up. By 15.30 hours the official 'Flit A' coded order came through, which was the signal for pushing off. Sally was left behind again to bring up the rear (I seem to remember he hadn't done much flying in the Squadron as yet and perhaps we were getting a little short of aeroplanes), and Billy Drake also stayed, waiting for his Hurricane to be repaired. It was a very quick move – we had had a little practice by now – and Doc Brown and I were the first to leave in my car, piled high with kit. Approaching Rheims we saw clouds of black smoke rising into the clear blue sky, but the city didn't seem to be damaged much, and as we passed the cathedral we both must have had the same thoughts. It had only just been restored after the shelling it had suffered in the last war and now it looked as though it would get another battering. We soon found that the smoke was coming from burning hangers on the Rheims Champagne aerodrome, which had collected a few direct hits, but 73 had arrived safely and not before – I discovered later – smacking a few Germans down on the way.

Arriving at our village, Pontevert, where we had had a short stay a few weeks previously, we met The Bull outside the Mess (the same bungalow) looking a bit white in the face. He told us how the Squadron had arrived at Berry-au-Bec aerodrome and were resting when a Dornier came over and dropped a stick of small bombs within a few yards of the boys, but none of them were hurt. A farmer and his son and two horses were killed on the edge of the aerodrome (Paul had to put one of the horses out of its misery with his pistol). Mourmelon had received some heavy stuff, which was no wonder, but apart from the hangars, little damage had been done. No 88 were still

177

there and one of our aircraft repair units used two of the hangars – one of which I used to visit when I was scrounging 'bits and bobs'. It had been the equivalent to our Central Flying School before the war and the concrete hangars could been seen for miles as there was never any attempt to camouflage them. This was our first experience of bombing, although I had missed it myself, and the aerodrome was visited several times later on. There were supposed to be two French Fighter Squadrons hard by, but nobody had ever seen them flying.

From now on, in addition to my official job, I found that I was also the Squadron Intelligence Officer once again – this time in earnest. I now had more opportunity than most to try and piece together the general progress of the war, that is, strictly from the war in the air point of view. The Bull received all Intelligence matters direct and I was left with the daily debriefing of the pilots. From the information collected, I compiled Combat Reports which I 'phoned through to Panther (HQ) every night whenever possible. On this not-easily-forgotten day of May, for instance, things were so hectic that it was impossible to get a true picture and no Report went through; more similar days were to follow. No 73 had been trying to keep at least two aircraft in the air throughout the day, as had No 1 but sometimes the Wing could only manage one aeroplane between the two Squadrons. The odds were, of course, overwhelming; working out roughly at one Hurricane to every ten to fifteen enemy aircraft. 'Ginger' Paul of 73 attacked eight Dornier 215s single-handed and saw one roll on its back and hit the deck. Because 73 had been much nearer the German border they had been ordered to flit at 07.00 hours and by the time they had reached Rheims Champagne (where they had been before for a while) they had brought down four enemy aircraft for the loss of one Hurricane and pilot. But even before this, at 5.00am, and before leaving Rouvres, Flt Lt Lovett and Sgt Humphries had chased eleven Dornier 17s and got one, though Lovett's plane was shot up so badly he had to make a forced landing. He had only moved a few paces from his aircraft when it blew up. Nos 1 and 73 accounted for sixteen enemy aircraft that day for the loss of four Hurricanes and one pilot. Still on the same day – although the details didn't reach us until a day or so later – the Battles had been doing their stuff, but with dreadful losses. German mechanical units were bombed by eight Battles – two lost; eight Battles bombed German troops and a large convoy of lorries – four lost. Again, from one Battle Squadron eight aircraft were launched on a raid; four were shot down and the remaining four were so badly damaged that they had to be written off after landing.

At the outbreak of war Bomber Command were only permitted to drop paper leaflets on German territory and only bomb German shipping and their Navy. Even after the German breakthrough on 10 May, General Gamelin would not allow the bombing of German positions, thinking that by some sort of gentlemen's agreement the Germans would refrain from dropping anything on France. Our Air Staff very soon realised that the French, with no experience of controlling a bomber force of their own, were incapable of carrying out their commitments and would have to be relieved of the responsibility of directing Bomber Command. This extended to the refusal by us to bomb useless targets selected by the French, knowing with certainty that our losses would be great. One could be excused for thinking that some of the French were ready to hand over France to the Germans by arrangement on 10 May. Thank goodness other Frenchmen had different ideas and at least kept fighting for a further five weeks until 16 June when France capitulated. Air Marshal Barrett took control of the small AASF bomber force, and looking back it might well have been he who moved Nos 1 and 73 from the three week stay at Le Havre up to a sensible front line position. The French l'Armee de l'Air seemed to have practically no fighters

11 June 1940 – my last day with No 1. Dopey Shaw, Colin Birch, the Author, and Moses who was to become a pilot in No 1, with a fin and rudder from a Me 110, the victim of Paul Richey.

and what few they had – a few Curtiss Hawks from America and Morane 406s, both inferior to the Hurricane or Messerschmitt – were mostly kept on the ground as aerodrome defence. The picture would have been brighter had the RAF the same number of Hurricane squadrons in France as we had Battles, but naturally Air Chief Marshal Dowding wanted to keep what fighter force he had in England to defend the country, as he would have to do as soon as France fell. Seldom does one event in itself ever win or lose a war, but there is no doubt that the eight months of 'Phoney War' during which Hitler gave us time to build just enough extra aircraft and train sufficient pilots to win the Battle of Britain was immeasurably important in our final victory.

The next day – 11 May – Rheims was bombed, and just to show that Ribbentrop had not forgotten the champagne firm he used to work for, the Germans had a crack at Panther, or its civilian home in the Château Polignac. Actually they wouldn't know what they were dropping their bombs on and they only wrote off a few MT vehicles parked in the yard of the Château. It was another busy day – 'A' and 'B' Flights carried out patrols in the morning and Paul Richey got a Me110 but got shot up himself and had to bail out. Billy Drake attacked five Dorniers single-handed and was wounded and had to bail out. Everybody was in the thick of it from first light and I can't remember how many Combat reports I managed to ring through that night, but of the few I have kept scribbled hurriedly in pencil, here are two for 11 May, the first day I found myself doing this strange new and rather unpleasant job. I think the reports are of general interest but two points may be missed. The first one (No 3), is timed at 3 o'clock in the afternoon while the second (No 5), at 7.15pm the same evening. I have mentioned that Billy and Paul both had to bail out after a scrap. Billy is not mentioned in either of the two reports, so I must have done another to cover his activities; also as Paul appears in Report No 5 and I make no mention of him having to desert his Hurricane in mid air it means that sortie was covered by yet another report and that Paul must have found his way back to the Squadron in time to take part in the 7.15pm show – in another aeroplane!

COMBAT REPORT No 3

No 1 Squadron	11th May 1940

'B' Flight Leader	Flt Lt P P Hanks
No 2	F/O L R Clisby
No 3	P/O P Mould
No 4	P/O Stavert

Time: 15.00 hrs   Place - 3 Miles NE Rethel   Height - 17,000 ft
Defence Patrol - Right Line   EA Type - Me110

Enemy formation – numerous – being attacked by Hurricanes – unknown, probably No 73 Squadron. Climbed – dived down from sun – attacked three Me110 aircraft. Flt/Lt Hanks (No 1) with first burst – starboard engine emitted white smoke No 3 attacked second Me110 out of enemy formation, and starboard engine put out of action. No 3 broke off attack and No 2 continued attack on same EA, and put port engine out of action. No 4 fired at third EA and saw large pieces falling from tail plane and fuselage. Nos 1 & 2 fired on second EA which dived towards ground – both engines out of action; EA force-landed one mile W of Chemery. Two crew taken prisoner. Nos 2 & 4 then attacked third EA together. EA was last seen diving down, one engine turning but out of action – other engine emitting white smoke at 10,000 ft, 5 miles SE of Rethel. No 2 then fired at first Me110 which was last seen diving down with starboard engine and wing in flames. Flight returned to unit – no casualties.

The highlights of this little encounter are that an 'enemy formation' generally consisted of anything up to thirty aircraft and on this occasion when 'B' Flight arrived on the scene, the enemy were being attacked by a Flight from 73 whose successes were unknown to us, the scrap then being continued by No 1. These four professional pilots had no hesitation in tackling an enemy vastly superior in numbers *and* fire power (four 20 mm cannons per Me110), knock down three of the German aircraft and, having used up all their ammunition, break off the fight and return to base. Neither pilot claimed individual victories, each telling me his version of the action as he saw it.

COMBAT REPORT No 5

No 1 Squadron	*11th May 1940*
'A' Flight Leader	*Flt Lt P Walker*
No 2	*F/O Brown*
No 3	*F/O P Richey*
No 4	*F/O I Kilmartin*

Time: 19.15 hrs   Place - W of Meziers   Height - 7000 ft
Defence Patrol - N end of Patrol   Line EA Type - Me 110

Formation of about forty EA (bombers) in sections of threes in line abreast formation, escorted by fifteen Me110 EA. From patrol formation turned W in Vic formation, attacked escort and bombers turned N. Approaching left flank of escort as they were more staggered. On sight Me110s turned to face our aircraft and a dogfight followed. No 1 attacked the first EA from rear and first burst had no effect. The EA got on to No 1's tail and our aircraft changed the position and got on EA's tail and gave one burst as EA did climbing turn. EA burst into flames – pilot jumped by 'chute and EA was seen to crash in wood.

No 1 then attacked a second EA and deflection shooting had no effect. No 1 then got in a slight deflection shot with remaining ammunition, and the second EA was seen to roll on its back and dive towards the ground from 4000 ft. Was not seen to hit ground. Position E of Vervins.

Six EA turned to form a right-hand circle. No 4 turned right followed by No 2 – opening found in circle and dog fight followed. EA appeared to favour a steep climb and turn, as an evasive action. No 4 got on tail of third EA which went into a spin and hit the ground – position not known. No 2 picked out fourth EA and followed in a tight turn and on straightening out fired at EA. Flames issued from front and tail of EA and No 2 broke away for further engagement. No 2 gave several short bursts into a fifth EA from rear, and at the same time found an EA on No 4's tail. No 4 dived, pulled out, turned and reversed the position and got on EA's tail. No 4 opened fire and EA continued on shallow diving turn, No 4 using up all ammo into EA (200 rounds per gun) down to 500 ft. EA disappeared into wood. No flames. No 4 then returned to unit. Position E of Vervins.

No 3 got on tail of sixth EA and attacked on starboard bow and gave short burst. The EA broke into pieces in the air. No 3 then dived onto a seventh EA and after a good burst, EA rolled over on back and dived straight down into a wood. No 3 then climbed for height and then attacked an eighth EA out of a bunch of five, but a short burst may or may not have had any effect. No 3 then saw four EA round one Hurricane so dived to assist and fired at one EA but ran out of ammunition, so returned to unit. Flight returned to unit – no casualties.

So this second isolated account of part of an evening's entertainment put paid to seven – possibly eight – enemy aircraft. There was no doubt that the Germans were losing a lot of aircraft, thanks to the guts, determination and skill of the vast majority of the RAF pilots, but in proportion we were losing more – bombers, not fighters. If only we had more fighters; if only the French had – well, anything. It seems incredible looking back now, but all the help that could be spared from England (apart from home-based sorties across the Channel) was the dispatch of ONE extra Hurricane Squadron – No 501 (County of Gloucester) Auxiliary Air Force, which I used to visit at

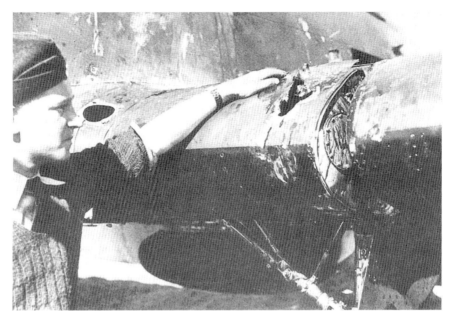

Cannon shell hole in Hanks' oil tank following a head-on attack on a Me110.

their home station at Filton, Bristol. Neighbouring 73, of course, had not been idle on this second day of real war. We heard that Fanny Orton, Cobber Kain, Ian Scoular, Graham Paul and Sgt Pilkington collected one each of a bag of two Ju88s, two Me110s and one Do215; this no doubt being the result of just one episode in their day.

On 12 May, the following day, No 12 were picked to put six Battles up to bomb the Maastrich bridges and do the job the Dutch sappers had failed to do in their hasty retreat. There were plenty of volunteer crews for the raid and six aircraft took off – one turning back with engine trouble. The remaining five met up with their fighter escort – THREE Hurricanes; thirty three would have been enough and, as predicted, the eight aeroplanes were set upon by thirty or so Me109s. The Battles pressed on and one bridge was destroyed for the loss of two Battles, but on the return flight the remaining three were shot down by anti-aircraft fire. Out of a total of fifteen aircrew of No 12 taking part, only one member survived and two received the Victoria Cross – the first posthumous awards of this decoration in the War. I have no record of the fate of the three Hurricanes, but they were not from No 1. There was a second similar raid made by the Battles, or it is possible this was the same as the one that No 1 was detailed to escort – perhaps with 73, but due to weather they never found their Battles. The Bull, Hilly, Leslie, Killy, Lewis and Sgt Soper went and there was a seventh member whose name I failed to record. They met heavy anti-aircraft fire at a low altitude and Lewis was hit and set on fire. There were some horrid few minutes when he failed to bail out and all the boys shouted at him, but still nothing happened. At last, the Hurricane was seen to roll over on its back and out fell Lewis. Afterwards he said he thought he was over enemy territory and was just making sure he would land on the right side of the lines. It was some days before he got back to the Squadron. Meanwhile, we heard stories that he had been captured and then recaptured by the French. I can't remember confirming this story – Lewis, a quiet Canadian boy did not survive France. Of the others on this sortie, The Bull had to make a forced landing in Belgium and had a pretty hair-raising hike back. Hilly was shot up badly but got back unhurt although his Hurricane was a write-off. Leslie going flat out as usual, got one Me109 and two He111s.

The Bull did the Combat Report himself when he returned and was not at all pleased with the results of his leadership. It had not been a good day; a total of thirty-two of our bombers made sorties and only twenty returned. May 13 was the same picture all over again. Perfect weather and defence patrols were continued, as two more short Combat Reports will show. The first one took place at 5.20am: young men were fighting for their lives while most people had not yet come to life.

COMBAT REPORT No 8

No 1 Squadron	*13th May 1940*
'B' Flight Leader	*Fl. Lt P P Hanks*
No 2	*F/O Lorimer*
No 3	*P/O Goodman*

Time 05.20 hrs   Place Right Patrol Line   Height 7000 ft.

Reached patrol line at 07.00 hrs at 5000 ft. Saw two He111s at 7000 ft. All attacked and No 1 brought one EA down one mile W of Chermeny. No 2 was damaged during the attack and had to force land at St Loup-Terria. Nos 1 & 3 return to base.

The day is still young – note the time of the next report and reflect on the impossible task of keeping up this pace. One 'authority' in later years considered the performance of the RAF in the French Campaign *"was not impressive"*.

COMBAT REPORT No 9

No 1 Squadron	13 May 1940

'B' Flight Leader	P/O Mould
No 2	F/O L R Clisby
No 3	P/O Goodman

Time 06.40 hrs   Place Defence Patrol   Height 12,000 ft.

Right patrol line at 12,000ft. Saw 15 He111s escorted by 6 Me110s proceeding towards Rheims. Dived on the Me110s from the sun. No 1 attacked one EA (Me110) which immediately went down in flames. No 1 then turned on to a He111 EA which had broken formation and turned to the East. Both engines of EA put out of action and EA force landed 15 miles W of Verdun and five of crew were seen to get out of EA. No 1 circled EA until French surrounded crew. No 1 then returned to unit.

No 2 attacked second Me110 and after several bursts EA dived in flames and seen to crash N of Minancourt, NW of Menehould. No 2 then attacked a second He111, and both engines put out of action issuing white smoke. No 2 broke off attack owing to Potez 63 (French) attacking from rear. No 2 thought Potez 63 was a Me110 but did not attack. Proceeding to return to unit on gravity tank. At 3000 ft sighted third He110 below. No 2 attacked and gave one short burst putting both engines out of action emitting white smoke. Followed EA down until it force landed with wheels up at Coulonnes-et-Marqueny. Attracted attention of French. Ran out of petrol so landed by side of EA and captured five prisoners – the entire crew, and handed them over to the French authorities at Boureq. No 1 and No 3 returned to base as did No 2 pilot.

The exploits of Leslie Clisby – that likeable Australian – were written up in the books of the day in various different versions but, were he alive today, he would be the first to admit that this little incident sounded foolhardy. Actually there was nothing else he could do, having run out of fuel and chosen the best landing area – which the German pilot had also done, and finding his Hurricane parked near the He111. You will have noted that young Goodman was a little busy before breakfast – two patrols in just over two hours.

It was about this time Paul Richey had a lucky escape from the fate which befell quite a few pilots in those days. The unpressurised fighters could reach altitudes where the pilot could 'black-out' for lack of oxygen, with tragic results. This happened to Paul at 27,000ft and in the resulting dive his engine

185

F/O Paul Richey made a perfect dead-stick landing after blacking-out at 27,000 feet due to lack of oxygen. Over revving in a dive, his wooden prop exploded with a bang!

over-revved to the point where his wooden propeller exploded. Luckily he came-to in time to regain control and then proceeded to find a suitable field and make a perfect dead-stick landing.

Our little Mess was very comfortable but we really did not have time to appreciate it. The boys were doing so much flying that they were always dog-tired when they got back in the evenings and all they wanted was food and sleep. Unfortunately they did not get enough of the latter and it was obvious that they could not keep up the flying and fighting all day long with little rest. As time went on we all – even the non-flying personnel – became a little jumpy. One evening this was brought home to us rather forcibly. We had left the ante-room and were about half way through our supper when we suddenly heard a voice shout *"Take cover!"* followed by another *"Take cover!"*. With one accord, we all jumped up and rushed out of the dining room only to find that someone had left the wireless on. We went back and finished our meal rather sheepishly. The programme was from England where they were apparently still light-heartedly putting on plays about air raids and war – perhaps to remind the populace that there was one going on.

One evening just before dark a Frenchman came rushing into the Mess and said that a parachutist had landed in a field close to the village. Led by The Bull about seven of us, who happened to be there at the time, grabbed our pistols, jumped into the Humber brake and, directed by our informant, made across the fields to a small lake surrounded by bushes where the enemy was supposed to be in hiding. We surrounded the spot and closed in, but having beaten up all the bushes, we found nothing. Maybe it was a good thing we didn't have to start shooting as we were more likely to hit each other on either side of the pond. This was the first of a spate of parachutist rumours going round about this time and apart from those dropping all over the place the thing we really had to take note of was the threat to capture the aerodrome. So more sleep had to be sacrificed to mount a night guard, although it mostly involved the ground personnel.

Robbie (a retired RAF pilot), our new Adj, did great work in organising our own 'RAF Regiment'. The aerodrome scare had by then turned to the next threat and that was of assassination of personnel of the Squadron. Rather than have the pilots scattered around the village in their various billets, The Bull ordered all officers to sleep in the Mess – a reversal of his original plan. This meant that we were going to be slightly crowded but everyone found some floor space somewhere. Lorry Lorimer put his camp bed in the room I shared with Donald Hills, leaving literally no floor space at all. Poor Lorry was very tired and nervy and slept with his gun in one hand. I had to stay up late doing Combat Reports and went into my room several times and each time I entered Lorry sat up and pointed his gun at me and said he would shoot the next person who came into the room. I felt he wasn't fooling. When I finally went to bed, I opened the door first and went in well afterwards! That night we all slept with our pistols under our pillows. Lorry slept badly and must have had numerous nightmares as he made strange noises throughout the night. He should have been rested for a few days but couldn't be spared and, in any case, he was determined to keep going with the others. The following day neither he nor Leslie returned from a patrol and we never heard of either of them again.

We had little time for relaxation those days and I only went into Rheims once. I had to look up 73 and as Johnny and Ducks had a few hours stand-down they went with me. No 73 were hard at it and being on Rheims Champagne aerodrome they were troubled by more bombing than we were at Berry. After I had been round their aircraft and seen their Engineer Officer, we went on into Rheims to have a much needed bath; the only one I had while at Pontevert! We went to the Lion d'Or, where the 'Bald Headed Old Bastard' (the manager, who the Press people, who lived in the hotel, swore was a fifth columnist), told us there was no hot water and generally made things awkward. Anyway, we eventually had our baths at twenty francs a time and the air raid sirens went twice while we were soaking off the dirt but we did not hear any bombs fall. Our aerodrome at Berry-au-Bec was the main attraction for the German bombers on several occasions, but we had no casualties, and the ground crews were magnificent. They went on with their work and only took cover when things started to fall. Once, Ducks had to add to the number of times he had to bail out through the enthusiasm of his ground crew (each aircraft and pilot had a rigger and fitter to maintain his aeroplane and engine). Some Germans had just passed over the aerodrome and Ducks knew it really wasn't worth the long hard chase, and by himself; but his two keen lads with their enthusiasm persuaded him to have a go. Ducks caught up with them all right but was caught in cross-fire and shot down himself. He arrived back at the Mess looking very sorry for himself with bloodshot eyes and soaked in glycol – minus aeroplane. He had had the terrifying experience of being unable to bail out as he, firstly, could not see for fumes and glycol in the cockpit and, secondly, could not open the hood. He was very scared but eventually he was able to roll on his back and drop out.

My Combat Reports were by now becoming very incomplete and I know I wasn't at all popular, often having to wake pilots up from an exhausted sleep in an armchair in the Mess to get their story. I quite expected someone to blow his top sooner or later and tell me to go to Hell, but nobody did. Reports were still important, not necessarily for keeping a check on how many enemy aircraft were shot down, but to note the tactics, formations, numbers, speed and armament of their aircraft, and whether our pilots found different kinds of attacks better than others. Finally, the lads got so tired that they sometimes could not give me a coherent story and I just had to piece together what I could, or rely on individuals to write their own if they happened to have a stand-down period after a morning's work. Here is the last one with no date or particulars, which Killy wrote for me, probably in mid May, around the time the others were written.

"I was No 4 in the flight led by F/Lt Walker. On sighting the enemy formation we swung in behind them and slightly above after a fairly long chase we eventually caught up with them and the Me110 escort fighters with the formation broke away from the main body to engage us. Six of them turned right and began to climb, and I turned right to meet them, and stop them circling in behind us. I attacked one of them on his starboard bow, and gave him a burst. I saw him break up in the air and go down in a spin. I pulled up steeply, and then half rolled out on my back and dived down on the tail of another. When within range I gave him a good burst and saw him roll over onto his back in a surprisingly leasurely (sic) manner, and go straight down towards a big wood. As things were getting a bit hot for me I was not able to keep my eye on him all the way down. I climbed for height again, and then went into a bunch of four or five of them. I singled out one, and gave him a burst, but I doubt if I did any serious damage to him. I had to break away to save myself from the others and then discovered that I was by myself. I saw

14th May 1940

I was No. 2 in the flight led by F/Lt Walker. On sighting the enemy formation we came in behind them & slightly above. After a fairly long chase we eventually caught up with them and the escort fighters (Me 110) with the formation broke away from the main body to engage us. Six of them turned right & began to climb and I turned right to meet them & stop them circling in behind us. I attacked one of them on his starboard bow and gave him a burst. I saw him break up in the air and go down in a spin. I pulled up steeply and then half rolled on to my back and dived down on the tail of another. When within range I gave him a good burst and saw him roll over on to his back in a surprisingly leisurely manner and go straight down to [crash] on a big wood. As things were getting a bit hot for me I wasn't able to keep my eye on him all the way down. I climbed for height again and then went into a bunch of four or five of them. I singled one out and gave him a burst but I doubt if I did any serious damage to him. I had to break away to save myself from the others and then discovered that I was by myself. I saw four of the enemy milling round a lone Hurricane and dived down to help him. When I got within range I opened fire but after about a couple of seconds my guns stopped firing. As I had no more ammunition I returned to my unit.

J. J. Kilmartin
F/O

Copy of the original Combat report written by F/O Kilmartin.

four of the enemy milling around a lone Hurricane and dived down to help him. When I got within range, I opened fire but after about a couple of seconds my guns stopped firing. As I had no more ammunition, I returned to my unit".

J I Kilmartin F/O

Selecting and reading these unpolished, almost verbatim accounts so many years later, brings those mad days back with a rawness and immediacy which is still affecting. They are very real, true stories of life, and death, and should not be forgotten.

One afternoon when the Squadron was resting Sqn Ldr Tommy Wisdom, then working as an official Air Ministry correspondent, and 'Glorious' Devon, the AM photographer, came over to see us from Panther to get any stories or photographs which might be of interest for publishing in the British press. Ducks told them of a Me110 which he had shot down that morning which had landed all in one piece in the same field and quite close to a He111 the Squadron had bagged the day before. *"It is only about thirty miles away",* said Ducks casually, and Glorious immediately got the idea of taking a photograph of both aircraft in one shot. It was decided that we should make a trip to the two German aircraft and take photographs and bag what useful parts we could from them. We had numerous trophies of bits of German aeroplanes in our Mess, but a few more wouldn't hurt, so I armed myself with a hammer and a hacksaw and, directly after lunch, off we went. Our route lay in the direction of Rethel and Mezieres, which we knew was in the path of the advancing Germans, but we did not know exactly how far they had got. The Belgian refugees were on the roads in never-ending streams, but they seemed to have thinned out a bit during the last few days. We were mistaken. The further we went along the Rethel road, the more crowded it became, and soon our car was crawling along at a walking pace. The lucky people with cars or motorcycles had already gone south and we were now meeting a procession of farm carts of all descriptions laden with what was left of a home, with the old people and babies riding on top. Bicycles, hand carts and perambulators added to the pathetic stream of listless, tired and frightened humanity; each following the one in front, to – they knew not where – anywhere away from the ruthless invaders. Now our progress was still more hampered. Small bomb craters appeared at the side of, and on the road, and seemed to be the result of anti-personnel bombs, designed to break into hundreds of small pieces, and spread fan-wise, killing or wounding any living creature within fifty yards.

On either side of the road wagons had been abandoned, the dead horses lay still harnessed; their owners continuing to struggle for survival on foot. Cattle lay dead in the fields where they had been grazing too near the road and had caught bullets or shrapnel meant for the civilians. It gave us an uneasy, and rather guilty feeling: here were all these poor unfortunate people fleeing for their lives and we were driving in the opposite direction souvenir-hunting and looking for anything that would make a good photograph. We felt like turning round and giving some unfortunate a lift but there was no turning back now and all we could do was to push on as best we could and try to get down a side road. We came to a village which was packed with people, tired and hungry; but the food resources had long since given out. A crowd had gathered round the steps of the church and some were kneeling as the priest said prayers, while some French soldiers were attending to the wounded.

Our driver took us off down a side road intending to bypass Rethel and we hadn't got far down the road when we heard the roar of aeroplanes. We stopped the car and jumped out into the nearest ditch. There they were, a mixture of Dorniers and Heinkels flying as low as 1000 ft, in no particular formation – they had the sky to themselves. As they came directly over us, Tommy Wisdom was making notes, while I counted them for him. I got as far as 67 and then heard machine gun fire. On looking round we saw that three Dorniers had broken away and were strafing the road we had just come along. There were no French soldiers on that road when we passed through – only civilians. There was no opposition whatsoever and during the whole afternoon we didn't see a single French fighter. We were longing for our boys to come along, but knew they wouldn't as it was their afternoon off and, in any case, they could not be everywhere at once. The 'crumps' of exploding bombs were going on all round us and it appeared that any road, wood or village that could shelter soldiers or civilians was being attacked. We drove on, but only for a few minutes, before hearing the roar of another wave coming over. The road we were now on was practically empty except for us and the only thing for it was to leap into a ditch as each wave came over. I was scared all right, but I think the feeling of helplessness made one more annoyed than anything else. Instinctively we held our pistols in our hands, which must have looked very silly, but subconsciously we wanted to hit back somehow and our pistols were the only weapons we had. Glorious had given up all ideas of taking any photographs by now and his camera was left in the back of the car every time we made a hasty exit. Someone ironically suggested that a whisky and soda would go down rather well just now as we were all a little dry in the throat. By this time, we had decided to give up and get back to Rheims by a roundabout route, but this was easier said than done.

The bridge across the river in the next village we came to had been bombed so another detour had to be made. A few more civilians appeared on another road we came to and when any aircraft came over, they took not the slightest notice. They were so weary that we could not persuade them to take cover with us. They had reached the stage when they just didn't care any more. Now we seemed to be making progress and the road was clear ahead. I was in the back of the car with Glorious. I suppose we were travelling at about 60 mph when I casually looked round through the rear window as if to wish the scene of the past hour or so 'good riddance', when I noticed an aeroplane which I could not identify, banking and lining up on our road – deserted save for our car – in a shallow dive. I thought, perhaps wrongly, that if I shouted to our driver to stop the car at that speed, and we had attempted to dive for the ditches on either side of the road, there was more chance of us being hit with stray bullets than if we kept together. So I said nothing – just sat and waited – and waited, and after several seconds ventured to look round again. Nothing; the sky was blue and empty. If I had told any of the others they probably would not have believed me so I kept my mouth shut. The first drinks we had at the Lion d'Or when we eventually reached Rheims evaporated as they went down our throats!

It seems strange looking back now that after some two hundred and forty days in France in winter weather, living a cold and rather boring existence, all the past had been temporarily forgotten, and one's sorely pressed memory could only span the five days since the invasion. Hence my paradoxical diary entry for 14 May started with *"... seems to be turning out like all the other days... It is reported that one fighter squadron had destroyed 27 EA in four days, but nobody could be bothered to find out which squadron it was. No 1 perhaps"*. Four Hurricanes attacked a large formation of more than 50 Me110s after which all the EA turned and made for home, but two Hurricanes were lost. I only know that No 1 did not lose two aircraft on the 14th so it might have been 73. We also heard the report that Leslie Clisby had been credited with a total score of 16 by getting three more He111s and had landed beside the third Heinkel. This actually happened on the 13th (see Combat Report for that date), but I suppose it was after midnight by the time I had 'phoned it through to Panther. This news was obviously the work of the Press people in Rheims as individual scores were never discussed in the Squadrons – or even known. Another piece of – perhaps unofficial – intelligence for the same day was that the estimated enemy losses were now 100 aircraft per day – no mention was made of ours.

On the evening of the 15th, The Bull told us to prepare for a rapid move as the Germans had got through Rethel, and were getting a little too close for comfort, while there was little resistance in their way. We all packed up and turned in as early as we could, but got little sleep as The Bull woke us up at about 1.00am and announced that we were off. There was no particular hurry for most of the pilots as it would not be light for another few hours and, of course, they were flying the aircraft. Paul and Pussy were, however, spare pilots so it was decided that Pussy should come with me in my Renault and Paul was to go in the Hillman van with Moses to assist him with the navigation. Within half an hour we were off, Paul leading our little party and Pussy sitting beside me with a German machine gun he had collected off one of the Dorniers he had shot down. The gun was in working order and Pussy had a drum of ammunition mounted and, with the dangerous end pointing through the rear window, we were ready for the whole Luftwaffe! We vaguely knew where we were making for, but at night with no lights to speak of, it was no easy job and after Rheims we knew we had to take the Chalons road, but the minor road turn off was obscure. The main road was packed with French military vehicles – mostly driving without lights, too fast of course – and we saw one or two nasty crashes. There was a fire in Rheims which appeared to be coming from the railway station, and we passed one French car on fire and another which had been burnt out. Thank goodness Paul and Moses were leading as with their excellent navigation and helped by the approaching dawn we eventually arrived at Conde-sur-Marne, the village we were making for. We parked under the large wooden roof of the open market in the village square – and waited. Finally The Bull turned up in the Humber and we carried on to look for the aerodrome. It was occupied by No 114, a Blenheim Squadron, which had been in a rather sorry state. Apart from the aircraft they lost in action, the aerodrome had been attacked on the morning of 10 May by five Do215s, which bombed it and then carried out low level machine gun attacks and made rather a mess of the Blenheims. Sixteen aircraft had been all bombed-up ready for a raid, but after the Dorniers had gone there were only about two Blenheims serviceable. They had got replacements by now and were waiting to push off somewhere but, as far as I can remember, they were still there when we moved on again. No 114 Squadron had done some good work and we could see that some of them were a bit shaken.

Led by Johnny, the Squadron found our new aerodrome and – once the Hurricanes had been parked on the other side to that occupied by the Blenheims – we repaired to a small café a few miles away, which the 114 pilots used as a Mess. Here we had a well deserved breakfast of eggs and bacon and the bomber chaps put themselves out to make us as comfortable as possible. All through that day enemy bombers were raiding all around and from time to time we heard the crumps and screams of the bombs. About the closest town to us to receive several visits was Chalons-sur-Marne and once when some 'whistlers' came a little too close, we lay on the grass until we felt rather stupid. By now the job of fixing billets automatically fell to Moses and myself so the afternoon was thus spent. Any light relief was always welcome and one tended to exaggerate the smallest incident so I mustn't forget the drama that took place that morning just before lunch. Most of us were hanging around the café waiting for our meal, when a cloud of dust was seen coming down the road. When this had cleared a little, we saw a French civilian jump off a push-bike and shout something very excitedly which nobody could understand. After he had cooled down a little he told us he had seen a German pilot, a spy, a fifth columnist, and a parachutist, all in one and the same person, and this terrible fellow was now proceeding towards the café on a push-bike. Well, one against all of us should cause no difficulty, so several of us took up positions on either side of the road and waited. A second cloud of dust approached down the road and out of it emerged poor unsuspecting Moses, who had tired of walking so had 'borrowed' a cycle. The Frenchman had not recognised his own country's L'Armee de L'Air uniform!

Moses and I then set off in my Renault to organise billets in a nearby village called Vraux, a reasonable distance from the aerodrome. It was a tiring job wandering from house to house with the mayor all the afternoon, but the strange part of the whole proceedings to me and Moses was that all through the afternoon German bombers were coming over quite low and nobody was taking the slightest notice of them. After all, they weren't playing games and the enemy by this time knew exactly where we were all the time so it was reasonable to suppose that a few bombs were made for us. One house we came to had a wine cellar and the owners were sheltering there, but somehow we had the feeling they were more concerned about their stock of wine than anything else. (I chose this billet for myself and Paul Richey!). At last all the billets were fixed and after supper we all turned in early for a good night's rest. In our room there was only one bed – a lovely big double one – and I won the toss so Paul had to use his camp bed. I felt I had been on my feet all day and, as Paul had been resting, for once I felt I deserved it. Paul got the better of me in the end, for at midnight we were awakened and told that we were off again! As Paul was flying on this move, he did not have to get up until later, so the ready warmed bed was his for the remainder of the night.

CHAPTER FIFTEEN

Fresh surroundings

After a hasty consultation, it was decided that Moses and I should be the first away in my Renault, find the aerodrome we were taking over and get things fixed up in the way of billets in the nearest suitable village. The Bull was going to follow on an hour or so later in his Humber after he had got the Squadron organised. So on 17 May 1940, just a week after Hitler's invasion, Moses and I found ourselves setting off into the night, having got all our gear packed into the car less than an hour after we had been wakened. A lovely moon made driving easy at first, but soon the traffic built up and slowed us down. Thank goodness Moses knew the country pretty well as by myself the drive would have been a nightmare. We kept to the north side of the River Marne until we were nearing Epernay and then crossed by what we thought would be a fairly quiet road. Approaching the bridge we found it presented a perfect bottleneck and before we could turn round and get out of the stream of traffic we were packed in like sardines. Refugees with every kind of vehicle under the sun were trying to get South, while French military lorries and equipment were trying to get North. Hours seemed to pass and nothing moved, and the whole situation appeared stupid and rather pathetic. The bridge, bathed in moonlight and packed to overflowing with humanity and vehicles, must have made a lovely target especially as the French were not particular about blacking out headlights. Actually it must have taken us all of half an hour to get across but once over the traffic eased off considerably and we were able to make up a bit of lost time.

By this time we were dog-tired and felt we just had to snatch an hour's sleep so we parked up in the large woods north of Epernay, mustered all the coats and blankets we had and slept under the trees. It was about three o'clock in the morning when we camped under the stars and the next thing I knew was that the sun was up, there were a lot of aircraft overhead, there were the crumps of bombs being dropped in the distance and I was cold and stiff. I woke Moses and we set off again. But for still feeling tired, dirty and cold, and the presence of enemy aircraft overhead, it would have been a lovely drive through the woods on that beautiful Spring morning. France was a lovely country, but the scenery could do nothing for our hunger so on reaching Sezanne we stopped at thc Hotel de France and had an early breakfast of ham and eggs. Apparently there was a raid on at the time and we heard a few rather close crumps but by the time we had finished our meal the all clear had gone. We found our aerodrome, Anglure, fairly easily as we saw three Hurricanes on it which turned out to belong to No 501 (City of

Bristol) Squadron. We found an officer from 501 who had no idea what had happened to the remainder of his Squadron and had no idea that No 1 was supposed to be arriving as well. There was no sign of The Bull so we tried to get through to Vraux on a field telephone but had no luck. We seemed to be wasting time so we selected a nearby village on the map and found that Pleurs would be very suitable for our billets and the mayor was quite agreeable. The only snag was that a French Potez Squadron had taken over the local château so the village really belonged to them. However, we paid our respects to their CO and all was arranged for us to start allocating billets after we had had lunch. Moses was by now asking himself the same question that was in my mind, *"Where were all the Potez aeroplanes belonging to this squadron?* The aerodrome was empty save for the three Hurricanes.

A little one-roomed café, which might easily have been the spit and sawdust of an English village pub, supplied us with more ham and eggs for lunch. This café was to become our Mess later when the Squadron eventually did move, but we were not to know at that moment that we had been sent on a wild goose chase. By early afternoon the Squadron had still not shown up, so Moses staked a claim on the village, found a nearby wood suitable for parking the Motor Transport (MT) and, as the aerodrome was still devoid of our aeroplanes, we decided the only thing to do was to return to Vraux. Arriving back at the Mess we found all the boys sitting around as if nothing had happened and when we tumbled out of the Renault looking a little part-worn they all thought it a great joke. Apparently on the previous day it was quite on the cards that the Squadron would move and we were told to hold ourselves in readiness. All through that night The Bull had waited for the flit order to come through from HQ but hearing nothing, he tried to get in touch but found that communications had broken down (not for the first time). He, therefore, thought that we might be cut off so took things into his own hands and authorised the move himself. The Bull must have passed us as we slept in the wood, as he had actually arrived at the new aerodrome before us, just in time to receive the signal telling him to return. The cancellation reached the Squadron before they moved, but they did not have a quiet day after all, and Moses and I were now eager to hear all about the day's events. Johnny, Killy, Hilly, Pussy and Sergeant Soper had a party with the usual large formation of Me110s. It was some time before Pussy returned and when he did, late in the afternoon, he was minus his aeroplane. After accounting for one Me110, he in turn was shot down but managed to bale out – for the second time to date – and had the extra frightening experience of being fired on by some French soldiers who thought he was a German. As the German pilot we had entertained to dinner at Neuville told us, the French didn't seem to want to take any prisoners. Sergeant Soper got two Me110s but his Hurricane was so badly shot-up that it was a write-off.

Thank goodness we were not losing as many pilots as we were aeroplanes; and we seemed to be getting replacements, often flown out from England by young pilots who had only just finished their training. This was all before the ATA (Air Transport Auxiliary) had been formed for ferrying new aircraft to various theatres of war. Amy Johnson was one such among many girls who joined the service. To finish off that day, Johnny, Killy and Hilly got one German apiece.

The following day Nos 1, 73 and 501 were required to take turns in covering a combined bomber force made up of French-based RAF aircraft augmented by Squadrons from England. In the event, when it came to No 1's turn, the weather for a change was so poor that they never saw their bombers, but they did meet twenty-five Heinkels. In the scrap that followed Paul got three, but was hit in the neck and leg and temporarily paralysed. His hood was jammed so he couldn't bale out, but after a terrifying period – which must have seemed like an age – he managed to land and was eventually picked up by the French and taken to a hospital near Château-Thierry, and then on to the American Hospital in Paris. Of the remaining Heinkels it was doubtful whether more than a dozen reached Germany again. So much seemed to be happening in such a short time and the following day we had the official order to move so off we set again, but this time Moses and I made straight for Pleurs and felt our labours of the day before had not been in vain. Not a bit of it: we found that during the night a French Army unit had taken over the village and there wasn't any room for us. This was one of the occasions when Moses would borrow my raincoat to cover his uniform so that nobody could see what rank he held – which strictly speaking was none at all – and persuade any rank in the French Army he happened to come across that he had the authority on behalf of the RAF to – well, get what he wanted – almost! On this particular occasion we finally dealt with a French major who agreed to move his men into one corner of the village. So the whole afternoon Moses and I went round with the mayor arranging billets and by 6.00pm we had completed the exercise and staggered to our café for a drink. By this time the boys had established themselves, had got the café organised and we had a good meal of omelettes. We had only just finished our meal when The Bull and Moses were called into another room and a bit of a row ensued with some French Army people who insisted that the village belonged to them. Their attitude suggested to The Bull that their billets were more important to them than fighting a war, whereupon he told them they could keep their village – we would camp in the wood with our MT.

That night we slept under the stars again, and on the morrow we pitched our tents and generally turned the wood into a provisional home. Moses and I spent all next day, 19 May, in going round the local villages trying to find a suitable one for us to live in. No 73 were lucky in having a different aerodrome with a village nice and handy which nobody else wanted, and they did themselves very well. At last we found one which we thought would be ideal for the Squadron, but when we took The Bull round he turned it down so it was back to the woods for us. He, of course, had his own reasons, but we felt this was the last straw and then and there I chalked 'BRASSED OFF' on my tin hat. Arriving back at the café (which we still used as a Mess), I showed my feelings by taking it off and throwing it on the floor, much to the amusement of the boys. A short while later, when Air Vice Marshal 'Ugly' Barrett inspected us on the aerodrome – still at Pleurs – I had forgotten the inscription on my tin hat. When he walked along the line and Pembers (who had taken over the Squadron) introduced me to him, he kept staring at my hat all the time he spoke to me and I couldn't understand why. It was all the adjacent boys could do to keep straight faces and afterwards I had my leg pulled unmercifully. However, nothing was said so maybe Ugly had a laugh to himself. For nearly three weeks we made the wood our home and although a camping holiday has never appealed to me since we did get used to the little discomforts; after all, we were young. Actually we remained under canvas for the remainder of the French campaign.

That evening – of 19 May – Moses, Leak and I went into Sezanne for a bath and some food. On the way we suddenly heard the drone of aeroplane engines and by this time we knew better than to just drive on hopefully under such circumstances so stopped the car and jumped out. They were making a fairly low approach so we didn't see them until they were nearly over us. Imagine how we looked at each other when we saw that they were Battles, very likely coming back from doing their stuff over the lines. We passed through the village of Gay where 73 had dug themselves in and saw Sqn Ldr Hank More's Hillman being loaded up with the boys so we guessed we would be seeing them later as Sezanne was the nearest town. We had fairly hot baths in the Hotel de France where Moses and I had had our breakfast a couple of mornings previously. The management didn't seem very pleased to see us, but we got what we wanted after a few threats from Moses. While I was in my bath the sirens went, but the bath was too good to leave so I just lay and soaked and hoped for the best. I must have been frightened – I left my very nice shaving brush behind. We forgathered with the 73 boys and had an excellent but expensive meal. They certainly put the prices up for us. Arriving back at camp we found that all the tents were full so it was under the stars again. The next day 'A' Flight was on early turn, but there was no action, so in the afternoon the Squadron was released and most of the boys went into Troyes where the HQ people had set up shop. I spent the afternoon going round the aeroplanes and doing odd jobs to my car. One enemy aircraft came over and dropped half a dozen or so bombs fairly close

– close enough for us to find ourselves assembled in the one and only ditch near our wood. In the evening Hank, Ian, Cobber, Scott and a new boy came over from 73 for a snifter but a party did not develop and they returned early. Sometime during the day Leak left the Squadron and went over to Wing HQ.

On 21st we learned with mixed feelings that most of the old boys from the two Squadrons were being posted home to England for a rest. Of course nobody doubted for a moment that they had earned it. In fact we ground 'dead beats' felt that they could not have carried on much longer at the pace that was demanded of them. We couldn't help feeling though that the old Squadrons would never be the same again, at least from a personal point of view, and of course the new members joining could not be expected to have had the training and experience. Everyone felt that they – especially the pilots – had been through so much together and now the friendships were being broken up and, of course at this stage, there was no knowing whether any of us would meet each other again. That the newly peopled No 1 and 73 Squadrons would keep up the great work and live up to the high standards set by the boys who were now leaving was never in doubt; the new boys, however, would have to learn in the hardest of schools – in actual combat with an enemy vastly superior in numbers, but in numbers only. It must be recorded that out of the original members of No 1 Squadron who went to France in September 1939 only one pilot had been lost (Leslie), one made a prisoner of war (Sgt Albonico) and two replacement pilots had been lost (Lorimer and Mitchell). No 73 had lost slightly more, but together the Squadrons established a record that was never equalled.

The twelve replacements duly arrived the same day we heard the news and on the whole they seemed a good keen bunch. They had been picked from Home Squadrons, but only two of them had seen any action. That evening The Bull, Johnny, Ducks, Hilly, Boy and I went over to 73 at Gay to have last drinks together. The Bull, Johnny and Ducks left fairly early and the party then developed into a sing-song. Cobber, Hilly and Boy passed out but, under the leadership of Graham Paul, the party continued far into the night. Strange coincidence I suppose – the former three survived the war; the latter three did not. I lost track of Graham Paul. We eventually poured Hilly and Boy into my car, and getting back to our camp, Hilly spent what remained of the night on the back seat while I managed to supply the legs for Boy to reach his tent.

During the next two days the new boys got quite a bit of flying in and on 23 May F/Lt 'Fritz' Walkup took his flight over enemy AA fire at 2000 ft, but no Germans were encountered and only two of the Hurricanes were slightly hit. Sergeant Clowes chased a He111 and, having closed to 200 yds, the Heinkel shot out from its tail what appeared to be four wire nets, which only had the effect of putting Clowes off, but this secret weapon was not encountered again. The Bull had pushed off to England the day before and in the late afternoon the boys who had been chosen to go home collected in the wood and packed into one of the coaches, which was to take them on the first leg of their journey. It was a touching scene and I found it very moving to say goodbye to each of the boys in turn. Hilly who was staying behind, couldn't face it and did not show up. As the coach moved out of the wood with Johnny, Ducks, Pussy, Stratters, Boy and Sgt Soper on board, the airmen gathered round and gave them three cheers and every cheer had feeling behind it. There were lumps in many throats. I followed the coach to Gay with Lewis, who was also homeward bound, there to pick up Dicky Martin, Graham Paul and two Sgt Pilots – for some reason Cobber elected to follow in a day or so. More goodbyes followed, and then Cobber, Doc Outfin, Willy Williams and I followed the coach in my car to the outskirts of Sezanne. Meanwhile Hank More had taken off in 73's Maggie and proceeded to bomb the bus with bags of flour and scored some direct hits! My car companions and I had the odd noggin in Sezanne then it was back to 73 for some supper, after which I returned to No 1 where there was only Hilly, Peter Matthews, Colin Birch, Donald and myself left of the old bunch, not forgetting Pembers who was now CO of the Squadron. In 73, Cobber, Ian, Willy and Doc Outfin were the only ones left.

The history of the Squadrons was now being formed around new names with some old. There were days when nothing seemed to happen and the Fighter Squadrons were kept on the ground, as their role had now changed and they were too valuable just to send off on a regular patrol basis. Their job now was to escort our bombers and if there were no raids being carried out the fighter boys took the opportunity of resting while the new arrivals practised their attacks and general flying. My diary for the next few days gives a fair idea of how the tempo of the last couple of weeks had now slowed down somewhat.

24th May   *One flight did a cover patrol at 4000 ft and met vigorous enemy AA, but no enemy aircraft. Matthews and 'Dopey' Shaw got plenty of shrapnel in their aircraft, and Peter Boot – a second replacement pilot – went and taxied into a trench on landing. A few bombs dropped around our district, and shrapnel from French AA guns rained down on our wood.*

25th May   *Spent the day with No 501 Sqn (they shared our aerodrome). Had a chat with the CO Sqn Ldr Clube, and Mr White the Engineer WO. An odd reccy aircraft came over very high.*

26th May   *Went over to 73 (at Gay) for a general check up. One or two enemy reccy aircraft over. The only opposition rather poor French AA.*

27th May   *Donald goes to Paris to try and find Billy Drake who is somewhere in hospital. Colin Birch arrived back from leave having taken 14 days in trying to find the Squadron. Spent the morning with 501 pilots; afternoon No 1. Another reccy comes over. Surely they know where we all are by now.*

28th May   *A spot of rain for a change. 'B' Flight did a 'blood bath' (a term born out of the dirty job of flying low over enemy AA to draw the fire from the bombers – running the gauntlet without being able to fight back) in the small hours of the morning, and did not return till evening. Don't know where they landed in between times. All get back OK and they didn't see a sausage. Spent the day with No 1 organising 'anti-high-temperature plates'.**

A lot of machine gun shooting around this evening – may be parachutists. Shepherd arrives back in the evening; forgot I hadn't noticed him around; back from leave or being shot down – the former I hope. He was one of our first replacements and is a kind of link with the old boys of the Squadron – a quiet and charming young Canadian. The day has been a good one for 501. They sent up 9 Hurricanes and bagged 12 He 111s out of a batch of 29 which were escorted by Me 110s, the latter clearing off and leaving the Heinkels to their fate. We took this success with a pinch of salt. Perhaps six counted twice, or maybe just Squadron rivalry!

* We had found that in cold weather a high speed climb and chase 'froze' the oil in the cooler matrix and effectively blocked the oil cooling system which caused the remaining oil to overheat. As the Hurricane oil cooler inlet was permanently open, I had experimented during the winter of 1939/1940 with partial blanking and found that a removable blank over the centre third of the matrix was enough to prevent the problem without leading to overheating. This dodge was adopted by Fighter Command for the winters of '41 and '42.

On 29 May things were quiet as regards my various jobs; all those engines not damaged by enemy action were serviceable, so I decided to make a quick dash over to Bar-le-Duc in the Renault as one or two things had to be cleared up there. When we left on 10 May for Pontevert, we had all thought it would be a temporary move and we would be returning before long, so there were some outstanding bills to be paid and laundry etc to be collected. I went alone because everyone else seemed busy and as there was a lot of scattered bombing going on I wasn't sure how far I would get. Bar-le-Duc, being close to the Maginot Line must surely have been a target – especially as there were three hospitals there, these being an added attraction if the German treatment of other hospital concentrations was anything to go by. It was a lovely day as usual and I had an uneventful run as far as Vitry le François, meeting only large numbers of French convoys consisting mostly of commandeered private lorries of all shapes and sizes with half of them just about ready to give up the ghost. Vitry had been bombed badly and approaching the town I could see the horizon on the other side, broken only by chimney stacks and the remains of a few buildings which had survived. I had known Vitry well enough before to find my way about, but now it was a strange town, and made several wrong turnings. St. Dazier was in much the same condition and on the aerodrome, which used to be occupied by a Potez 63 Squadron which we visited occasionally, there remained about three Moraine fighters well covered with tarpaulins and not exactly ready for any kind of action. Not a soul could be seen on the aerodrome and it struck me it was just asking to be landed on by German troop carriers. I persuaded myself that it was now a minefield.

Bar-le-Duc was approached with mixed feelings. Surely it had not been spared and I was going to hate seeing a place we knew so well in ruins. To my surprise, as I dropped down into the town, there was no sign of damage anywhere. Everything seemed exactly the same – brighter in fact, as the sunshine was something we had seen little of the previous winter. I decided to go straight on to Neuville and return to 'le Duc' and the Metz Hotel for lunch. Driving along the road to Neuville, which I knew by heart, I found myself dawdling and looking round with astonishment. Here was the miserable patch of country we had known so well in winter, now lovely and green, basking in the sunshine. I forgot all about the war – the countryside was at peace – no aeroplanes, no guns, no bombs: what the boys back at the Squadron were missing, and I felt it would have done them a power of good to be here. Had it not been for the fact I was driving on the wrong side of the road, it might well have been in England where I imagined it was still quiet and peaceful. Neuville now seemed a pleasant little village, cut off from the world, and no longer damp and cold as we had known it; yet there was Germany just over the way. I saw the same faces in the village and I wished a more genuine member of No 1 was in my place. Whenever my car was recognised (we had long since camouflaged it in a fetching fawn and green paint with a large RAF across a front wing, after which I was never stopped by the French) folk came up and jabbered away much too fast for me to understand. It was a little embarrassing when I gathered what it was all about. They were glad to see me back because I was a link with the Squadron they had got to know so well. They hoped I was the first one to arrive back and the remainder of the Squadron were following. *"No, we were not coming back just yet"* I said, or tried to say in my bad French, *"but the Squadron is somewhere else doing great deeds, and when the Boche had been driven back, we would return"*. Poor things – none of them seemed to know the awful truth and the sleepy little village was still at peace. A French Squadron was now quartered in the village, although I saw no signs of it, and apparently it hadn't made itself very popular; they were not as clean as we were! What a contrast to when we first arrived at Neuville. Then, the people did not want any squadron in the village at all, but if they had to have one, why couldn't they have a proper French Escadrille? I eventually got to my old billet and my landlord was overjoyed to see me and immediately the bottle of home-made Kirsch was produced. Unfortunately Madame was away, so I never saw her again. I collected a suitcase I had left there and, after numerous farewells, made my way back to Bar-le-Duc still thinking of the joys of life and oblivious to war.

The Metz Hotel was brighter than ever I had known it and full of people eating excellent food and drinking the best of wines. Madame Jean was rushing about as usual, but found time to shower me with greetings. She wanted to know about everyone in the Squadron, and especially if I had any news of Leslie. (Leslie had been missing for about a fortnight now and somehow all our friends had heard about it). I had an excellent lunch in the – to us – famous dining room and collected smiles and a few words of greeting from the regular customers who I knew at least by sight. Madame Jean sat at my table and we talked about everything: she knew alright how the war was going and how black things looked. One of our replacement pilots who had not been in the Squadron for many days had got shot up on a patrol and had been seen to make a forced landing on what passed for an aerodrome near Verdun. We knew Dibner would be picked up, but we had had no news of his whereabouts except that he had been wounded. Imagine my surprise when Madame Jean told me he was in one of the hospitals in Bar-le-Duc. Apparently poor Dibner had got a nasty piece of cannon shell in his thigh from a Me109 and was taken to hospital at Verdun. He was pretty miserable there as he could not speak French and none there spoke English and his leg was getting worse while nobody seemed to be doing anything about it. Goodness knows how he heard of Madame Jean but directly she found out she had him removed to Bar-le-Duc where the shrapnel was removed immediately, but by then septicaemia had set in and he was in a bad way.

After I had blown myself out with the marvellous lunch provided by Madame Jean, we went round to the hospital together, taking fruit and what few English cigarettes I happened to have with me. Dibner was glad to see us, but was in a lot of pain, so our visit was short. Madame Jean had been going to the hospital every day taking him fruit and had her own doctor look after him. I was glad to get away from the ward he was in; it was full of French soldiers and some of them were in an awful mess and in great pain. How the nurses can stand that kind of work I do not know but suppose one can become hardened to almost anything in time. Now I knew where Dibner was we could keep in touch and send him what he wanted. Actually shortly after my visit he was removed to Bordeaux by train – presumably to be shipped home and we lost touch with him. What happened to Madame Jean and her husband, we never heard but we at least saw to it that they had enough petrol stored away to reach the South if ever they had to make a quick getaway. The next task was to settle a number of personal bills and collect some laundry which had been left, and this was soon accomplished. Reluctantly I then said goodbye to Bar-le-Duc later in the afternoon and could not help feeling I would not see it again. Nearing St. Dazier I woke to reality; there was still a war on – a war that had only just started, and it looked like being a long one: somehow it had completely bypassed our old stamping ground. The next day things appeared to be back to normal as the following two diary extracts suggest:

31st May   *Boys released at 3.00pm and three parties of us go into Troyes for a feed and a bath. I took Barber (new Intelligence Officer), 'Fritz' Warcup and Doc Brown. We had haircuts and a long wait at the public baths which were not clean, but excellent meal afterwards at the Restaurant au Gare. I met Ross and a few more of the 'Battle Boys' from No 142 Squadron. They have been having a rough time. Troyes seems a decent little town, but did not have time enough to see much of it.*

1st June   *Boys had a 'blood bath' today. They flew to Rouen early this morning and operated all day from there. Hilly thinks he got a Me109 when his flight met nine of them. Shepherd had a squirt at one but got shot down himself. Aircraft caught fire but he bailed out OK. Sgt Clowes fetched him back in the Maggie this evening. Snow Shoe (Peter Boot) got a bullet in his head-rest, passing his ear. Sally got his sights on a Me109 only to find guns wouldn't fire for lack of compressed air. Went over to 73 in the afternoon with Dopey. A spot of bombing going on around.*

The Battles were still being asked to do impossible tasks – again to try and stop the German advances. How many aircraft remained in the Squadrons by this time it was hard to say but for one big show, either on 14 or 15 May, they must have put half of their remaining force into the air with, no doubt, some Blenheims as well. It was the usual slaughter; 71 aircraft were used during the day, and of these, 40 failed to return. Other figures quoted, presumably for the same day's work, were 35 aircraft lost out of a total of 67 put into the air. Who was supposed to be escorting them I certainly didn't know, but No 1 were not involved. In A H Narracott's book, *War News Has Wings*, in talking about the losses of the bombers and the conditions and morale of the RAF pilots, he says *"Losses did not shake the RAF men's resolve to do their best to turn the tide – and a wonderful best it was. The pilots and crews thought nothing of themselves or of their rest. They just put everything they had into their job. Their faces became pale with fatigue..... It was the same with the Hurricane pilots"*. When I had seen No 218 Squadron leaving its home station of Boscombe Down in September, eight months previously, I had hoped that they may return. The Air Council not only knew that they would not; they had already been written off as expendable and, when the British Forces finally evacuated France in 1940, it was a great surprise to the powers that be that there were any Battles left capable of being flown back to England. Air Marshal Dowding, C-in-C Fighter Command might well have had the same thoughts when he was coerced into letting more Hurricanes go to France as the situation became more and more desperate.

Of the total number of Hurricanes sent to France only a quarter – slightly over sixty – saw England again. Charles Gardner borrowed the now well known words used on many British endeavours, but their sentiments were fully justified when he wrote in his *AASF* of the RAF crews: *"Bravery which has always gone far beyond the needs of duty"*. It is a pity that the size of the score – the number of enemy aircraft destroyed – must be used to gauge the value or rating of a fighter pilot; leadership, tenacity, bravery etc must, anyway in part, be accepted. The heavy bomber pilot's world is a very different one: a small fish in a large pool. Long hours of cold, dreary – and more often than not – frightening flying, relying on the quality of his crew as much as his own; not only successfully to reach and hit the target, but hopefully to return home with his aeroplane and crew. The recognition of his prowess and skill – also in part – must be the number of missions he has been able, or lucky enough, to complete. The Battle Boys had not yet experienced this technical stage of warfare and were still flying single-engined aeroplanes not dissimilar to the fighter of the day. They were carrying out comparatively short daylight raids which were just as frightening for all that – though the exposure time to the fear was shorter! It was the later generation of bomber pilot who had four Merlins in front of him instead of only one, who really carried the war to the heart of the enemy.

The Hurricane, Battle – and Blenheim – pilots in France were unheralded

– the real 'First of the Few'. So many of them would never grow old while the rest were growing up too quickly.

CHAPTER SIXTEEN

Last days in France

The next day, 2 June 1940, our stay at Pleurs was to end abruptly, as was now the normal procedure, and we were off again – still in the wrong direction. The signal to flit didn't come through until late afternoon so it was 6.00pm before Moses and I got away. As it was rather a long step to Châteaudun we planned to spend the night in Orléans; it would have been easy to cover the hundred and thirty miles or so, but searching for an aerodrome in the dark would have been time-wasting. As usual our job was to get as much prepared as possible before the Squadron arrived the following day, and Sally Salmon was to follow almost immediately bringing the Doc in his Lagonda. Sally by the way, had completed a Short Service Commission and was rubber planting in Malaya when war broke out, so he drove his Lagonda home to rejoin the RAF, but for some reason had got his car only as far as France, where it was now proving very useful. Moses and I reached Orléans about 9.00pm and booked rooms at the Hotel Terminus as we were determined to have at least one night's decent rest, but found it hard to get a meal. It had been a lovely drive and the roads were quite clear of traffic: we had quite expected to meet a lot making South out of Paris, but this was to happen later on. As usual, the little Renault had gone like a bird, and the country was lovely and as yet untouched by war, Moses pointing out things of interest as we passed through. My first impressions of Orléans were formed as we entered the town in the dusk and I was struck by the lack of war precautions. Life seemed to be carrying on as usual; the street lights, although painted with the standard French blue blackout paint, were brighter than any other town I had been through at night, and cars did not make much attempt to shade their headlights. We came across a few bomber boys who were also passing through, but met nobody I knew. Sally didn't show up as arranged, so Moses and I had a comparatively early night after lovely hot baths. After my camp bed a real one with sheets should have been savoured for hours, but alas, our pétit déjeuner was brought up to us at 5.15am.

We arrived at Châteaudun aerodrome at about 7.00am to find the Squadron had already landed, but there was a spot of bother afoot over where our aircraft should be parked. The hangars which stretched for about a third of the perimeter of the aerodrome had been bombed, a couple being completely written off, while several French aircraft of varying types lay burnt out, or on their backs, or both. There was little room for dispersing the Hurricanes, but eventually Pembers and the French CO decided on the east side of the 'drome and, aeroplanes having been parked, we foregathered in the French Officers' Mess for a very good breakfast of eggs and bacon, coffee and toast. Retiring to the ante-room we talked to some of the French pilots and pretended to read the magazines; we were human again – just for a while at least. The boys returned to their aircraft while I took Pembers over to the nearby château which had been leased to us. It was about four miles from the aerodrome and was approached by a long drive up an avenue of trees. This looked promising though I could see from the state of the flower beds, overgrown box hedges and the asphalt tennis court sprouting its selection of weeds that the place had been badly neglected for some time. One could imagine how lovely the gardens must have been years ago and although only a few of the château's twenty-four rooms were now in use they contained some priceless Louis XVI furniture, lovely carpets, and many paintings – relics of happier days. To my horror, after having looked round the comfortable living that was in store for us, Pembers announced to the caretaker that we might damage the furniture, so that all we would be requiring was one room for a dining room, a second for an ante-room, and the kitchen. The ante-room was the billiard room, so I thought we could at least use the table for a game of – perhaps, snooker. Again I was wrong. The French must have thought us crazy. Here was an empty château with its owners living in Paris and we were going to camp in the grounds and just use the place for feeding in. The French Services just took a house when they wanted it, whether it was occupied or not, and an empty château was too good to be true. Or was it too good? It certainly made an excellent landmark and target as No 12 Squadron learned later when their château was bombed, though not very successfully. So, having decided to camp the whole Squadron under the trees in the drive, we retraced our steps to the aerodrome to announce our CO's decision to the rest of the boys. Actually many of us felt that a long line of trees sheltering the whole Squadron would be a perfect marker for a low bombing attack and we would be just as vulnerable.

Shortly before lunch three car loads of us made our way to Châteaudun to see what the town looked like and to have a meal. I took Pembers, Moses and Doc Brown in my car and while driving along on an open stretch of road with no other vehicle in sight a piece of something fell out of the sky and made a hole in the windscreen right in front of my nose. Being toughened glass it was impossible to see through the screen until we had knocked it out, but a Renault agent fitted a new one while we waited. What looked like the best hotel in town faced the market square and the restaurant looked inviting. I sat with Pembers and the Doc. Next to our table were two middle-aged men and a woman. Directly they saw our uniforms they started to speak to us in perfect English, saying how glad they were to see us there, and to me they were a 'link with home'. But Sqn Ldr Pemberton was not going to be fooled by anybody, and we had to be rather rude to them by saying we would rather not talk to strangers. Pembers was quite right; by now we had a pretty good idea of the widespread Fifth Column movement working throughout France and you could not trust a soul. A few days later a story went round the Squadron that somebody had found a piece of paper on the floor of a tobacconist's shop in the town saying that No 1 Squadron was at the Château. What we couldn't help noticing after a while was that in town the air raid sirens always seemed to go after the aircraft had gone instead of before!

The remainder of that afternoon was spent in organising the camp at the château and the maintenance tents on the aerodrome. We got the kitchen range working but as yet had no food, so off to town again in the evening. I took Robbie and Colin Birch and we joined up with Moses and Donald for a drink and a meal at the hotel. Our reception by the local population was mixed; some obviously resented us being in the district, while others appeared to welcome our presence. This attitude varied to a degree in different districts; some people being very friendly – a few being almost hostile. Some of the French had no intention of fighting for their country, while others were flat out to wipe out the traditional enemy once and for all. The downfall of France was inevitable. Apart from our initial contact we saw little of Châteaudun once we had organised our food supply and we felt it was best to keep away, but the history of the town would have been interesting. It seemed to have been involved in many of France's wars with street-to-street fighting during a previous invasion of earlier Germans – and others.

The following day, 4 June, the boys were at it again. The whole Squadron took off early in the morning, leaving one very lonely looking Hurricane on the aerodrome. I never found out where they set down that night, but they did not return until the following evening. That afternoon Madame, the Château owner, turned up and we invited her to dine with us. There were only a few of us in the Mess and Pembers and Robbie did most of the entertaining, as their French was quite good, while Madame's English was quite bad. The following day the boys were off again at dawn, led by Pembers, in order to operate from Rouen. At 6.30am they met up with one hundred enemy bombers on their way, it was assumed, to bomb Paris and escorted by a large number of Me110s. In the usual way, the eleven Hurricanes attacked and bagged five bombers, Hilly getting a Do17 and Peter ('Snow Shoe') Boot got two others. The Squadron were not without losses, however, and poor little Shepherd failed to return. This was a great blow to the Squadron as by now he was an old timer – a link with the original members. Shepherd and Lewis had joined the Squadron together, shared the same billet and tent, and were both Canadians. They both did great work before they were killed.

Our tents being pitched on either side of the Château drive were more pleasant than when in the wood at Pleurs, as we got more sun and fresh air, yet still had the protection of the trees. I shared a tent with Moses and Barber (Intelligence), and it was pitched right outside the gates of the Château. Opposite, on the other side of the drive, was the CO's tent which he shared with Robbie at first, and later with the Doc. We used to shout cutting remarks at each other at night. I can't remember when Robbie joined us as the Squadron adjutant, but it must have been when nobody else had time for the job. He was a great character, being a reserve pilot in peacetime, and had kept a pub in Wales. By the time war broke out he was too old for flying but was determined to do something useful. He soon got the nickname of 'Fish Hooks' simply because he used the term in place of a swear word. My 'dressing table' consisted of a four-gallon petrol can nailed to a tree just outside the tent. This was quite satisfactory, except that every morning my shaving tackle was covered with an unpleasant species of tree bug, which Moses told us was quite common round those parts. I bought a small methylated spirit stove in Châteaudun, which did all the work that the common Primus stove one is used to in England, could do. Apart from heating shaving water, on one occasion it had to work overtime. Dirty clothes were getting a bit of a problem and I must have had three week's worth saved up so decided to devote one whole day to domestic affairs. To start the day I heated one petrol tin of water and started on myself by having a good soak in my camp bath (the last one I had enjoyed was at Orléans on the way from Pleurs); a second boiling absorbed all my 'smalls' plus half a packet of Lux and a third tin of water was used for the actual wash. A rinse in a fourth petrol tin and some hand-wringing was followed by hanging the now, slightly smaller and bluish green, garments out to dry on string stretched between the trees.

We were often awakened by aircraft or gun fire at night and on one particular occasion an aeroplane kept circling overhead and seemed to be fairly low. I took little notice of it at first, but it was so persistent in its circuits that I couldn't sleep, when suddenly its engine cut and at the same time there was a dull thud. I jumped into my flying boots and rushed out of the tent to see an aeroplane burning on the ground not far away. It had wakened several of us and before long an ambulance was rushing to the spot. It looked like a Battle but no pilot or gunner could be found, not that it was possible to get near the machine. In the morning it was confirmed that it was a Battle which had been on an operation but, before reaching its objective, the pilot had noticed his oil pressure dropping so had turned for home, then he and his gunner decided to bail out. Well, the poor old Battle flew on without a pilot, circled above our heads for a while losing height gradually until it crashed into a farm building only a mile and a half away from its own aerodrome!

When we moved to Châteaudun, 73 and 501 went to Le Mans aerodrome with our Wing HQ (No 67 Wing) quite close to them in a neighbouring village. This was some ninety miles from us so contact was infrequent – in fact, my first visit was on 6 June when I took Moses as a companion for the two and a quarter hour trip over some indifferent roads. The country was lovely, well wooded with pine, reminding one of Surrey, and of course the sun was still shining brightly. We drove straight through the town of Le Mans out towards the aerodrome and famous motor race track, passing a Scottish regiment on the way. They were the first British troops we had seen in France and they were singing and full of spirits and were camped, as we found out later, on the other side of the aerodrome alongside an Indian regiment. Apparently their white tents were neatly spread across a clearing in a wood which the boys used as a landmark to direct them to the aerodrome when coming back from patrol! Following a field telephone line which had obviously been put up by our signals people, Moses and I were able to find the village where the Wing had hidden themselves. I saw the CO again – W/Co Walters – and had lunch with the staff and then pushed off to find the aerodrome. When we arrived 501 had just returned from a 'do' and W/O White, the Engineer Officer, was rushing around much too busy to see anyone. No 73 were still in the air, although there were eight spare aeroplanes on the aerodrome, so maybe only one flight were up. I drove round the track to W/O 'Jumbo' Neil's office, which turned out to be one of the pits for the racing track. 73 were having no mechanical trouble with the Merlins, so we carried on to the village where they were billeted. Ian Scoular, Henry Hall and Willy were the only three Officers there, and as it was nearly lunch time we repaired to their Mess, which turned out to be the famous Hippodrome Café, well known as a landmark synonymous with the Le Mans 24-hour road race. It wasn't big enough for a proper Mess but the boys were able to feed there, and a few lived in.

Cobber joined us and it was after our meal that I found myself sitting with him drinking coffee under the orange sunshades in front of the café. We were both in reflective mood, thinking about the war, when a flight of Hurricanes took off and passed over our heads on their way to another 'David and Goliath' fight with the Luftwaffe. From the Hurricanes our gaze fell onto the long tarmac road shimmering in the heat of the sun, when Cobber remarked in a rueful voice, *"There has been a lot of British skill and courage displayed on this road over the years, but that was for the love of sport. The same breed of men are now meeting the Huns in the air, and the odds are about the same – one to ten, but it isn't sport"*. Ian and Cobber had been left behind in 73 to run two of the flights when the others had gone home for a rest and, now that the new pilots were getting settled, it was not long before HQ informed them both that they could go back to England. However, the day for their departure had been put off so many times that they were almost resigned to staying and were getting restless. Although many have now forgotten his name with the passing of time, Cobber was famous then and was the first RAF hero of the war. The public needed to have one, and a hungry Press was always waiting for him to add some more enemies to his score; he was expected to continue to be an inspiration to the young pilots, or would-be pilots of Britain and the Commonwealth. As we sat together outside the Hippodrome I sensed he realised this and he seemed very tired of it all, especially as he shunned publicity. I never saw him again and back at No 1 we could hardly believe the news when we heard he had been killed in a flying accident during his last flight in his Hurricane before going home. I wondered whether this would have happened had he remained just F/O E J Kain. His recorded score was seventeen enemy aircraft.

Panther was now at Blois, or rather a little village just beyond, on the South side of the Loire. It was a pleasant enough spot but the comforts of Rheims were sadly lacking and the HQ people had to lump it for a change. There didn't seem to be the same co-operation as there had been and when you could find them – hidden away in some obscure spot – nobody seemed interested in talking aero engines or offering any help. Circumstances were now more difficult but it had been a very different story when W/Co Benson and Sqn Ldr Tuttle were running the Engineering branch. They were always keen to see anyone from the Squadrons; listening to suggestions and getting first-hand information.

Although he wouldn't tell me when I asked him the direct question, I was sure Moses came from these parts. He came with me on my first visit to Blois and seemed to be very much at home. In a village by the river people seemed to know him and he bought me one or two souvenirs; I felt he was about to take me to his home but then changed his mind. We had a chance to nip into Orléans one afternoon and look round the shops, but hadn't time to see much of the town. We ran across Peter Matthews who had force-landed on the aerodrome and was out for a drink with some Spitfire Boys. Unbeknown to us there were half a dozen or so Spitfires operating from Orléans 'doing special work', so we asked no questions. One of the pilots, Wilson by name, had had a beer with me in the Crown and Thistle at Abingdon before the war. Abingdon was quite near Benson, the Photographic Unit which used Spits, so perhaps that was what they were doing – taking snaps. It was while we were having a drink at the café opposite the Hotel Terminus – where Moses and I had spent the night – that we received news that Italy had entered the war. We treated it as rather a joke then and everyone wanted to go south and have a crack at the Italians. Of course one was not allowed to forget Joan of Arc in this town – ash trays, pictures, trinkets of all descriptions and replicas of the bronze figure on horseback which stood in a prominent place in the city.

There was now a lull in activity and we had time to reflect on the storm that must be brewing – in whatever shape it might take. The French were being pushed back towards Paris day by day and there were rumours that they were about to throw in the towel. The Squadron was standing down more frequently and for a change we had time on our hands. Time enough to discover a small village on the road between Châteaudun and Blois with a pub whose gardens ran down to the Loire. We had a couple of swims in the river and the same number of excellent meals in the hotel. It was not long before it was eaten out of house and home with swarms of people coming through from Paris on their way south. This we discovered the hard way when our excuse for a meal was to celebrate my promotion to Flying Officer, which Pembers had put forward and had been approved by Panther. It was intended that I would take over the Maintenance Section as a separate Flight – but it was not to be, as I was recalled to England before it was organised. We found time to look around the remains of the château gardens and Pembers and I found an overgrown strawberry bed. In spite of the lack of attention it had received, there were quite a number of lovely strawberries which we managed to dispose of. On 10 June, Moses and I paid Le Mans another visit. We went round the aerodrome before lunch to see how things were going, and discovered that No 17 Squadron (Hurricanes) had arrived from England and planned to visit them in the afternoon. We had lunch with the 73 boys who were still very cut up about Cobber, especially Ian, who now had to go home by himself. We had barely finished our meal when a signal came through that I was to report back to No 1 immediately, so the little Renault was driven flat out back to Châteaudun. What was this all about? Moses and I came to the conclusion that the Squadron had received orders to move immediately, but when we got there everything seemed normal and there was no hectic activity. I went straight to Robbie, our adj, who told me some shattering news. Panther had signalled that I was to report to them immediately, prepared to return to England. My heart sank. Why must I leave the Squadron at this time – just when things were bound to liven up again? I had been with them right from the start of the French campaign and had always assumed I would stay until some final result of our efforts had been reached.

Having got used to the fact that I was really going, I started packing up my belongings thinking I might at least take some of my things – including my civilian clothes – home. That evening I went round to the Sergeant's Mess tent to have a few last drinks, but alas a major calamity – all the beer had run out and they were short of spirits. I had a few drinks with the boys in the Château but somehow nobody could work up a party spirit and it fell rather flat. The next day, 11 June, I got all my kit packed into the CO's Humber and, having bid farewell, was driven over to Panther. Whatever my mode of travel for the remainder of my journey at least the first leg would be in comfort. Arriving at Panther they repeated that they had been signalled from the Air Ministry to send me home immediately, but beyond that they had nothing to suggest as to how I would get there. I hung about for the remainder of the morning and then in the afternoon the local Army Transport Office made an attempt to fix up vague transportation arrangements. This Captain started by saying I would be lucky if I got a train from Blois to Le Mans where I should change and catch another train to Cherbourg – but he wasn't sure whether any trains were running! Having collected all my papers I got into Pembers' Humber again and made straight for the Squadron.

Now that the wholesale evacuation of Paris had started, the train services were in chaos and there was as much chance of reaching Cherbourg by train as the proverbial pig had of flying there. We were told that the Germans had taken Le Havre and were still pushing west, and Cherbourg was about the last Northern port from which to evacuate, so my papers were made out for any boat leaving from there and it was up to me. Getting back to camp I transferred my kit to the Renault and drove to the aerodrome where I hoped to get a lift in the Anson, which was still coming in daily from England bringing equipment etc. I had no luck, however, and in the middle of my dilemma the AOC had to turn up, so Pembers, Hilly, Fritz Walkup and I had to brief him and try to look efficient and respectful. The obvious thing for me to do now was to drive to Cherbourg but I was most reluctant to leave this little car, which had given such faithful service, to the first passer-by. I suggested to Pembers that if I could borrow a MT driver to come with me and bring the car back for the Squadron's use, all would be happy. Returning to camp I got the Renault ready for the return trip – tank full of petrol and eight gallons in two tins on the back seat. Pembers, Hilly and Fritz agreed to join me for a meal out of camp on this my final last evening, so we went into Crois – the village where we had found the hotel by the river – but the Parisians had beaten us to it and there was not a scrap of food left in the place. Foiled again!

On the following morning, 12 June, I was up by 4.00am and had a quick wash and shave with the aid of my little stove, which I now left for Moses. My remaining belongings were packed into the Renault and by 5.15am Corporal Larkin and I were on our way to Châteaudun. Even at this early hour the roads were packed with refugees on their way south as, of course, they travelled by night and day in a continuous stream. I had mapped out a route of by-roads to try and avoid the main stream, which was just as well, but even then in one small village we passed through a traffic jam held us up for some time. Near the village of Nogent we came across a crowd of civilians and French soldiers milling around in an aimless fashion looking for – presumably any vehicle they could lay their hands on – and I am sure we would have been stopped had I not accelerated past them. We didn't dare stop and gathered from some less excitable walkers that we were stupid to proceed north 'as the Boche was just over the hill' but I suspected that they were more interested in me turning round and giving them a lift south. I was, however, a little concerned: before we had left camp there were rumours that the Germans were moving across the Northern part of the country in order to trap the AASF and, while I could probably get through to Cherbourg, I felt some responsibility for Corporal Larkin who had to make the return trip. Suddenly the traffic dwindled to nothing as nobody wanted to travel north and by the time we reached Argentan the road was ours and we sailed through Falaise as if everybody was still in bed. Passing through Caen I remembered that the tomb of William the Conqueror was in the cathedral, and while the invasion of 1066 turned out to be the renaissance of England, it was hardly likely that the benefits brought by the Norman king would be repeated by the 'Corporal from Austria'. It seemed inevitable that sooner or later France would fall and here we were scurrying home to defend England and make sure that 1066 would not be repeated. We breakfasted off omelettes and coffee in a small café on the outskirts of Bayeux and, while contemplating the history as told on the Tapestry, felt by now we were well out of bowshot of the advancing Germans.

We were now on the neck of land on the end of which is Cherbourg and the whole area seemed to be virtually taken over by British troops so we were continually being stopped at check-points and asked for our passes. Long convoys of Royal Artillery (RA) transport were now coming towards us from the port and it seemed that Britain was making a desperate effort to reinforce the French. Here I was going home and yet we were pouring war materials into the country: so there really did seem a hope that France would hold on. A Squadron of Hurricanes flew over us several times, apparently covering the convoys but I could not see the lettering to identify them. We entered Cherbourg without further incident and having reported to the Embarkation Officer in the town I drove along to the rest camp. Here I handed over my automatic to Corporal Larkin as it would be more useful to him than me, although had I hung on to it I don't suppose it would have been missed though I wasn't really entitled to it. I wished Larkin luck and said goodbye to my Renault which had served me so well.

I had lunch at the rest camp which was full of exhausted Army Officers, and not a single RAF man, save myself. The small beach was crowded with British soldiers who were resting after their long marches and many seemed all in. I felt a little ashamed of myself as I appeared to be the only officer there who wasn't hot and tired and dirty. A newspaper corespondent told me that the RAF's name stank with the Tommies, and later this was fully brought home to me. The Army Officers, however, seemed to know the true facts and I had a chat and a drink with several of them. The harbour was full of ships of all shapes and sizes and with the troops on the beach the Germans could hardly have had an easier target. The raiders were in the habit of attacking just before 10.00am and it was now getting a regular practice. They had already completely wrecked a small aircraft factory near the docks and had hit a few ships. I had dumped my kit in one of the huts holding about a dozen beds and when I went round later for a quick nap it was occupied by some Canadians who had just landed. They were the first to land in France and were in fine spirits and eager to get going against Hitler. Seeing I was in RAF uniform they thought that I was a dare-devil of the skies and when I explained that I had hardly been up in an aeroplane at all they thought I was just being bashful. A bottle of Scotch was soon produced and when I could see a party looked like developing I excused myself and went: I had to keep my wits about me to make sure of getting myself onto a boat. So here were British and Commonwealth troops arriving in France while others were waiting for boats to take them home; the latter of course being tired out and demoralised. I was told some had marched the 300 miles from Dunkerque, which I found hard to believe. I managed to get all my kit transported to the wharf, where there were one or two Battle Boys I knew who were also homeward bound. Gillman and Keys I had known in peacetime at Andover and Harwell and were now Squadron Leaders, so I flung them a smart salute and the odd 'Sir'. They had lost most of their comrades and did not want to talk. On the other hand 'Spike' Hughes was also there in good spirits at the thought of going home. He had a DFC ribbon up and was still in what was left of 218, and had been the only one to return from one of their raids. There were also a few airmen on the docks from 105 Squadron which had lost nearly all its aircraft – and pilots – and they were going home to re-form the Squadron.

We were eventually put aboard the *Prince Albert* and managed to get a bunk each. There was no food available; but the 218 boys had brought plenty of rations with them, which they generously shared. The large majority of passengers were soldiers, who ignored us completely – *"The RAF let us down"* they said – so it was a natural reaction. Ten o'clock came – and went; lying on my bunk I kept thinking my watch must be fast, and then we were out in the Channel without a single goodbye from the Luftwaffe. It is ironic that it was going to be four years to the month before the Allies were to return and claim Western Europe back for democracy.

It was about 5.30am after a good night's rest that I awoke and washed and shaved in cold water. From somewhere eggs and bacon were produced for breakfast which was cheering as we had been told that there was no food on board. We hung around in Southampton Water for some time and eventually docked at 11.15am. England looked good, but nobody seemed to know there was a war on. We had passed other troop ships on their way to France and the men shouted at us in light-hearted manner that we were going the wrong way. The RAF were ordered ashore first and as the few of us walked along the deck towards the gangway a soldier shouted in a loud voice, *"Come on RAF – when we want you, we can't find you"*. Once we had tied up everything worked like clockwork; no customs or luggage checks – I just followed my kit onto the London train, for my railway warrant was made out for RAF Warrington. This didn't thrill me a bit and I had visions of being stuck up there for days until somebody found out what to do with me.

What happened to the rest of the RAF men I don't know, but now I found myself alone in a first class compartment in the only expensive coach on the whole train – the remainder was completely filled with soldiers. My heart was heavy and I felt rather alone. There was plenty of time in which to reflect and think back over the past nine months to appreciate the value of friendships made, which in peace would require as many years. It was rather like coming to the end of another sea voyage – leaving friends behind, and again for a time England seemed a strange country – not yet at war. I was comforted by the thought that a lot of the old originals of No 1 and 73 were now in England too and I would no doubt meet them again some time. The horizon of one's future had been no greater than a day-by-day existence – at least for the last month so I now found it hard, or even unnecessary, to think of what lay ahead. It was even more difficult to judge the wisdom of my acceptance of Rolls-Royce's offer to go to France initially. But then I wouldn't have missed it for the world! I also wondered how history would treat the endeavours of a handful of the best pilots in the world, who had shown immense courage against overwhelming odds. Nobody would claim that the Battles or the Blenheims had been very effective, nor could anyone expect anything different without the massive fighter cover which they never got.

What I didn't know until after the war was that the situation had been anticipated by the Chiefs of Air Staff who had written off the Battle Squadrons and their pilots as expendable even before they left England; even as I had watched 88 and 218 leave Boscombe Down that morning in early September. They were no doubt astonished that any of the sturdy old Battles were in a fit condition to be flown home to England. The Hurricane had proved itself an ideal and efficient fighter, which had successfully operated from rough aerodromes little better than fields and had there been enough of them, a very significant dent could have been made in the Luftwaffe. This was reflected in No 1 Squadron's record which by the end of the French campaign was 155 enemy aircraft confirmed for the loss of six pilots excluding one prisoner of war, and No 73 Squadron's tally was only slightly less. The shortage of Hurricanes and pilots merely brings us back to politics, politicians, and maybe high-level strategy.

One thing was certain and clear to me as I continued the lonely journey to London: the war had now certainly started, but it would be a long time before it ended. Arriving in London I tore up the rail warrant and bought a ticket for Somerset – RAF Warrington must still be waiting for me! Whoever authorised my hasty return from France I will never know but the timing was about right. I would not have enjoyed a trip on the ill-fated Lancastrian – although a Hurricane from No 1 shot down the Heinkel that had dropped the bomb down the ship's funnel. After a few days at home, the welcome I received from Rolls-Royce was not what I had expected. They were surprised to see me and having received no news for some time had begun to give me up for lost. My boss asked me how much leave I had, not knowing I was home for good. The majority of people in England didn't realise how near France was to throwing in the towel. Two days later she capitulated and on 16 June the AASF started pulling out.

The family of one of my schoolmates illustrates, in perhaps extreme form, the human cost of conflict such as this. Harold Deck also went to Blundell's School in Devon, though none of us knew his Christian name in those days. Because of a slight nervous tic in one eyelid he was known to us, for no logical reason, as 'Corkeye' Deck. The family's home was at Westleton, Suffolk, but on finishing his schooling he joined his father on an estancia in Uruguay, to be followed by his younger brothers, James and Charles. By the outbreak of war their father had died and the three bothers returned to England to fight for their country, Harold bringing his young Uruguayan wife. All three joined the RAF, Harold becoming a navigator flying Bostons from Swanton Morley. On the night of 27 July 1942 young Mrs Deck's husband took part in a large raid on Hamburg and never returned. James was flying a Typhoon when it was thought he was overcome by fumes from the Sabre engine and never recovered consciousness. Mrs Deck senior had by now lost her husband and two sons, but she still had Charles, a Spitfire pilot. That was until just before VE Day when he was shot down and his body never recovered. If you go into the church at Westleton you can see the two memorial windows put up by Mrs Deck senior, one for her husband and the other for her three sons. This story is of course not unique, but this must be one of the greater losses to any one family and makes one wonder how many people today remember, or have even heard of, such sacrifices made in those days.

CHAPTER SEVENTEEN

Back in England

During the 1914-18 war a tract of flat open land known as The Downs, situated roughly equidistant between Cirencester and Stroud, was taken over by the RFC. They named it Minchinhampton Common, which was hardly sensible since the genuine article was not only several miles on the other side of the sprawling village of Minchinhampton, but the original, real common, was undulating and crossed by six roads meeting at Tom Long's Post which is said to mark the burial ground of a highwayman. (Strange how the word conjures up romantic awe – almost reverence, yet we despise the modern highwayman be he called bank robber or hijacker). When this old aerodrome situated high on the southern end of the Cotswolds was resuscitated by the Air Ministry in the mid '30s, they renamed it RAF Station, Aston Down. While hangars and other brick buildings were put up, making it a permanent establishment, it was created as a storage depot or Maintenance Unit (MU), and the Minchinhampton villagers, who kept very much to themselves, were not unduly disturbed by those aircraft which occasionally flew in for storage. This changed suddenly early in 1940 when it was decided to make full use of the aerodrome by establishing it as a Fighter Command Operational Training Unit (OTU) in which battle-experienced pilots could pass on their hard-won knowledge to newly qualified pilots before they were posted to operational Squadrons.

It was now July 1940 and I had been back from France barely a month and, having had some leave at home, was catching up with new engine developments at Derby. This educational interlude was interrupted when my boss sent for me and instructed me to proceed to this RAF station called Aston Down, somewhere in Gloucestershire. Being sent off at a moment's notice 'to look after the Firm's interests' was not unusual, but this time it all seemed a little vague and I got the impression that there was some reluctance to letting me go, almost suggesting that an unwelcome order had come from higher authority. The sudden departure from France and having to resign my Commission on return to Rolls-Royce – who had practically written me off – had unsettled me and I seriously considered leaving the Company and joining the RAF permanently. Probably wisely, I decided against the latter course and this new posting bucked me up and I looked forward to it – whatever the future held. It seemed strange that I was to cover one station only and it turned out to be a bit of a holiday.

No 5 OTU was barely in being when I arrived. A complete new camp had been built out of wooden huts on the north side of the aerodrome near the

Cirencester–Stroud road, well away from the MU. The only brick built structure, used by all personnel, was the Guard Room to which I now reported. When I was escorted to the CO's office and saw W/Co P Halahan DFC on the door, it all became clear. The Bull had been given the job of forming the OTU and was proceeding to collect as many of the old No 1 boys as he could wangle and it was nice of him to think of me and give my string a little tug. My presence – at least at that time – was quite unjustified, since the unit's strength was about four Hurricanes and one Maggie, there being no other station within miles using Rolls-Royce engines. The Bull took me over to the Mess where I found Johnny, Ducks, Leak, Paul and Boy, and great was the rejoicing. This was indeed a pleasant surprise and our lunch that day was very late – if we had any at all! The Bull instructed the Messing Officer to fix me up with one of the larger bedrooms in a hut near the Mess and to detail a 'quarter' of a batman. This was going to be a very pleasant time and after ten months in France I felt not the least bit guilty at the prospect of not being exactly overworked for a month or so. As it turned out, little time was wasted in supplying aircraft; Hurricanes, Spitfires, Blenheims (fighters) and Masters – even one or two Defiants, with more instructors to match the increasing number of pupils. Few daylight hours were wasted that summer in flying and thousands of engine hours were accumulated. The initial slack period enabled us to explore this very pleasant, but rather isolated end of the Cotswolds. Petrol rationing meant that apart from an evening drink at The Bear or perhaps The Amberley, we seldom left camp. Later on, when a few of the local inhabitants invited us to their homes (Gloucestershire was a very 'county' county in those days), social life became more interesting. Meantime, an occasional spot of shopping in Stroud with perhaps a picture show, or in the Cirencester direction, a game of squash in the borrowed court belonging to the Royal Agricultural College (where my father had trained to be a farmer) was the extent of our social life.

There were not enough pupils to start organised courses during the first weeks so in between times the boys took me up in the Maggie for a spot of dual – generally when all the other aircraft were safely on the ground! Leak took me up one day and we paid a visit to RAF Hullavington, just north of Chippenham. I flew the Maggie most of the way back, which seemed to dispatch him into fits of laughter. The failure to disclose the cause for this outburst of mirth did not make me think that my inability to handle the aeroplane was in question – though it should have – I was just impatient to share the joke. Leak eventually told me it was the situation we were in that tickled him. Here was a civilian with no flying instruction to his credit, quite happily flying a RAF 'plane, with no authorisation, we weren't lost and what was more, he was keeping the aircraft straight and level in rather bumpy conditions. He was of course being kind, but I was having fun. Later I managed to get a couple of flights in one of the Masters, which was more of an aeroplane, having a better performance, while one had a retractable undercarriage and a constant speed propeller to cope with. One day, flying with Stanley Grant, who later rose to AVM, with CB, DFC and Bar, I formated on a Defiant from the camp which I thought terribly clever, when on the other side a dirty great eagle-like bird had the nerve to formate on us, and take a good look before peeling off. Unfortunately an over-enthusiastic Polish pilot (several Poles came on a conversion course later in the summer) dived that Master at too great a speed and the wings came off.

I hadn't been at this new 'home' very long when one morning Moses suddenly turned up out of the blue. He told us nothing about his escape from France or how he had found us. He seemed well enough, but had practically no clothes, no money and nowhere to live – and, of course, no job. We were able to supply all his immediate requirements but it wasn't long before he was off again. Moses was determined to join the Free French Air Force which was being formed and I think The Bull had a hand in arranging a meeting for him with one of de Gaulle's people. I loaned him a suit and the Mess funds supplied a ticket to London. In no time at all he was back full of joie de vivre: he had been accepted into the Free French Forces. It was long after I had left Aston Down that I learned at least part of the story of Moses'

Early in 1940, a quantity of Miles Masters Mk I (Kestrel XXX) advanced trainers were armed with six guns and armour plating fitted as an insurance against excessive loss of fighters.

escape from France but still wonder why he couldn't have come out with the ground personnel from No 1. Apparently he had left it too late and found himself on some RAF aerodrome hoping to get a lift. The only aeroplane left there which was anything like serviceable was a troop carrier, which was going to be abandoned as it had a broken tail wheel and there was no pilot to fly it. The stranded RAF ground crew repaired the damaged tail wheel after Moses had told them that he would have a go at flying it and them to England – although he had not flown an aeroplane for five years. All went well and as most of the RAF lads seemed to come from Yorkshire, Moses put the aeroplane down 'somewhere in the Midlands'. It took some time to confirm his identity and I think The Bull had to come to the rescue in the end. Moses went off to a Flying Training School (FTS) to get his hand in again and before long he was back at Aston Down officially, where he flew a Hurricane for the first time. Later, he became one of the fourteen Frenchmen who took part in the Battle of Britain, even getting into No 1 Squadron as a Flight Lieutenant, which must have made him very happy. It wasn't long before more personnel arrived – instructors from other operational Squadrons, and pupils – mostly Sergeant Pilots, but also a few Officers who had been Cranwell-trained, or had joined the RAF with Short Service Commissions before the outbreak of war.

I never understood why it was necessary to have such a senior member of the Engineering Branch to take charge of Aston's Maintenance though, of course, it was most important at the time to have a good record of aircraft and engine serviceability, but when Wing Commander McKenna arrived we both hit it off immediately and worked well together throughout the period. No 5 (later No 55) OTU was at Aston Down. He was also a pilot and used to keep his hand in on the odd Hurricane or Spitfire, with the excuse that he really ought to test fly all aircraft after inspection before they were handed back to the Flights. I think he went on to Boscombe Down and worked with Grp Capt Sam Wroath about the time that the latter was flying the slip-wing Hurricane biplane. Sam later joined Rolls-Royce and became Sales Manager – Military, with the reference Wro. The only times we disagreed were when we experienced engine snags which I knew would take time to rectify. He was all for stripping everything down to investigate the trouble, while I wanted to change the offending part or even engine and get the aeroplane into the air again as soon as possible then find the cause and cure it later. I generally won, as while we were discussing the problem I knew that the maintenance staff under the very efficient Flt/Lt Hunt was getting on with the job my way. Later McKenna was killed in a flying accident, a great shame. Many of the Station's other functions were covered by older regular or reserve personnel and in a short time all the characters seemed to blend into one happy unit. Strangely enough we had no contact with the permanent

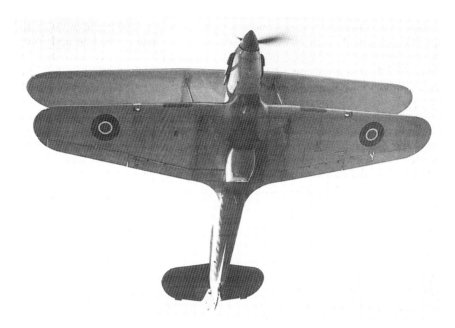

Group Captain Sam Wroath (Wro, Sales Manager – Military) flew the slip-wing Hurricane at Boscombe Down. The expected increase in the rate of climb was lacking so the project was dropped.

station establishment, the Maintenance Unit, and I can only remember the Station Commander visiting our Mess on two occasions. Occasionally an ATA (Air Transport Auxiliary) pilot would join us for a meal in the Mess when delivering or collecting an aircraft from the MU. One such was Jim Mollinson who nobody went near as his aftershave was a little too strong.

The catering side of the Mess was run by local contractors, so the daughters of several of Minchampton's residents volunteered to wait at table and it was through these girls that we were eventually invited into local homes. Some twenty WAAFs were posted onto the Station to take on signals and various clerical duties and one of their two or three officers was Flight Officer Veronica Burleigh, RA – known to us as 'Knickers'. After the rush of summer flying and during some of the snowy winter days she kept her hand in by painting portraits of Stanley Grant, Pikey and myself, and another whose name I have forgotten. The other three were excellent likenesses, but although I patiently endured several sittings, she never managed to get a good likeness on canvas – a task that even cameras often fail to achieve!

It has been stated that five thousand RAF personnel were killed in training

Flight Officer Veronica Burleigh, RA… kept her hand in by painting a couple of us: she considered my portrait a failure.

before they ever saw Squadron service. While the majority of casualties must have been in the initial stages of training and not at OTUs, accidents will always happen, though many can be prevented. I don't know how Aston Down's record compared with the other OTUs but I can only remember three or perhaps four casualties. One was the Pole already mentioned and the second – a multiple one – was due to an error of judgement on somebody's part; a useful phrase which covers most accidents. I was talking to W/Co McKenna in his office when we heard an explosion on the aerodrome, followed by a column of black smoke. We rushed out to the scene on foot; a fire tender and an ambulance overtaking us on the way. We had no idea what had happened, except that it appeared that more than one aircraft was involved. We never reached the burning pile, being abruptly diverted from our objective. How McKenna felt I don't know to this day, but I think after the initial shock the only thing that prevented me from being sick was the unexpected weight of the human head we picked up from the grass of the aerodrome. I don't remember whether we spoke at all; we just turned towards the Flight huts – for my part in a slight daze – not quite knowing where we were making for with our gruesome burden. I suppose instinct makes one clutch at any grain of comfort or relief at such times – 'it might have been worse' attitude – and I remember thinking how lucky we were, or at least I was, when I saw that the pilot's eyes were covered by goggles or something, though his oxygen mask had been torn away from his helmet. I was shaken enough by this macabre scene without having to look at the face. Apparently a flight of three Spitfires was taking off in formation when a Blenheim, which had just landed, taxied across their flight path. The port wing of the left hand Spitfire sliced through the cockpit of the Blenheim. The Spitfire pilot also died. Later in the Mess we spoke of other things over our double whiskies.

Although now a civilian again, The Bull invited me to don my uniform for specific occasions, which in our little isolated world worried nobody. About this time somebody started a leg pull by addressing me as Wing Commander – generally outside the camp, but it caught on and continued, until after a while I began to wonder whether someone knew something I didn't and I was about to be whisked off somewhere on a new job. It didn't happen in camp, but whenever we went to a party or the like in a new-found friend's house, I was introduced as Wing Commander Henniker. On one occasion two wives of middle-rank Air Force Officers visiting from some other part of the country must have had the same thoughts on being introduced to me. They both opened our conversation almost in unison with: *"Aren't you very young to be a Wing Commander?'* in voices mixed with hurt and jealousy! Anticipating that sooner or later I would be confronted with some such situation, I had rehearsed a few stock replies. *"Yes, true"*, I said, *"but if you are very lucky and very good there is no reason why one should not get quick promotion".* We then discussed the weather!. On another occasion six or seven of us were returning from one of our frequent evening visits to The Bear in an RAF Hillman van, singing along with a portable radio and no doubt making a bit of noise. We had reached the open ground of The Common, when suddenly our vehicle was stopped by an Army Captain with a number of soldiers who ordered us out of the van and demanded identity passes. It was a pitch black night so nobody could see anybody else, and thinking they must be the local Home Guard having fun, the senior among us told them politely to buzz off. Things started to get a little tense, so Ducks – I think it was – said he wanted proof that they were in fact members of the British Armed Forces and, by the way, could he – Ducks – introduce the Captain to Wing Commander Henniker (who was in civilian clothes – wasn't he!) The atmosphere suddenly changed and phrases like *"Terribly sorry, sir"*, *"Had to check up you know"*, *"Do carry on"* and from within the van in my best Wing/Co's voice *"Think nothing of it old boy"*, *"We all have a job to do in this war"*, *"Goodnight – nice meeting you"* and off we went back to camp. We never found out whether we were having our legs pulled or not, but we certainly frightened them whoever they were.

We seemed to be free of enemy aircraft except perhaps at night, which made our part of the country ideal for training purposes. A stray He111 flew over one day and one of the armed Hurricanes, which apart from training had the dual role of aerodrome defence, gave chase. Before it came down one of its crew bailed out, but his parachute failed to open and he fell fairly near the camp. The Poles became very excited and we thought them a bit blood-thirsty, but as they explained, we had not experienced what the Germans did to their women and children. The Summer wore on and the OTU kept supplying the Squadrons with operational pilots (although their training was not as long as it should have been) and no doubt some of these took part in the Battle of Britain. Some of the old No 1 boys were still there too – Killy (who at the beginning of the war was actually in 43), and of course 'Hilly' Brown who seemed never to be posted out of No 1. He had joined as a Pilot Officer and was promoted right through the Squadron to Sqn Ldr and the command of Squadron, which must have been most unusual. At one stage three Army Officers spent some time training prior to transfer to the RAF, but they seemed to lack the temperament and we heard that once they reached operational Squadrons they only lasted a few days.

As the long winter evenings approached entertainment became important and while The Bear, and less frequently The Amberley, received more visits than during the days of long daylight, it was essential to organise amusements in camp. By now there was a small WAAF establishment whose

The audience enjoying *Me and My Girl*.
Author – top left (face partly hidden), Flt/O Veronica Burleigh RA – top centre (facing camera), Crusoe (middle centre), F/O Grant (retired as Air Vice Marshal) – far right.

members, apart from the Officers, were on occasion allowed to come to our dances as civilians. In addition many of the married officers had found accommodation for their wives near the camp, so with the girls working in the Mess there was no shortage of partners for our dances. These were generally preceded by a cocktail party which abruptly finished when the very efficient Station dance band struck up. The supply of professional entertainment was sparse; the two most memorable and contrasting evenings were provided by the cast of a current London musical on one hand and a solo artiste on the other. Perhaps it is an exaggeration to say that Lupino Lane brought the whole cast of *Me and My Girl* down from the Victoria Palace for our benefit, but there seemed a lot of them and I think the show had more of a *Lambeth Walk* theme. Anyway it was greatly enjoyed by the whole Station and a few local guests, after which the Mess laid on an amusing supper for the entertainers. The solo performer was Leslie Hutchinson – better known as 'Hutch' – who struggled to make the Mess piano sound as good as the one he played at Quaglinos, but had no difficulty with his voice. He sang and played for us far into the night and all the girls fell for him so, although I had never spoken to him before in my life, I was 'volunteered' to introduce them all in turn and this seemed to please everyone.

Johnny Walker and Boy Mould had their wives living nearby but lived in the Mess themselves, while The Bull was found a CO's house in the village, and he and his wife gave small parties for a few of us now and then. One such was after a Mess Dance when I found myself being pushed into the back of The Bull's Humber Snipe with his wife. Try as I may, I could find no objections to her throwing her arms around my neck and kissing me, but felt more than a little uneasy when The Bull shone his torch into the back of the car enquiring if there was room for any more passengers! I thought my number was up, but the little party went with a swing and the incident was never mentioned. Shortly afterwards there was another incident that was recorded – on the Mess noticeboard, for all to note.

A Flight Sergeant in Stanley Grant's section had just been promoted to Warrant Officer and before being posted to another Station, and to celebrate the occasion, he and our camp WO invited Stanley out for a drink. To balance the 'teams' Stanley asked me to join the party at The Bear. On our way we knew that the beer we would find waiting for us would be well-

A dance in the Mess at Aston Down. Partners were provided by the WAAFs who were allowed to turn up as civilians.

laced, while our hosts would be trying to look the picture of innocence. Now, it is almost a duty for an NCO to see that his superior is under the table before he finds himself there, but on this occasion Stanley and I managed to hold our own – as they say – throughout the evening. Our last port of call was the Sergeants Mess and the party   but not the whole evening – finished with Stanley, the WO and me pouring our chief host into bed, and Stanley and I seemed to be doing all the work. It must have been the change in temperature coming out of the Sergeants' Mess into the cold night that upset our sense of direction as we appeared to wander about in the snow for some time. There was never any difficulty in identifying a Sergeants' from the Officers' Mess. The one with the expensive cars parked outside was that of the Sergeants. But now we should have been looking for our own hut as it was high time we were in bed, which in our condition we had no intention of sharing with anyone else. Something, however, gave us the idea of giving the WAAFs a fright. Perhaps we were assisted by the moon shining on the snow, but somehow we found the hut of the sleeping beauties quite easily, whereas in broad daylight we would have had only the vaguest idea of its location. As we staggered through the whole length of the building and out the other end – without stopping – the reactions of the girls varied somewhat from giggles to exclamations of excitement (and hope?). By lunch time the next day there was an order on the Mess noticeboard saying in effect that *"Officers were not allowed..., and disciplinary action would be taken in future...".* By the afternoon a little fence had been erected round the WAAF's quarters.

It was at Aston Down that the 'Messerschmitt Knicker' was introduced to the British public by the peacetime manager of a womens' underwear manufacturing concern, whose name I forget. He was sent a few samples by his company which he distributed among us, and more were demanded, although the reactions of the girlfriend recipients varied somewhat. In those far-off days women were women, and a pair of knickers was large enough to support an embroidered message on each leg – similar to the graffiti we see on T-shirts today. They came in two colours – pink and pale blue – the little aeroplane on either leg being depicted in the alternate colour. The message on the right leg read *'The Messerschmitt Knicker',* while the blue (or pink) aeroplane was heading down the left leg in flames with the caption *'Comes Down Without a Fight!'.*

By early March 1941 it was time for everyone to move on, so reunited – as well as new-found – friends had to disperse again. Dickie Grice, who had been CO at Biggin Hill when I arrived there the day after the outbreak of war, had arrived to take over the OTU from The Bull, and I think he was by then a Group Captain. Most of the old No 1 boys had been posted back to operational Squadrons or Wings. A satellite aerodrome had been built at

Moreton-in-Marsh ('Much Binding in the Marsh?') and was to be used more in the future. Paul Richey by this time had written most of his book, *Fighter Pilot,* and was also posted back to a Squadron. The OTU was to move lock, stock and barrel to RAF Usworth, between Newcastle-upon-Tyne and Sunderland, and nobody looked forward to the prospect. We held a farewell dance in the Mess but it was not a happy one, and to finish off the evening I could not start my car to deliver various people to their homes. I had several gallons of paraffin in my office (for the oil stove) which I thought would be a pity to leave and had made the mistake of pouring some – too high a ratio – into my petrol tank. The following day it was goodbye Minchinhampton.

Who the new occupants of the station were after our departure I know not – nor did I want to know. Today the site is steadily returning to its original state with grass re-colonising the area. In time Aston Down will be just a faded memory of another age.

CHAPTER EIGHTEEN

On the move again

"All good things…" and Aston Down was bound to come to an end sooner or later. Looking after one Station when I had been covering whole countries in the past seemed to be going from one extreme to the other and I had started to get a little bored. Nevertheless there were attractive reasons enough not to complain at being stagnant in our Cotswold station, and for my part an occasional lift from one of the boys down to Weston-super-Mare for a weekend with my parents was a major one. Suddenly, in February 1941, No 55 OTU received its marching (flying?) orders to set up its new home at RAF Station Usworth, Castletown, Sunderland and with this move, and a radical range of personnel, the whole atmosphere of the Unit seemed to change. True, many of the ground staff had come North with the OTU with one or two of the instructors, including Leak, which made the place tolerable. Looking out onto mine dumps when you got up every morning didn't improve matters, and it was hard to choose between Newcastle-upon-Tyne or Sunderland when an evening out was called for. Being near the east coast and large towns meant that we were often disturbed by enemy aircraft – at night anyway. It was hardly the right spot for a training establishment.

One such night was when I had been into Newcastle with Peter Gardiner. On returning to camp and entering the Mess, we were faced with quite an eerie experience, and for a few seconds words failed us. The lights were full on, and in the ante room the fire was blazing in the hearth and playing cards lay scattered on one table. Smoke rose from a half-extinguished cigarette in an ash tray and unfinished drinks were dotted around on the other tables, while total silence made the scene more dramatic. Could this be a 'Marie Celeste' on dry land, a gas attack or had the air raid sirens gone during our return journey and everyone was now in the shelters? We guessed it must be the latter and thought we ought to join the others, but passing through the hall the silence was broken by what sounded like a running tap. It was, and it came from the sink behind the bar. We needed something to steady shattered nerves and this sound reminded us of a good remedy. Many free drinks later the all clear must have sounded without any bombs dropping but we hardly noticed the Mess suddenly return to life. It was said that the Mess funds took a dip that month!

The monotony of Usworth was relieved only by occasional visits to RAF Ouston, a neighbouring station, and RAF Acklington, a Polish stronghold flying Hurricanes. After three or four weeks I shed no tears on being recalled to Derby and said farewell to Usworth. The war was now well into its second

231

year and there were many more aircraft and engines in service on an increasing number of aerodromes around the country, and the build-up was accelerating. In fact, by D-Day, there were to be some four hundred and fifty RAF Stations operating around thirty different types or variants of aircraft with Rolls-Royce engines installed. At this time it could not be forecast how far the expansion would reach, but to meet the immediate needs the Company divided the country into four regions, each controlled by a supervisor having an appropriate number of service engineers answering to him, so relieving the head office at Derby. There was no empire building with office staffs during the war – this only came later – and the whole Service Department office couldn't have comprised more than twenty-five. I don't suppose my boss thought that it would go unobserved when, whereas my home was in Somerset, I was given the North West area to look after while John Martin, who had gone to France with me, was given the South West when his home was in Derby!

This required a move to Cheshire, a county I did not know at all, and establishment of my headquarters at RAF Cranage, Middlewich, a vast improvement on Usworth. Although I was away a great deal of the time travelling around the 'parish', the place still holds some amusing memories. I had three Service Engineers under me and, although we only covered some fifteen stations, they were rather scattered, the furthest north being Walmey Island, Barrow (target towing Henleys – a precursor of the Hurricane), and the furthest south, RAF Honiley, Kenilworth. The isolated ones I covered myself such as the North Wales coastal stations – Llandwrog, Caernarvon and Penrhos, Pwllheli and further down the coast Llanbedr near Harlech and Fairbourne near Barmouth, and then Towyn. On one circuit I was pleased to meet up with Paul Richey at Llanbedr, which was good. He had not been married long and insisted on me meeting his wife and spending the night at The Victoria Hotel where they were staying. The village was some way from the camp and when we reached the hotel it was dark, but it could not have been very late as we had not had an evening meal. This might have been some excuse for Paul charging up to their bedroom, bursting in and saying *"Darling I want you to meet an old friend of mine – you know ......"* But his wife was sitting up in bed reading a book at that precise moment, and the poor girl was somewhat taken aback at having a strange man ushered into her bedroom, so drawing the bedclothes up around her said *"PAUL! PAUL! how could you?"* Undaunted Paul continued, *"but you know, he is the chaacter you asked me about in 'Fighter Pilot'."* *"See you in the bar Paul"*, I said rapidly backing out of the room. It was quite some time before Paul joined me and I never did see his wife fully clothed!

Paul was in high spirits because he had just been given No 74 Sqn (Spitfires) with the acting rank of Sqn Ldr, and was looking forward to a rest

232

at Llanbedr while training and working up his new charge. He was too modest to tell me that because of his fluency in French he had been awarded the Belgian Croix de Guerre for helping five Belgian pilots of No 609 Sqn (where my cousin John Bisdee was a Flight Commander) while posted there from Aston Down.

To divert from the narrative for a moment, Paul's book *Fighter Pilot* was published anonymously around this time and a copy found its way to the C-in-C Fighter Command, Air Marshal Sir William Sholto Douglas. Having read it, Douglas demanded to know its author so his expertise could be put to best use. Much against his wishes, Paul was immediately pulled out of 74 and posted to Fighter Command HQ for six months to introduce his ideas on fighting tactics learned the hard way in France and expressed in his book. His only consolation was that by chance his old colleague, Peter Matthews from No 1 Sqn, was posted to No 74 as his replacement. Paul did not like his desk job at Fighter Command and the moment the six months was up the C-in-C granted his wish and posted him to No 609 Sqn as the CO, where he found its Spitfires had been replaced by Hawker Typhoons.

Meanwhile, *Fighter Pilot* had taken off in a big way (with numerous reprints amounting to ten editions, the last published in 1990). Unfortunately the wealth, which proceeded from his book, and more, was later used in fighting a case against those he considered had plagiarised his work. In 1988 a book entitled *A Piece of Cake* had been written by Derrick Robinson, followed by a six-part TV series on LTV with the same title. I have not read that book, but did see the series and the story was obviously based on the activities of the Hurricanes of the AASF in France in 1940. While some of the scenes were certainly very realistic and nostalgic, on the whole, it was a bad portrayal of the truth. By choice or chance, the expert selected to advise on the making of the TV version was Group Captain Peter Matthews, but the director seemed to have been given unlimited licence to stray from reality. Paul immediately started breach of copyright proceedings on the author, the publishers and LTV, alleging that many incidents were taken from his book and that many of his comrades had been grossly misportrayed.

Paul died in March 1989 at the age of seventy-two, leaving his wife to carry on with the legal battle. When I last spoke to her in the summer of 1994 she was desperately short of funds and had sold everything of value except Paul's medals and his log book, and was arranging with Spinks to put even these up for sale. I understood her wanting to carry out Paul's wishes, but at this point I lost contact as I felt that things had gone too far, and anyway it was none of my business. It seemed that some lines of Sqn Ldr John Pudney's poem from *The Way to the Stars* were rather appropriate:

"Better by far for Johnny the bright star,
To keep your head and see his children fed"

Some time later the papers reported that the Imperial War Museum had paid £10,120 for the medals and log book and that Mrs Richey was very pleased with the outcome of the sale.

There were two stations on the Isle of Man, Ronaldsway and Andreas, to which I paid the occasional visit. The official way of getting there was by means of a civil de Havilland Dragon operated from Manchester, which had all its windows blacked out to prevent anyone checking up on shipping in the Irish Sea. This was no way to travel, but I had a piece of luck by meeting a Flt/Lt who had the dreary job of testing radar equipment installed in Beaufighters. He flew from RAF Sealand near Chester, out over the sea and often to the Isle of Man. He was only too glad to give me a lift and have some company at the same time. This arrangement worked well: he used to ring me up at Cranage, or leave a message, telling me when the next aircraft would be ready for test. I would drive over to Sealand and have an exhilarating trip to Andreas. After flying in a Maggie the take-off and climb was terrific, but the journey was too short. My 'chauffeur' would call for me the next or following day.

There was little entertainment to be had in Douglas and it appeared to be a prisoner-of-war camp for Italians, but the night five of us motored in from the camp for a drink, the boys seemed to have no difficulty in finding a pub on the north side which was open. On this particular night the landlord decided that he had run out of beer long before normal closing time, which caused a bit of an upset, but we managed to obtain a crate of a dozen bottles. It was very unfair of us to take our revenge on the community of that pleasant island but by the time we had reached Andreas, some sixteen miles away on the north tip of the island, all the bottles had been emptied and disposed of. I am afraid the fighter boys had converted to Bomber Command for this exercise, and as each couple of bottles was emptied, the command *"bomb doors open"* was heard loud and clear, whereupon windows were wound down on either side of the car and only closed again after the empty bottles had been heaved out with the confirmation of *"bombs gone"*. From the food supply at Andreas one would hardly know there was a war on. There seemed to be a shortage of nothing and at every meal there was a cold buffet on the sideboard in addition to the menu.

I was a little taken aback when I found that, because I hadn't submitted travelling expenses for these trips to Andreas, the Company – or I suppose my boss – doubted whether I had made any more than the first journey so he sent someone to check with the RAF, Isle of Man. I also learned another interesting fact of life which I could see occurring again and again during the remainder of my employment with the Company. Your superiors are apt to forget all about you unless your name crops up from time to time – and it doesn't necessarily always have to be for good reasons. Contrary to what one might expect, anyone who is working away from the factory in the field has a march on his equals who are lost among the thousands that go to make up a factory community. He has the right and freedom to send as many reports back to HQ with his name at the top as he thinks fit – provided he doesn't overdo it, when his dispatches become worthless. My mistake was that I failed to report troubles of little consequence when no assistance was required from Derby, the problem being solved by the RAF personnel with a little help from our Service Engineers. The fact that we had the best record of serviceability in our region might have been good for the war effort, but not for me personally; only trouble made news. The Company doubted our record so, much to his embarrassment, Pat Bate – who was now senior to me since I had gone to France in his stead – was sent to check up on me. I think I reached the Service Department office before Pat had had the opportunity of reporting his findings. After I said what I had to say, I felt better, and on my way back to Cranage, wondered what I would be offered on this occasion to keep the peace. It wasn't long in coming.

I made more friends than I deserved at Cranage as I was one of the lucky ones with a car and enough petrol for an occasional trip into Knutsford for a meal at The Royal George or a drink at The Rose and Crown. Closer to hand was The Bells at Peover (delightful name), where – if you got to know the landlord well enough – a bottle of champagne would be produced from his cellar. One day Stanley Grant (ex Aston Down) turned up with his Spitfire Squadron from somewhere up North on their way to Manston, where they were to refuel before doing a sweep over the Channel. That evening Stanley, Joe Cooper and one or two other characters piled into my car to go over to The Whipping Stocks at Knutsford for a drink and the fact that we had a bit of a dust-up with the Army in the pub had nothing to do with our journey back to camp. In the black-out I could not be expected to see the Austin 7 parked well into the road with no tail light, and my Standard 'Flying Twelve' gave it a good one up its tail. Out of the Austin came a man and a very shaken girl, but nobody was hurt, so we all repaired to the nearest cottage to await the arrival of the police. Our surprised but accommodating host produced tea for us while we told our story, but the Austin owner sat and said nothing, whilst his partner appeared to become more and more agitated. The man continued to sit in sullen silence till the girl resorted to tears and I suggested Joe might go across and try and comfort her. This he did and after a few minutes disappeared from the cottage, returning with a grin on his face and handed something over to the girl. This immediately cheered her up. In her haste to evacuate the Austin after the bump up its tail, an intimate article of her clothing had been left on the back seat. I wonder if my car was ever accused of being the father of the girl's child.

It was very late when station transport landed us back at the Mess, for the Standard was rather bent in front and was undriveable, and by now we were hungry so we raided the kitchen. Half way through our hastily prepared meal one of the boys noticed that I had a rather badly cut lip of which I was unaware. Apparently during our slight shunt the steering wheel had got in the way of my lower lip, and before I could protest the others had decided I must see the camp doctor. Before long he and an orderly with needle and cotton arrived and ten minutes later the others had finished their meal and I had four stitches in my lip. The last time I was stitched up in cold blood, six stitches were necessary, so this was an improvement. Early next morning Stanley came into my room (so he told me later) to see how I was, and seeing quite a lot of blood on my pillow quite put him off the sweep he was about to take part in. At breakfast, not only did I have difficulty in eating, but the Gentian Violet all over my lip advertised my plight, and I had my leg pulled badly. I was now without a car so laid low until the stitches had dissolved and then got a lift to Derby where I borrowed a Company car for the remainder of my time at Cranage.

Driving round the country in a private car in wartime, one was occasionally stopped by the police who checked your papers and the reason for your journey. I think it is reasonable to suppose that during such a period there are more important things on one's mind than routine details like renewing one's driving licence, which had to be done regularly in those days. The policemen seemed rather pleased to note that mine was at least three weeks out of date, which encouraged them to exercise their right to search my car and, of course, my brief case. Ah, ha! – a spy at last. What else could I possibly be – carrying all kinds of details of Rolls-Royce aero engines? I was beginning to wonder how the food in the local gaol compared with that of Cranage, when the two arms of the law decided that it would not be necessary to ring Derby 2424 (the Works 'phone number in those days), which I had suggested. I don't know how many times the local Middlewich Constabulary cycled out to the camp to deliver the summons, but it appeared that he called week after week, always finding me out, until at long last he found me in, after about the fifth week. So while the 'Stanley Grants' of the RAF arrived over France to deliver an attack on the Germans, 'PC49' was arriving at Cranage to deliver a private letter to me On His Majesty's Service from the Justice of the Peace for the county of Stafford. While this member of the 'Force' rested on his cycle – and his laurels, I read the following:
"… Information has been laid by Henry Jones Superintendent of Police for that you on the 18th day of August 1941 at the Parish of Wall in the said County of Stafford unlawfully did drive a motor vehicle on a certain road

there called Watling Street Muckley Corner" (dirty work at the Roman crossroads), *"when you were not the holder of a licence so to do, contrary to section 4(I) of the Road Traffic Act, 1930... summoned to appear... at the Guildhall of Lichfield..."*. Was I really expected to waste time and petrol to drive the hundred miles or so there and back from Lichfield for what was so obviously an oversight? It might have been appropriate for me to have arrived on an ass, but instead I got one of the Cranage inmates who happened to be a solicitor in peacetime to get some practice in and draft a letter for me. He relished getting his hands on even such a trivial matter, so wrote two letters for me – one on the attack, and the second he guaranteed would bring a reply on tear-stained paper. I am sure Justices of the Peace don't cry, but I really must make a point of having a look at the inside of the Lichfield Guildhall one day.

Of course, I was not the first Company employee to receive a summons. For instance, one was sent to a certain Ernest Hives, c/o C S Rolls, Lillie Hall, Earls Court, London, which commenced with the usual – *"Information has been laid by... for that you on the 3rd day of August one thousand nine hundred and three at the Borough of Worthing... then being the driver of a Light Locomotive then used on a certain highway there situated to wit the road leading from Findon to Broadwater and did drive the same at a greater speed than twelve miles an hour contrary to the Light Locomotive on Highways Order 1896. You are therefore summoned to appear before the Court of Summary Jurisdictions... DATED the 4th day of August. One thousand nine hundred and three"*. I wonder how much the fine was – if any – and whether the future Chairman of Rolls-Royce had to pay it himself. If I know anything of Lord Hives he would have questioned the accuracy of whatever method of speed measurement they had used those ninety years ago.

I was never sure whether thumping the table on my visit to Derby after Pat Bate had been sent to check on me resulted in the offer of a job in the department's office as a technical assistant or whether they just wanted the firm's car returned. However, it was clear that it was high time I moved on, and I would not get anywhere if I continued roaming round the world for ever, much as I liked the life and job. So at the end of October 1941, I packed my bags and said goodbye to Cranage after a stay of some five months to start a chair-bound career. The M6 now runs through the middle of the aerodrome, so I am told; another fading memory!

CHAPTER NINETEEN

All at sea

Soon after getting back to Derby in October 1941, I began to wonder whether I had done the right thing. I had been on the 'outside job' for barely seven years, and although I had packed quite a lot of experience into a comparatively short time, there was still a lot more to be learned. For a start, there were still thirty-six years to go – assuming I stayed with the Company – and had given up my freedom where I was my own boss and was to be confined to offices for the remainder of my working life. However, our office (actually a wooden hut) at Belper, eight miles north of Derby, where the total staff of twenty-five was gathered together in the name of the Service Department, was at least centrally-heated and winter was nearly upon us.

After a while it became clear that things were not going to be as dull as had been anticipated as I was making quite a few visits to nearby Hucknall, the Company's Flight Test Establishment, and to the factory on the south side of Derby. Later when I was established in the office and had my car back on the road, I began to be looked upon as the office travelling 'trouble-shooter' and welcomed the opportunities of answering calls for help from our men in the field. It was good to get out and about for a few days and I always managed to return with the problem solved. In fact, our Service Engineers generally knew what the trouble was and merely wanted a little backing to convince the Station engineering staff that they were right. Somebody coming direct from Rolls-Royce always sounded impressive! As time went on and the RAF expanded, this kind of exercise became commonplace and the Air Ministry even suggested at one stage that if one or two of us from the office were taught to fly, they would supply an aircraft so hours of road travel could be saved and we could reach distant aerodromes quickly. The aeroplane would be kept and maintained at Hucknall and, while our department would have first call, it would not be for our exclusive use. After giving the idea some thought, however, it was decided that while it would be useful in the summer, it might even be a handicap in the winter as one could nearly always get through bad weather by car, while a return flight could be grounded for a day or so. My second chance of obtaining proper, formal flying tuition, came to nought. Having written and sent many hundreds of reports to the office as a Service Engineer, it was interesting to read other people's narratives, and to learn how to analyse them, circulate the key information internally, write replies in answer to queries, and many other routine office duties. I was all at sea to begin with, but I had only been in the office a few weeks when I was sent on a job which was literally all at sea.

The Admiralty asked the Company for an engineer to accompany a new aircraft carrier, while on her deck landing trials: it was all very secret. I was to proceed to Liverpool docks on a certain date and report to a specific officer who would give me further information. I was not told the name of the ship, the type of aircraft or what my duties would be, but for this exercise I was to be made an honorary Flt Lt RAF. This was puzzling as, although I knew next to nothing about the Royal Navy, I at least knew that they treated the 'Junior Service' with a certain amount of contempt, and if rank was supposed to give me some status or respect, I would have thought it best to leave me as a civilian. However, it had its amusing side whatever the future held, and I reminded myself that this would be my fifth official, or unofficial, rank since by this time I had dropped everything else save my genuine status as Private in the 12th Battalion of the Sherwood Foresters Home Guard!

HMS Indomitable was a large aircraft carrier which had completed her sea trials and had just been commissioned. When I eventually found her, she lay in Liverpool docks having a few last-minute alterations. They could not find me a cabin until she put to sea and the trials – whatever they consisted of – were ready to commence.

Since an aircraft carrier and its aircraft only become a war machine when married together, this may be the point where a description of this 'other half' would be useful. The 23,000 tons displacement *Indomitable* was laid down in December 1937, the last of a class of four vessels (*Illustrious, Formidable and Victorious* being the others). This timing enabled her to incorporate modifications pointed up by her sisters: a longer flight deck (745ft), a second hangar to accommodate additional aircraft and a larger forward lift to enable non-folding wing aircraft to be struck down in the upper hangar. She had three Parsons three-shaft geared turbines, to give a total of 113,250 shp. Her airborne weaponry comprised 18inch torpedoes, 1000 and 500lb AP (armour-piercing) and general-purpose bombs, depth charges, 20mm cannon and .303 machine-gun ammunition. Two important innovations introduced on this Illustrious class of carrier were the strengthened flight deck and the armoured hangar protection. Neither the American nor the Japanese carriers had this, and suffered major damage and many sinkings from gunfire, bombing and Kamikaze suicide attacks as a result, while these four survived similar incidents far better. During her service, *Indomitable* suffered; holing below the waterline by a German bomb, two armour-piercing bombs piercing the flight deck, a torpedo hole below the waterline and a glancing Kamikaze strike. She was eventually scrapped after going into unmaintained reserve on the Clyde in 1953. Her high-point was as Flagship, Home Fleet in 1947.

Pending completion of the alterations to this brand-new fighting ship and

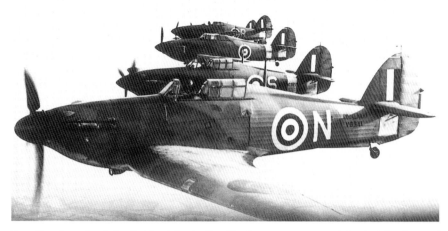

Resulting from the *Indomitable* trials, the Sea Hurricane was converted for deck landing and as above Catafighters for convoy duties, catapulted from merchantmen with no deck to land on, so no arrester hooks.

in her ability to accommodate this mufti-clad pseudo RAF-type, I stayed at The Adelphi Hotel and as the car had been left in Derby, the Navy promised transport to and from the docks each day. Sure enough, every morning, sharp at 9.00am I was met at the hotel by a battleship-grey Hillman Minx, and every evening the announcement echoed through the ship that *"Flt Lt Henniker's liberty boat is now alongside"*. It was a pity that the pretty WREN driver had to waste the Nation's petrol by returning to the ship each night, only to come back in the morning to pick me up, there being adequate berthing in the hotel car park for a liberty boat to rest at anchor overnight!

Apart from getting to know the Fleet Air Arm officers with whom I would be dealing, and finding my way round the ship, there was nothing much to do until we sailed. I discovered the large hangars which seemed to take up most of the two upper decks of the ship and last, but by no means least, the aeroplanes housed therein. The Albacores with Bristol engines were of no concern of mine, but the Fairey Fulmars were, and – what was this I saw? – what on earth were these Mark 1 Hurricanes doing here? I was among old friends and, in fact, they were the reason for my being in the ship. This was an experiment to find out whether Hurricanes, fitted with catapult spools, arrester hooks and with no major reinforcement, were suitable for deck landing. I soon discovered that the operation was actually more of a confirmation exercise, since the Royal Aircraft Establishment had already completed some convincing tests on a marked-out simulation of a carrier deck at Farnborough. Later in the war the Sea Hurricane became established in various rôles, but this would be the first time they had formally put to sea. The Navy had never seen one before and wanted to be sure the trials were not held up by any lack of knowledge of this mark of Merlin and engine installation. It will be noted this affair was intended to be a more civilised and drier business than that planned for a less fortunate batch of Hurricanes, and their pilots. Some fifty more Mk Is were being converted into Hurricats then Catafighters for catapulting off converted merchant ships to help protect the convoys in which they sailed. The volunteer(!) pilots became known as the Atlantic Suicide Squad, and once launched into the air, their sortie ended in them either ditching or dangling on the end of parachute lines. Whichever they chose, they landed up in the drink. Now I knew what the job would be, I returned to Derby for a few days to report progress.

Our General Manager Production, H J Swift, and my boss had decided they would like to see over the ship and permission, with the necessary security clearance, came quite speedily. The three of us were driven up in a Company car and I took the opportunity of explaining to my landlubber superiors the correct etiquette when going aboard one of His Majesty's warships. As we were civilians (I was not in uniform) we could not salute the quarterdeck, so the form was to raise one's hat instead. My boss seldom wore a hat, but one was produced for this auspicious occasion and we duly arrived at the foot of the appropriate gangway. I never did discover where the quarterdeck is located on an aircraft carrier but it was certainly nowhere near the 'hole' in the ship's side which swallowed the top end of our gangway. Prudently I let my seniors precede me, duly wearing their hats (I carried mine). These were raised as instructed while eyes were elevated looking somewhere aloft, towards the bridge, of which there seemed to be several. The sailor on watch did not pipe us aboard, neither did he salute; he reacted by raising his hat and gave me a wink as I passed him. No words were spoken – looks said it all!

At last all was ship-shape and Liverpool fashion and we put to sea. I had no idea where we were making for or for how long, but I had been allocated a nice cabin, the food in the wardroom was excellent and gin was three old pence per tot. However, at this stage, I felt a bit of a loner and wasn't going down too well with the permanent members of the wardroom. Though I was not the only one new in the ship, at least everyone else was in uniform and no doubt this civilian (or Flt/Lt) was a bit of a mystery. About the third day out I was minding my own business in the wardroom when a call came over the tannoy – *"Would Flt Lt Henniker please proceed to No 1 hangar at the double?"* (At the double indeed!). This sounded a simple enough exercise and some action at last, but on a strange ship the size of the *Indomitable* you could get lost in a hangar alone, not counting the false turns taken in finding your way there. Two underground 'car parks' full of aeroplanes instead of cars, would be a reasonable description of the hangars. When at last I found the cause of all the excitement, I realised that the wretched engine fitter – if that is what they called them in the Navy – really didn't know much about his charges and it was the first time he had set eyes on a Hurricane. There was nothing seriously wrong – a small three-minute throttle control adjustment put things right – but this had been holding up the whole flying programme for the day. While doing this job I was a little surprised to see the matelots tramping all over the aeroplanes as if they were battleships. I stayed with the Hurricane to make sure it was OK and then returned to the wardroom. Here to my surprise, the atmosphere had suddenly changed. I had done a great job apparently and was almost a hero – pink gins all round! No leg pull – my mess mates were being serious – I had solved the problem. I never did find out what all the fuss was about, but suspect there was some professional jealousy somewhere along the line and that the little problem had been through several hands until some senior person had told those concerned to send for me 'at the double'.

From then on I was accepted as a 'Goofer', that is, I was allowed to watch all the flying from the 'Island' which afforded a grandstand view and made we wonder why, given the choice, anyone would prefer to join the Fleet Air Arm, rather than the RAF. As a flyer in the senior of the three Services, one has the dual role – a pilot as well as a sailor – which may have its attractions. However, it was apparent that the Air Arm people were treated as second class citizens. It did not seem to have sunk in that were it not for the aircraft and their pilots (not forgetting the airborne and shipborne support crews), there would be little point in having this very costly lump of iron floating around the oceans. The ship's captain was not an aviator – very definitely 'steam' – and I got the impression that it was a little infra dig to be a pilot of aeroplanes rather than of ships. The Naval airman (or observer-radio operator etc) could not show the insignia of his achievement or acumen by wearing his wings or half-wing proudly on a conspicuous place on his uniform as do pilots of any other Service, of any other nation. He has to hide them on his left arm, just above his stripes of rank.

After seeing a television documentary on the *Ark Royal* one would conclude that the Ship's Captain ran the whole shooting match, which seems to make sense. This did not seem to be the case in the *Indomitable*, where the Ship's Captain handed over to the Captain Flying once aviation exercises commenced, and as soon as flying was over the roles were reversed. I could be mistaken but it did seem strange and likely to lead to misunderstandings during an engagement.

The Fleet Air Arm pilot was not allowed to forget that he was still a sailor (not that he would wish otherwise) and still had his part to play in the running of the ship. This would seem perfectly reasonable at times, other than when the ship was in action, and I doubt whether even Nelson would expect every man to do two duties. Assuming that a pilot has carried out his mission – dropped his torpedo for instance – and is lucky enough to be still alive with a serviceable aeroplane underneath him (and an undamaged observer/navigator), it is quite a feat to locate his relatively tiny floating aerodrome which is maintaining radio silence in a great ocean, and to make a successful landing on its usually pitching and tossing air strip. After picking up his arresting cable and not overshooting into the crash barrier, so denting himself and his aeroplane, one would think he was entitled to splice the main-brace, or have a meal, or go to his bunk, or all three. Not a bit of it, he is a sailor again and part of the ship. If the time of day coincides with his watch duties (four hours – or whatever) – he has to get on with his ship's duties. Whether he was supposed to be fit for more flying duties after however many hours, my informant didn't enlighten me.

Having put to sea, we remained in home waters for obvious reasons and cruised up and down the Irish Sea looking for suitable wind conditions and dropping anchor each night in the Firth of Clyde or Solway Firth. It was summer and there were some lovely sunsets – quite romantic from the flight deck facing aft as the Ensign was lowered in the evening. In 1941 I doubt whether any films depicting aircraft carriers in action had been made for public showing. Today with television, the exercise of deck landing is fairly widely understood, thanks to the feast of wartime films and documentaries. At that time I had never seen, or had much idea of what it was all about, so what I witnessed from the island was most interesting.

Here we had what was really a floating aircraft hangar with its private landing strip on its roof; a veritable powder keg with its self-contained arsenal of torpedoes, bombs, ammunition etc. In addition were storage tanks containing fuel oil for its steam turbines and petrol/paraffin for its aeroplanes, the whole very vulnerable to attack by even the smallest of 'proper' warships. Apart from its own aircraft, all this investment relied upon a few clusters of pom-pom guns for defence. No wonder these hybrids were always escorted wherever they went. This was the picture I visualised once the ship was fully operational and was on active service. Scrambling a Squadron of similar-sized land planes dispersed round an aerodrome seemed like child's-play compared to the palaver which takes place at sea, at least prior to the deployment of the Sea Harrier with its vertical take-off and landing capability. Of course, I did not witness the real thing – a carrier in action – but what I did see during these trials gave a good insight into what seemed a really amazing performance.

To launch aircraft these must first be brought up from the hangars on the aft lift and ranged at the stern with wings still folded and engines warmed up and checked. Once all the aircraft to be flown have been ranged and the signal given for flying to commence, the deck hands (my nomenclature) would bring each aircraft forward with the crew already strapped in. Wings would then be unfolded and locked into flying position and the plane mounted on the catapult, situated forward of the island. When the pilot is ready for take-off, he opens up his engine to full throttle and signals for the catapult to be fired. Before catapults were developed the whole length of the flight deck had to be utilised for take-off and even with the carrier steaming into a stiff breeze many an aeroplane has gone in over the bows and been run over by the ship. This process is repeated until all the aircraft are launched and, of course, no aircraft can land back until the completion of the launching. This can be embarrassing for any aeroplane in trouble after it has taken off. If for any reason an aircraft has to abort – engine refuses to start or a major snag – it has to be dealt with immediately as it is holding up the whole operation. The aft lift cannot be used to 're-hangar' the lame duck as this forms part of the flight deck, so if space cannot be found at the side of the deck, the only alternative is to push it over the side – 'ditch it in the drink'.

Having gone through the exercise of launching your 'birds' with some relief, sooner or later the more difficult task must be faced of landing them back safely when they come home to roost. And of those that can make it back to the ship there is always the likelihood of some being damaged in battle, so making life just that much harder. In those days only the aft half of the flight deck was utilised for landing-on, so leaving the forward half free for the forward lift to be used for returning the aircraft to the hangars. Wheel brakes would be quite inadequate to slow the aircraft down on such a short landing run, so towards the tail of the aeroplane an arrester hook is attached under the fuselage and lowered by the pilot at roughly the same time as he lowers his undercarriage and flaps. Provided the pilot approaches at just the right height above the pitching, rolling deck, his arrester hook picks up one of the several cables or 'wires' as they are known, which are stretched across the aft deck at intervals, and brings him to an abrupt stop. While the cables have a certain amount of (hydraulic) 'give' in them they still pull the aeroplane up with a jerk. This is when all the many 'ifs' must be right if the pilot is to make a success of getting home. Having located the carrier in the first place, if you remember to carry out all the necessary drill correctly – undercarriage, flaps, arrester hook etc, if you approach at the right speed, at the right angle, at the right height, remember the pitching deck!, throttle your engine just at the right moment, and if luck is with you – all would be well. But you have several alternatives, like landing short and crashing into the ship's stern, going over the side or hitting the crash barrier head on. The

HMS Indomitable during deck-landing trials in 1942 of four Hurricanes. The Merlin of one is being run up on the aft lift. The other three are parked fore and aft of the island.

latter used to be a steel wall which was raised across the centre of the deck to prevent the most expensive of all accidents, namely landing amongst all those other aircraft waiting to go down on the forward lift. Hitting the crash barrier – by missing all the arrester wires – was no good at all as the aeroplanes were generally written off and the pilot did himself a bit of no good.

While on this trial the Hurricanes performed without a hitch, every sortie being carried out successfully and there seemed nothing to stop the type being modified for carrier use. One incident fully demonstrated what can happen in the middle of flying-off a number of aeroplanes. A Fairey Fulmar had signalled that it was in trouble soon after take-off and, as it circled close to the ship, the aircraft seemed to be covered with oil. The pilot had to continue doing circuits until the remainder of the aircraft had been flown off or moved forward of the crash barrier. How the wretched pilot made a good landing was a mystery, as he could only see by looking out of the side of the cockpit and without any goggles. When they helped him out of the cockpit his head and shoulders were drenched in thick black engine oil and it took two fellow officers most of that afternoon to clean him up. One of the mechanics had failed to tighten up the oil tank filler cap situated just in front of the cockpit. When it unscrewed itself, the oil was sucked out and blown backwards, the pilot becoming drenched as he had to slide the hood back in order to see anything at all. The sailor was no doubt keel-hauled and transferred to destroyers!

Now the subject of the Fulmar (Merlin VIII) has arisen, a few remarks may be appropriate. It was the first time I had seen the type and it did not impress as a fighter. It looked like a shrunken Fairey Battle but was heavier and slower due to the Navy's requirement for physical robustness (deck landings) wing-folding, extended endurance (petrol tankage and ammunition capacity) and an ability to withstand use as a stamping-ground by sundry matelots, as I had already witnessed.

Under extreme circumstances, unrehearsed feats of take-offs and landings have been made on carriers ever since their inception. Perhaps the very name encouraged the Services to make more literal use of these vessels than was originally envisaged by the Naval Architects. When the Germans invaded Norway in 1940, a small force of Hurricanes and Gladiators (the last of the biplane fighters in the RAF) was sent in with the British Forces. No 263 (Gladiator) Squadron was one of the units selected for that ill-fated

One of the Hurricanes landing on.

A Fairey Firefly F1 day fighter (Griffon 12) lands on.

campaign and, on 21 April, the Squadron embarked on *HMS Furious* and the Gladiators were flown off the carrier to their 'aerodrome' – which consisted of a frozen Norwegian lake. After one glorious day of fighting, the Luftwaffe sneakily bombed the lake and the whole Squadron was lost through the ice. A new base was selected and operations renewed, but overwhelmed by the might of the Luftwaffe, the few remaining aircraft of the re-formed Squadron flew out to sea on 6 June and, joined by the remaining Hurricanes, landed without further loss on *HMS Glorious* after persuading her reluctant Captain to accept them. This evacuation and the successful landing-on of the much faster Hurricanes without any arrester aids by RAF pilots, who had never attempted such an exercise before, gave birth to the idea of using this type of aircraft as a Navy fighter – hence the trials on the *Indomitable*.

Other occasions when the Navy had to play host to the junior Service were when on 2 August 1940, 12 Hurricanes were flown into Malta from the carrier *HMS Argus* to relieve *Faith*, *Hope* and *Charity*, the three remaining Gladiators which had defended the island so valiantly. Then, eighteen months later, the first 15 Spitfires arrived from Gibraltar, flown from the deck of *HMS Eagle*. These were led by Stanley Grant (ex Aston Down) and Prosser ('Ducks') Hanks (also ex Aston Down and No 1 Squadron) my old colleagues. Cyprus was also supplied with Hurricanes from one of these

A de Havilland Sea Hornet long range fighter (Merlin 133/134 – 'handed' engines) lands on. Converted from the RAF Hornet by Spec N5/44, it and night fighter versions (NF21) later embarked on the *Indomitable*.

'Carter Patersons' or' 'Pickfords' of the sea. On her maiden voyage *Indomitable* herself not only took part in the battle for Singapore but, well before she reached the area, the Hurricanes which she had been bringing from the UK took off from her deck to fly to the aid of that great Naval Base.

It was interesting to learn more of Navy attitudes to the flying business, once the ice had been broken in the wardroom. One was on the old air- or liquid-cooling question. The Engineering Officer (EO) had had some experience of the Hawker Osprey (Kestrel VI) and Nimrod (Kestrel V) in pre-war carriers and personally preferred liquid-cooled engines, but the Navy generally favoured the reduced workload involved in operating air-cooled engines. Perhaps the installation efficiency of water-cooling was not as important in the generally lower performance aircraft often operated by the Navy. Our talk also reminded me of a subject which had embarrassed me on a number of occasions before. He told me of a new engine my own Company was working on, long before our own grapevine had brought me the news. This was the 24-cylinder, air-cooled sleeve-valve Exe, proposed for the new torpedo bomber, the Barracuda. I learned later that the Exe had been abandoned, but the message was clear: Company reps needed a formal briefing back-up on what was happening outside their own strict field of activity if their credibility with the Services was not to be compromised. It was this that prompted me to launch the 'Aero Service Bulletin' as soon as I had the opportunity, to keep all the reps up to date. Tony Dunwell did a great job cleaning up my sketches before printing, some being coloured for clarity. The subjects covered ranged from 'Miss Shilling's Orifice' (the precursor to the Negative 'G' Merlin Carburettor) to the early jets, Welland and Derwent, on which there was practically no literature in late 1943.

There has always been rivalry between the three Services, and perhaps always will be. This is a natural side-effect of the espirit d'corps essential in a fighting unit, but it needs to be channelled and controlled if it is not to be destructive. The following is an example from this very vessel, *The Indomitable*, of how it can degenerate into pettiness and become counter-productive. One of the most serious problems during the Battle of Britain was the lack of operational fighter pilots, even if they were only partly trained. There were a number of accounts of rusty Squadron Leaders having to take over Squadron sorties and flying aeroplanes on which they had less than an hour's familiarisation. In some cases this involved leading pilots into battle for the first time, while some of those junior 'sprogs' under them had had at least a couple of days current battle experience and had fired their guns in earnest. The aeroplanes were now arriving in sufficient quantities – Lord Beaverbrook saw to that – but some had no pilots ready to fly them. To alleviate this deficiency the Fleet Air Arm came to the rescue by seconding to the RAF all the pilots they could spare at the time and a total of 12 actually served during the summer battles of 1940. ' Dickie' Cork was one such and won a Distinguished Flying Cross (DFC) for valour. After the Battle, where at one time he flew as Douglas Bader's wingman, he was posted back to naval duties on *Indomitable* and this RAF decoration did not meet with the approval of the ship's Captain, who refused to recognise it and instructed Cork to remove it. Had it been a Distinguished Service Cross (DSC), a naval decoration – all would have been well. Unfortunately for that idiot captain, Cork was involved in some kind of naval review soon after being decorated at Buckingham Palace. The King remembered Cork, as it was unusual for a naval officer to receive a RAF decoration, and enquired why he was not wearing it. Cork told the King what had occurred and the latter was not best pleased, his displeasure being conveyed to the offending captain. Cork told me that while he was instructed to wear the decoration again, he was fed up with the ill-feeling that had been caused, so he only had the ribbon on his 'Best Blue' – or whatever the Navy called their best uniform. I noticed a Lieutenant Commander on the ship wearing an Air Force Cross and assumed that either because of his rank or personality, no captain had dared to order him to remove his ribbon! I heard that Dickie

Cork was killed later in the war while flying a Corsair off *Illustrious* in the Indian Ocean.

Quite by chance I learned of a further twist to this story when chatting to a Navy Captain in 1944. He had served on *Indomitable* and confirmed Cork's account and told me that, unbeknown to the King, the Admiralty later went to the trouble of ordering Cork to hand in his DFC in exchange for a DSC! When the Army awarded the Military Cross (MC) to Air Commodore Whitney Straight (Rolls-Royce Deputy Chairman in 1970) for his services to the Army in Norway, one hopes the Air Ministry did not try to make him exchange it for a DFC!

CHAPTER TWENTY

More fresh air

During the summer of 1942 several excursions from the office provided welcome breaths of fresh air, but only two were interesting enough to recount. The first was a nice long spell of seventeen days of combined air, road and rail travel, meeting old friends, mostly in the North of England and Scotland, with a quick visit to Wales and the West Country. A not-easily-forgotten character known as 'Bush' Bandidt was a Wing Commander Engineer at Fighter Command and I first came across him soon after he had had the embarrassing experience which had befallen others before him. While with one of the Groups in Fighter Command he had complained – long, loud and bitterly – about shortfalls he was experiencing in the Squadrons for which he was responsible. Next thing he knew, he found himself posted to Fighter command HQ with an 'IN' tray on his desk, full of his own reports which he now had to action! He was also concerned with various Merlin troubles occurring at OTUs, chiefly in the north of the country. Bush considered these were caused by bad engine handling. He suggested doing a tour round some of the stations and, as I had some knowledge of OTU procedures gained from Aston Down, I was chosen to accompany him.

On 15 July 1942 I drove up to London, picked up Bush at Bentley Priory (Fighter Command HQ), left the car at Kings Cross, and by 1.00pm we were on our way to Carlisle, in a nearly empty train. Here we were met by transport from RAF Annan, (in Dumfries) where No 55 OTU had moved from Usworth, so it was rather like being home again. Most of those I knew had gone, but Bullock was still there, complete with his moustache. While at Aston Down we used to reckon that if ever he took to the air, he would fly left wing low, so one day we annoyed him by shaving half of it off! It appeared that none of the Mess catering staff had moved and they seemed pleased to see me and some came into the bar to have a drink with me. The following day Bush and I talked Merlins with the maintenance people and in the evening we repaired to the Sergeant's Mess where it was good to find many Aston Down/Usworth friends who were by now senior NCOs; W/O King, W/O Wilson, Flt/Sgt Wyman and Sgt Davis were a few names I now recall. A good party was had – with much singing and ale consumed.

The following morning we borrowed an old acquaintance – the station Maggie and flew over to RAF Crosby on the Cumberland coast to meet Flt/Lt Hitchins, ex-Aston Down, by this time a Senior Flying Instructor. It seemed strange but was actually natural to meet so many Aston Down people scattered around these parts. Aston was one of the first OTUs to be formed, so the valuable experience gained needed to be passed on to the new units being set up. Bush and I flew back to Annan and in the evening after supper we walked over to the WAAF Officers Mess, where I found Knickers – again ex-Aston Down. It was a bit of luck running into her again for Flight Officer Veronica Burleigh, RA was able to give me photographs of the paintings she had done of Stanley Grant, Pike and myself at Aston Down some two years previously. The next day we were due to fly to RAF Grangemouth, but the weather was down on the deck so we had to go by road; a most frightening journey scorching across Scotland to the Firth of Forth. After our talk with the Station Engineer Officer at Grangemouth over Merlin matters we entrained for Edinburgh where we were met by W/Co Simmons and F/Lt Coleman and driven out to another OTU. The aerodrome had been Scottish Airways' Airport, and the Officers Mess, hangars and living quarters were all in one block. This was contrary to the normal Air Ministry practice, as one well-aimed stick of bombs could wipe out the whole organisation. It was another pleasant surprise when we met the Station Commander, W/Co Walters, who was the first Senior Engineer Officer at Panther (Rheims) when I was in France. We had a long talk about the AASF and some mutual acquaintants and what had become of them in the intervening two years.

Bush and I then borrowed another Maggie and flew up to RAF Tealing to meet W/Co Preston, the Chief Technical Officer (ex No 9 Group). We were rather surprised to find the engineering was not up to scratch, especially as Preston always enjoyed having a dig at Rolls-Royce. Glasshouses and stone throwing! In the Mess I came across Colin Birch, ex-No 1 Squadron in France, who was now Senior Navigation Officer, so there were more reminiscences over our drinks. The next time I met Colin was in 1959 when he had a job as Floor Manager in Peter Jones, Sloan Square. Years later I wondered if he had been the inspiration for Captain Peacock, as played by Frank Thornton, in the TV sitcom *Are you Being Served?*, though in fact Colin was very reserved and non-pompous! The return to Grangemouth from Tealing was very enjoyable, as Bush let me fly our Maggie most of the way.

My travelling companion was a large man – a very amusing and jolly Australian, but a sound engineer who could be very serious when necessary, and I suspected many of our hosts on this tour were not exactly pleased to see us. I was enjoying the trip immensely but there was one slight snag. Bush was by way of being a shot putter and had represented the RAF in this event on several occasions. Apparently there was an Inter-Services athletic meeting due to take place shortly and Bush was not going to let a little tour of the country interrupt his training schedule. So he, I and a 'shot' travelled everywhere together and sometimes I didn't think the Maggie was going to take-off with all three of us, plus luggage. My job was to nurse the shot on my lap in the back seat, and at odd places where we stayed, Bush would practice while I was expected to throw the shot back to him, having marked the spot on his best effort. On one occasion I got a little tired of carrying the shot so I put it on the floor of the Maggie where it rolled about doing no harm. We suddenly ran into some very bumpy weather and the shot left the floor every now and again, only to fall back again with a crash. I couldn't bend down to pick it up without undoing my harness, which was the last thing I was going to do as I had no intention of parting company with the Maggie. I was sure the shot would eventually break through the three-ply wood of the floor and somebody would be hit on the head by a cannon-ball. In a way I wished the ball of steel would break through and be lost – but no, more practice. On the morning of 20 July we left Grangemouth by Service transport for Edinburgh and then on to RAF East Fortune. W/Co Robinson was the CTO. I knew him slightly, as on one occasion I looked after him and W/Co Don Findlay (the hurdler) when they visited the Rolls-Royce works at Derby. The aerodrome was large with long runways and had been used by airships in the 1914 war. The Officers' Mess was an old sanatorium (which prompted Bush to make a few sarcastic remarks) but it was very comfortable compared with the usual wartime wooden huts on many newer RAF Stations.

The weather on the morning of 21 July was bad, while we were due at Abbotsinch for a meeting. By mid-morning it was supposed to be brightening up and East Fortune offered us a lift in a Blenheim, our pilot being a Polish sergeant. Soon after take-off we ran into bad weather with low cloud and practically nil visibility, and our pilot got well and truly lost. I didn't know how Bush felt at the time as he was up front with the pilot, while I took the mid-upper (rear gunner) position, but he let me know his feelings when we had our feet on earth again. We spent ten minutes or so doing steep turns at pretty low altitude looking for a break in the cloud, and the first one we found I would rather not have seen. Looking down through the gap I distinctly saw several faces looking up and the winch of one of Glasgow's barrage balloons with its cable seemingly coming straight up at us. By now I had given up hope of ever landing in the orthodox manner, but presumably this glimpse told the pilot roughly where he was, and we back-tracked and landed at RAF Turnhouse, the home base of No 603 (City of Edinburgh) AAF Squadron. Bush was as shaken as I and said that communicating with the Polish pilot was not easy, but he thought the Sergeant felt his passenger was a VIP and had to put up a good show, so wouldn't admit that he was completely lost. The Station CO at Turnhouse, W/Co The Honourable A Guinness, gave us an excellent lunch in the Mess then took us into Edinburgh and showed us round the city before putting us on the train for Glasgow, where we arrived about 5.00pm. We found Works transport waiting to take us out to the Rolls-Royce factory at Hillington where we met Bert Millward (from whom I had taken over the 'Knuckleduster' at Shorts, some eight years previously). He was then running a small Service Department covering all the Scottish RAF and RN stations using Rolls-Royce engines. After talks on current engine problems and a tour of the factory, Bert took us into Glasgow and put us on the train to Carlisle where we arrived at 12.45am on 22 June. We had by now covered quite a bit of ground in the first seven days of our tour.

We were met again by Station transport from Annan and had a hair-raising drive back to camp. The driver kept dropping off to sleep and after I had once saved our skins by grabbing the steering wheel from the back seat of the car Bush took over the driving. Apparently the wretched airman had been on duty for about eighteen hours, with only one meal break, so he was hardly to blame. We didn't have much sleep ourselves that night, but a bath and breakfast refreshed us enough to discuss our findings with the Station Engineer Officer. The following day after an early lunch it was back to the railway station for the Derby train. Arriving at Derby about 7.00pm we were met by Bill Harker and were joined later by my boss, W P Calvert (Cal), at The Midland Hotel for dinner – where Bush was staying the night. My car was still in London, so Cal took me to my digs where I was able to get a change of clothes before setting off on the second leg of our journey. The following day Cal picked me up from my digs and Bush from The Midland to take us to the Main Works at Nightingale Road. Here we had talks with the design people, and then on to the repair investigation unit, which Alec Harvey-Bailey had set up at Agard Street in the centre of Derby. After lunch, Bush and I caught the train to London and reached St Pancras at 7.00pm. A meal at the Regent Palace Grill was followed by an early night in a RAF billet, and in the morning – 25 July, we reported to Fighter Command at Bentley Priory in North London, where we spent the day.

We were now concentrating on the training establishments in Wales and the West Country so 26 July found us motoring across country in Bush's car making for Aston Down where a new OTU had been formed. To my surprise, Leak was there. He had been posted back when No 55 OTU had moved from Usworth to Annan. In the evening Bush, Leak, Pip Le Fevre – who I hadn't met before – and I had a bit of a party at The Bear Hotel with some of the friends we had made in 1940 and finished the evening at the Minchinhampton Golf Club.

Llandow in South Wales was the next port of call and as accommodation seemed short, we stayed the night at The Duke of Wellington. Next day we called at No 32 Maintenance Unit (MU), St Athan – still in South Wales, then it was supper at Aston Down and back to London for 11.15pm. The morning of the 29th saw us having another conference at Fighter Command, finishing in time to catch the train to Chester where we arrived at 10.15pm. Station Transport took us to RAF Hawarden where we met Group Captain Tough, and stayed the night in Hawarden Castle which had been taken over for the Officers Mess. We had a look round the station in the morning then as we were going in to lunch, a voice boomed across the room, *"Henniker, you're under arrest – stay where you are"*. Looking round there was 'Taffy' Jones (one of the many). Once, four years previously, Taffy had had me removed from RAF Benson, Oxfordshire, where he was Security Officer, as he did not consider I had the required security passes. We had a drink on the memory, and others had to be told the rather long story and how he got a ticking-off from the Air Ministry for being too efficient! After lunch we departed from Hawarden – yet again by Station Transport – for RAF Rednall and arrived there about 4.00pm to meet Geoff Blount, the local Rolls-Royce rep, and F/O de Witt, the Engineer Officer. We held our usual meeting and stayed the night and next day we took the train to London. 1st August found us back at Fighter Command making our reports and that afternoon I drove back to Derby. It was good to get back as we had been rushing about rather a lot during the past sixteen days; we had visited Fighter Command four times, called at sixteen RAF Stations in England, Scotland and Wales, visited two Rolls-Royce factories and covered a lot of miles.

I had been back at our Service Department office for a month or so when it became necessary to pay a visit to RAF Tangmere – the old home of No 1 and 43 Squadrons, and from where I had left for France three years before. Since that historic departure, recounted in Chapter Ten, Tangmere had been badly bombed by Ju87 Stuka dive-bombers, as it was one of the main Stations in No 11 Group, Fighter Command, and host to the famous Spitfire Wing. Douglas Bader was the first to command the Wing, in March 1941, followed by the South African, 'Dutch' Hugo, and now it was my old friend 'Johnny' Walker from No 1 who had given me my nickname when we were in France.

This famous airfield was first 'discovered' in WWI, when a FE2b of the RFC force-landed there due to fog or engine trouble in 1916. Two years later the War Office bought the land and Nos 91, 92 and 93 Squadrons were posted there to work up before going to France. It was closed in 1920 and, at one stage, W O Bentley had visions of building a motorcar factory surrounded by its own test track on the site. In 1925 the Ministry took it over again, erected permanent buildings and posted Nos 1 and 43 Squadrons in.

On 10 June 2000 a plaque was mounted in the cottage by the Tangmere Trust Museum in recognition of the operations carried out by the Special Operations Executive (SOE) with No 161 Squadron.

TANGMERE COTTAGE

THIS PLAQUE COMMEMORATES THOSE OF 161
SQUADRON RAF AND THE SPECIAL
OPERATIONS EXECUTIVE WHO STAYED AT
TANGMERE COTTAGE PRIOR TO COURAGEOUS
MISSIONS TO AND FROM FRANCE
1940 – 1944

ROYAL AIR FORCE – TANGMERE

The Museum is also mindful of Violette Szabo (SOE Agent), who was dropped by Lysander into occupied France and for whom the coded poem "The life that I have" was written by Leo Marks.

Tangmere Cottage.

Perhaps the most romantic outfit to operate from Tangmere was No 161 Squadron, one of the Special Duties or 'cloak and dagger' units. Planned and controlled from the legendary 'Tangmere Cottage', their clandestine missions to France and the Low Countries they dropped agents and supplies and retrieved agents from under the noses of the enemy throughout the war. Gordon Scotter of Aero Sales in Derby made six such night trips. He was only the second pilot undertaking this type of adventure, flying Lysander T1508 each time, and was awarded the DFC for it. This dangerous work inspired the film *Dangerous Moonlight* after the war ended. Another romantic activity based there was record-breaking. Wg/Co 'Teddy' Donaldson captured the World Air Speed Record in 1946, reaching 610 mph in a Gloster Meteor 4 (two Derwents), with his engine servicing covered by Tim Kendall. In 1953 Neville Duke raised this to 727.63 mph in a Hawker Hunter (one Avon).

I had not been back on the Station more than a day when a 'phone call came through from RAF Hawkinge, a station on the south coast of Kent. To my surprise and joy, it was Moses who had somehow heard I was at Tangmere for a few days and said he would sent a Maggie over for me if I could possibly spend the night at Hawkinge. We had completely lost touch since the Aston Down days and I had no idea what he was doing except that he had been accepted into the FAF (Free French Air Force), and now here he was, in a position to send aeroplanes off to pick up his friends! Of course I accepted his invitation and on arrival was intrigued to find a very different Moses, dressed in RAF uniform with the rank of Sqn Ldr and a DFC and Croix de Guerre with goodness knows how many palms – nine for certain. He was CO of 91 Squadron based there, and it was marvellous to see him again. Hawkinge in peacetime had been the home of No 25 Squadron, which had done the same aerobatic flying with their Hawker Furies as did No 1. He was proud as Punch, happy and enthusiastic, and was almost child-like with, what he considered, his good luck. A veritable Anglophile, the same position in a French Squadron would have meant practically nothing to him. That evening we kept very much to ourselves, talking about old times (as if they had happened at least a decade ago!) and I hardly had a chance to meet or speak to any of the other officers, who were all English or came from the Dominions. I could see they all respected Moses and there was certainly no resentment at having a foreigner as a CO. They didn't know who I was – this civilian who their CO sends an aeroplane to pick up, but at least he must be worthy of a 'sir' now and then, especially as his meals and drinks were coming out of Mess funds! Moses would tell me little or nothing about himself or his achievements, but I found out afterwards that to his great joy he had been posted to No 1 Squadron (surely not a coincidence!) and had risen to be at least a Flight Commander with them, by which time he had fourteen enemy aircraft to his credit.

Moses had promised to get me back to Tangmere in the morning if I agreed to stay the night, but on the morrow the weather was right down on the deck, and only started to clear at 11 o'clock and even then it wasn't at all promising. However, along the coastline it was clear so it was decided to have a go though there was just one snag. At that period in the war the Me109s were coming in over the Channel at zero feet beneath our radar beams to drop a single bomb on any coastal town they saw before nipping back home again. Moses said he would notify the defence batteries that a Maggie would be proceeding along the coast, so all would be well – wouldn't it? Yes? I was reminded of an earlier trip in a Maggie at a time before some AA gunners had had much practice, but then this was England.

As the Squadron was at standby, the only pilot available was a young Sergeant with a CANADA flash on each shoulder of his battle-dress. While we were waiting for a final weather clearance I learned that he was really an American who found that the only way he could get into the RAF was to cross the border into Canada and join up in the RCAF. As Moses was introducing me as 'an old friend from No 1 Squadron', I thought to myself what a strange little scene this was, one that could not have been created in times of peace. Here was a Frenchman – a Sqn/Ldr in the RAF, instructing an American in the RCAF to make an unauthorised flight, with a civilian as passenger who, in turn, had no business being on the Station in the first place. As we climbed out over Folkstone to the sea I was not to know that I would not be seeing Moses again, and I felt I hadn't thanked him enough for the pleasant evening. My thoughts were interrupted by a voice coming through the earphones, *"Would you like to take over sir?"*, Yes, I would and did! I kept roughly to the coastline, except for Dungeness, where I went inland a little and I found it great fun flying past Hastings, Bexhill, Eastbourne, Brighton and Worthing etc at only a few hundred feet. I hadn't realised before that all the piers on the south coast resorts had been 'gapped' halfway along their length to prevent them being used by landing invasion forces. It appeared to me that these slices taken out of the piers were wide enough for a Maggie to fly through. The first must have been Hastings', or was it Eastbourne's, which I approached with caution and at first there seemed room enough to fly through the gaps. Luckily, we had time to see the cables strung across the openings to discourage such stupid pranks, and a few feet of added altitude were taken. I heard not a word from my co-pilot but at least he wasn't asking to take over again! Tangmere is just a couple of miles north of Chichester (commonly known as 'Chi'), and by the time we had reached Littlehampton, I thought it was time to turn right and miss RAF Ford – and I didn't quite know where I was. I was having fun, but I suppose it should have been with some relief when I heard my 'Canadian' Sergeant suggest he should now take over – and I agreed without any hesitation. By strange coincidence, I was coming back to Tangmere exactly three years to the day, 15 September 1939, after I had left the Station for France and one of the most exciting periods in my life. Landing back at Tangmere my pilot quickly checked the weather situation as it seemed to be deteriorating again, but he considered he would get back alright. I said goodbye and thanked him for letting me fly for a while, and he replied that he had enjoyed the little trip, and then added, *"Anyone can tell that you have been a Hurricane pilot"*. Before my moment of pride had turned to laughter, he had climbed into the back seat of the Maggie, an airman had swung his prop, and with a wave of his hand he was taxiing to the end of the runway. Of course he was pulling my leg; he must have been suspicious – perhaps at my performance. But then again he treated me with great respect and was not likely to have taken the liberty of being sarcastic. Then I remembered Moses referring to me as *"an old friend from No 1 Squadron"*, so perhaps it was an indirect leg-pull engineered by Moses. I shall never know.

After Hawkinge, Moses had several postings including one to No 11 Group with the rank of Wing Commander and received the DSO and a Bar to his DFC to add to his Croix de Guerre. A posting to North Africa was followed by a mission to Russia before he returned to France to become Deputy Commander of all flying training. He was killed in a flying accident while flying to England in bad weather in December 1945. His 21 victories were the second highest in the French Air Force. Moses was also decorated with the Legion d'Honneur, Ordre de Liberation, the US DFC, Croix de Guerre Belge and the Czech War Cross.

CHAPTER TWENTY-ONE

Guarding the home

Office life from now on became more prosaic and dull and, apart from the occasional escape, it was very different to that of my first ten years with Rolls-Royce. However, I must record a few adventures in the Home Guard and perhaps one last fling on a short trip to a hotter clime. In 1941, soon after becoming a Technical Assistant in the department, I joined the 12th Battalion Sherwood Foresters, Derbyshire Home Guard – one of the six battalions in the county. Come to think of it, I would have had to take the King's shilling later on one way or another in any case. On the whole, the ten of us from our department accepted it was something which had to be done. Actually we quite enjoyed the regular two (occasionally three) HG nights per week, as it meant we could leave the office comparatively early – at 7.10pm – in order to be on parade at the drill hall for 7.30pm (19.30 hours). We took it seriously and by the time I joined, about a year later than the others, the embarrassment of dressing up as soldiers had worn off and they were quite good at throwing a rifle about.

During the three years until stand-down on 12 December 1944, there was a lot of sweat and toil, but many amusing incidents and we were keen enough in our platoon to become quite proficient. Apart from being drilled by an ex-regular Sergeant Major, we had an excellent battle course, built on Army lines and the exercise – particularly in the summer – was all we had time for and kept us pretty fit. The early LDV (Local Defence Volunteer) days were long gone and there was no shortage of equipment. Apart from his uniform, every man had a rifle and bayonet, steel helmet, webbing equipment, gas mask and gas cape. Live ammunition was issued for target practice on the firing range and occasionally for battle drill. Automatic weapons – Bren and Browning – were few and far between, but most NCOs had a Sten gun and officers had .38 revolvers. Many of the winter evenings were spent in the drill-hall – drilling, map reading, lectures, exercises, weapon training etc, which got a bit boring after the first two winters. Discipline could have been tricky with no Confinement to Barracks (CB) or 'glass house' sanctions for extreme cases, but there didn't seem to be many awkward characters. Most of us had done more than a normal full day's work before we went on parade, so I suppose we had some grounds for not showing up – but we invariably made it.

There was still much to learn and room for improvement, and one evening soon after I arrived our CO decided we required a bit of smartening up, especially with saluting and respect for officers. The remainder of our platoon was made up of members of the Detail and Design offices which had been, like ourselves, evacuated to Belper from different parts of the Derby factory, so many were still partial strangers to each other. As I was the latest recruit I was even more alien. There had been some vague talk that I had been *"in the RAF or something"* and maybe it was this, or perhaps that the officers thought I was taking the Mickey by flinging them a smart salute when going on parade, but the upshot was that I was detailed to instruct all ranks – officers included, in the correct way (longest way up, shortest down) to salute the King's uniform. The only way I could think of spreading this exercise out for the whole of the parade was by making each one in turn march smartly, the whole length of the drill hall, halt in front of an Officer, salute, deliver some meaningless message, take two paces backwards, salute, about-turn and march back – then repeat it!. This could not have made the newcomer popular, but was the best I could come up with at short notice.

Soon after the saluting episode, the top brass began to realise that under my private's uniform was a young and vigorous potential war machine and I was to be promoted to a full corporal to allow me to give expression to all this natural talent! However, when the rumour got around, there was awful heartburning and jealousy. Some snide remarks were thrown my way and I almost had to move out of the 'spit and sawdust' and drink by myself in the saloon bar. In the end I was given one stripe and, as a compensation, I handed in my rifle in exchange for a Sten gun (Carbine Machine, Sten 9 mm MkII) instead. This little machine was great fun and during our various exercises, I found that I could fire off the 32 rounds contained in one magazine very quickly – and it was light to carry. Firing from the hip always seemed slightly cowboyish! A side-effect of the promotion mix-up was that Pat Bate, who had been offered the same rank, now had to solider on as a Private! David Huddie (Sir David) was our Squad Commander and I found that now I was second-in-command with a certain amount of responsibility, I was acquiring all kinds of literature on this soldiering business – *Home Guard Squad Commanders Hand Book*, *Infantry Section Leading*, *Squad Battle Drill Procedure*, *Aircraft Recognition Part I* etc and became an expert on the Browning Automatic Rifle, having to give lectures on it in the drill-hall during winter parades. This was most important, considering we had only one of these cumbersome weapons in the platoon! This exalted rank was a handicap at times as I often missed important instructional courses and parades due to having to make various sorties out to the Squadrons. This handicap did not seem an excessive price to pay.

On one occasion we were in a Battle Drill competition in front of some high ranking Army visitors and our squad was picked as the Rifle Group and were doing well under David Huddie's command. The only snag was that I

L/Cpl Henniker 12th Battalion, Derbyshire Home Guard with gas mask, tin hat, Sten gun and bayonet.

didn't really know what was going on as I had missed all the training parades! Those with rifles had fixed bayonets, the bomber had thrown his grenades, then panic! Huddie became a casualty (because he was ordered to!) and I had to take over. We were well under cover in a natural trench so the 'dead' Huddie and I crawled towards each other, and then with only a few seconds delay I shouted out the commands as Huddie breathed them into my ear. On the final command of *"bullets"* my brave men charged with more firing from the hip, and the enemy post was taken. We were not only praised for our performance but a special mention was made of the clear and concise words of command!

There was another little incident which could have been more serious, again because I had missed the instruction and the practice parades. It took place near an old country house. Through fire or neglect, it was virtually a ruin and it was our task to continue its demolition by practising our weapons of destruction upon it. I had never thrown even a dummy practice grenade (Mills bomb) in my life, and here we were under instruction by a regular Army Sergeant throwing live grenades at the outbuildings of this unfortunate old house. We threw in no particular order so I purposely stood back a little to watch the others have a go, hoping to pick up a few tips. That the bombs were either missing or exploding short of the target meant little to me until my turn came; I wanted to heave mine as far as I could. Unfortunately I had failed to observe that all the grenades in an open metal box had a liberal covering of grease, which the others had wiped off before throwing. This I failed to do. When the Sergeant called *"your turn Corporal"* it sounded as though I was expected to do better than anyone who had gone before. I did all the right things – held the grenade against my hip with my throwing hand and pulled the safety pin out with the other. My bowling action was quite stylish except that the grenade was so greasy it just slipped out of my hand and fell about four yards in front of us. Luckily we were standing behind a low brick wall and the remains of a moat around the house, and when the Sergeant shouted *"down"* everyone fell flat on the ground and the shrapnel went over our heads. I demanded another throw; perhaps spurred on by embarrassment or maybe the memory of my cricketing days came to the rescue. Either way, the result was a bulls-eye and the target was at least hit if not demolished. Whether we completely razed the house to the ground or not I can't remember, but on another occasion we furthered its end by blowing up its north side. I was not allowed to lay the charge but had the responsibility of making sure the area was clear, and hiding behind a large oak, touched the two wires of the detonation cable to the terminals of the battery. The branches of our tree were peppered with broken pieces of brick after the quite impressive explosion.

The night and weekend exercises had their lighter moments during the summer but there was little to laugh at during the winter. One of the biggest of these involved the whole Battalion and was held in the winter and lasted from Friday night until Sunday evening. We seemed to spend most of our time round the west of Belper – Shottlegate and Cowers Lane – and slept in a barn which was cold but dry. I am sure a lot of people knew what was happening but our platoon thought the whole thing a bit of a shambles. The only noteworthy part I played was when I took up sentry duty one night outside our HQ. The instructions were clear: I was not to let anyone by who failed to give the password when challenged. Sure enough an officer, who I knew, failed to answer correctly so I wouldn't let him pass. After a few remarks like *"Don't be bloody silly, you know who I am"*, I escorted him into our HQ, much to the surprise of the CO who was somewhat taken aback when I explained the nature of my action. After a slight, rather embarrassed pause, he replied with *"Very good Corporal, that will be all"*. However, my prisoner was not satisfied with this light dismissal of the matter and started to protest, mumbling about carrying things a little too far until I felt the CO was in the mood to agree with him. I knew that none of the officers had seen active service, so quickly interjected with a polite but firm reminder that it was my experience in France (always sounds impressive) that an example had to be set by all ranks and that orders must be adhered to and carried out by the letter. If the lower ranks are allowed to be discretionary, or form their interpretation of the orders when they are not in the possession of all the reasons for their implementation, disastrous errors can, and have been made. This little bit of pomposity seemed to take the heat out of the situation, dumbfounded the NCOs present and gave the officers little time to work out whether or not what I had said really made any sense! The result was an immediate *"Quite right Corporal, you acted correctly"*, and I was even congratulated!

Continuing with the lighter side, there was the night when four Sections had to capture the road bridge over the main London-Manchester line and

River Derwent at Whatstandwell on the A6 some five miles north of Belper. I never found out whether someone had a grudge against me or whether it was a leg-pull but I was detailed to approach the west end of the bridge and, for cover, lead my section through the thick wood there. I queried this folly but was assured it would take the enemy by surprise – which it probably would have done if we had ever emerged at the right spot. Had it been daylight or even bright moonlight, it would still not have been tactically sensible. On a near pitch-black night it was ridiculous. I had one advantage, even if I didn't know where I was going, when I whispered *"Follow me"*, I only had to hang on to a Sten gun, while the remainder had to cope with rifles. At first the crackle of breaking twigs and sticks indicated in which direction I was heading, but by the time the whole section was engulfed, the spreading racket indicated that the section was fanning out in all directions. Men were cursing as they ran into trees or extracted their rifles from the undergrowth. What a deep hole was doing in the middle of a wood I know not, but there was one, and a character by the name of Crumb found it the hard way. He was saved from vanishing down its hidden depths solely by his rifle, to which he clung desperately as it fell across its mouth. I had already started back-tracking and hearing the cries for help, reached the spot first and enquired the victim's name. Being by now a little shattered by the whole chaos I could think of nothing better to say than *"What the bloody hell are you doing down there Crumb?"* as if to imply he did it on purpose. Two of us lifted his rifle, together with the luckless Crumb attached! By the time we had extracted ourselves and reached the end of the bridge we were greeted by *Why are we waiting?* in a loud chorus from our transport, which had been waiting to move off for some ten minutes. I never did find out whether the bridge was held or whether it was captured and did not greatly care.

Interspersed with these episodes are flashes of memory: the Sunday morning Sten gun practice – advancing up a lane in line, each alternate man firing short bursts left and right to clear the cover afforded by the hedges on either side – and of the slightly misdirected bullet from someone's gun which went through the heel of my boot; of the revolver practice – what on earth was a L/Cpl doing firing a .38?, a weapon carried only by officers; remembering the grouping of five shots touching each other on the target at the .22 miniature range, followed by not quite such a good score at one thousand yards on the local rifle range; the unpleasant drill wearing gas masks and capes through the gas chambers and some marching while still wearing masks; crawling through a field of stinging nettles; trying to fox the enemy by crossing the Derwent on an inflated Lilo instead of the expected bridge. One last bit of amusement came at our stand-down parade. This was at the expense of one or two of our officers, when I saw a head or two turn and at least one frown. The cause was the sight of the 1939/45 Star Ribbon on the chest of a lance corporal fighting machine lined up in the ranks. At the end of the day it was a relief that there was no chance of promotion through the casualties that would normally occur after three years of real combat. I might have become a full corporal!

CHAPTER TWENTY-TWO

From birds to rivers

It took many years to get used to polishing the seat of an office chair day after day, so I jumped at any opportunity for a visit to an RAF unit or aircraft manufacturer. The only snag was that the result of the visit was often important enough to be circulated in a report, when I needed to catch up with the delayed normal office work. When Derby finished producing piston engines and took over the gas turbine work, which had hitherto been carried out at the old Rover factories at Barnoldswick, I was to start a 'jet section' in our office to cover the servicing. The educational period in Lancashire was enjoyable but back in Derby I had to set to and write an instructional booklet with pretty coloured diagrams since at that time there were no official Dunwell drawings or publications on the subject.

As D-Day (Europe) approached I had to make several rushed visits to Fighter Command stations in the south, to Biggin Hill for instance, where two Canadian fighter Squadrons were in temporary quarters on the other side of the aerodrome to that of the RAF. Their attitude to Merlin maintenance was strange indeed. Complicated tasks like coolant level checks seemed to be too much trouble for some of them. It was too late to make much of an improvement but I was able to show some of them how to strip a Sten gun, so the Home Guard training was bearing fruit at last! The atmosphere of their Mess ante-room was unusual; it was more of a café where a coffee or a rum 'n' coke seemed the normal choices.

Then, almost immediately on return to the office, it was off again on a run of some three hundred miles to RAF Predannack, situated between Mullion and the Lizard. The Merlins in their Spitfires had been boosted to a max 25 lbs/sq in to catch anything the Germans were likely to put into the air and they were probably expected to blow up as a result.

Memories are short, but by the end of the war the free world was beginning to appreciate the great contribution the Merlin had made to the war effort. One hardly bears to contemplate the outcome of a Battle of Britain without the Hurricane or Spitfire – not forgetting the Defiant, or a bomber force without the Lancaster or Halifax Mk 1, nor yet the twenty or so different versions of the Mosquito. As well as being the most famous aero engine of the war, the Merlin was certainly the most successful of all the sixteen different types of Rolls-Royce reciprocating aero engines produced. Even the great enemy of the Hurricane and Spitfire – the Messerschmitt Bf109, which first entered this world with a Kestrel under its bonnet, relied on the Merlin to finish its active career in the Spanish Air Force!

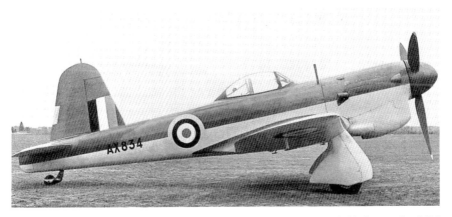

When in September 1940 the supply of fighters became critical, Miles built the wooden M20 to specification F19/40 with a Merlin XX Beaufighter II powerplant.

Of the fifty or so different makes and marks of single to multi-engined aircraft with the Merlin installed, some became famous while others were hardly heard of. It may be worth mentioning some of the latter.

Interesting and sometimes unexpected results came of contingency plans to cover events that did not take place or did not develop. Should the Hurricane or Spitfire production fall behind the demand, the Air Ministry had taken the precaution of issuing Spec F19/40 for a wooden aeroplane that could be constructed quickly wherever suitable timber was available. The resulting Miles M20 was designed, built and flown in sixty-five days from authorised release, by using the Lancaster, Halifax and Beaufighter Merlin XX engine and, in fact, a complete Beaufighter or Lancaster 'outer' power plant. The Beaufighter, in turn, only had Merlins installed in the event of there being a shortage of Bristol Hercules. The M20 turned out to be faster than the Hurricane even though it had a fixed undercarriage and the Merlin-Beaufighter was faster than the standard model. In August 1942, the Luftwaffe used a version of my old 'friend' the Junkers Ju86P, for high-altitude recce work, and to meet this threat the AM issued Spec F4/40 for a high-altitude single-seat, twin-engined fighter. Vickers produced two aeroplanes only of their type 432 (F4/41) with two Merlin 61 engines, but handling problems let Westland in and they received a contract for their Welkin, some 70 of which were made and fitted with Merlin 76/77 engines. The Westland contract was curtailed at that point and the aeroplanes never went into service when it was found that the NF Mk XV Mosquito (also Merlin 76/77), converted from the Mk IV bomber, could fly higher. After all that effort – or because of it – the Germans ceased their high altitude

The Westland Welkin (illustrated) and Vickers Mk 432 were built to spec F7/41 to combat the threatened Ju86R high altitude bomber. Only 70 Welkins were made as the Mosquito NF XV (Merlin 76/77) had a higher ceiling and the Junkers threat failed to materialise.

The French Avion Amiot type 356 was the fastest twin-engined bomber (Merlin X) just prior to the War. At 18,000 ft it was faster than the Hurricane.

reconnaissance flights.

The two best American fighters during the war – the Curtiss P40 and the North American P51 – were not inspiring until Merlins were installed, when they became the P40F Kittyhawk and the P51B Mustang. The former's performance was somewhere between the Hurricane and Spitfire, while the Mustang – whose design was possibly influenced by an escapee from Willie Messerschmitt's design office – shared honours with the Spitfire as the best fighter of the war. When two Merlins replaced the Gnome-Rhône engines in the Avion Amiot Type 350 series bomber of 1939, a speed of 330 mph at 18,000 ft was obtained (faster than the Hurricane of the day) but the war broke out too early for this Type 356 to be considered for production.

Later, when we were entering the gas turbine age, Spec T7/45 called for a trainer with a turboprop engine. Avro produced the Athena with a Rolls-Royce Dart engine installed and Boulton Paul made the Balliol powered by an Armstrong Siddeley Mamba. When it came to production both types were engined with Merlins! Perhaps the last aeroplane designed to be powered by a Merlin is the Tsumani which was first flown in August 1986. It was built privately in Chino, California, especially for the Reno National Championship Air Races.

Before leaving the Merlin, I must recall the day when the RAF effectively said goodbye to that famous engine. Between the wars it was not unusual for the Derby factory to be on its best behaviour, accompanied by a degree of

The Tsumani was privately built in California specifically for racing and powered by a Merlin.

spit and polish, to receive and impress VIPs, Kings, Emperors and Princes who came to be wined and dined and shown the manufacture of the new Rolls-Royce motor car chassis we hoped to sell them. There was at least one occasion when a mobile lavatory was kept handy in case the call came while said VIP was walking round the factory. Came the war and the production of cars ceased and with it the visitors calling for red carpet treatment.

This special day was 11 January 1949, a day the like of which had never before been witnessed in Nightingale Road. It was an impressive and yet enjoyable one which is not likely ever to be repeated. Rolls-Royce was host to Fighter Command for the unveiling of a memorial window by Marshal of the Royal Air Force, The Lord Tedder GCB, DCL, LLD, dedicated to the Royal Air Force and other pilots who took part in the Battle of Britain. The guests had breakfast on a special train from St Pancras and on arrival at Derby were met by official Rolls-Royce guides and escorted to the Welfare Hall for lunch with six directors of the Company and a quantity of Rolls-Royce workers. Amongst the eight members of the Air Council was Marshal of the Royal Air Force, The Viscount Trenchard, GCB, GCVO, DSO, DCL, LLD, ('Father of the RAF'). As one of the guides, I was pleased that amongst the thirty Wing Commanders present I found Killy Kilmartin and Paul Richey, and from the twenty-six Squadron Leaders Darkey Clowes and Peter Matthews – all ex-No 1. Strangely, no ex-73 pilots of my day were there. After lunch a welcome speech was made by Mr E W Hives, CH, MBE, the Company's Managing Director, during which he said *"… we workers of Rolls-Royce like to consider ourselves part of the RAF. We recognise that our efforts were more congenial and we were not called upon to display the courage and suffer the hardships and the sacrifices of the fighter pilots. Nevertheless, we hope we shall not be considered impertinent if we insist on our claims that we were a part of the RAF in the Battle. The very purpose of the Memorial Window which Lord Tedder has kindly agreed to unveil is to have a permanent record of the close association of the industry with the Services".*

The Rt Hon Sir Archibald Sinclair, KT, PC, CMG, then spoke in reply and extracts from his long and inspiring speech follow. *"…This is a most happy and imaginative gesture tinged as it must always be with wonder, for the heroic Polish, French, Belgian, Czech, American, Dominion, but mainly English, Scots, Welsh and Irish pilots who fought and won the most decisive battle of the last war – the Battle of Britain. I have seen those young men enduring both the boredom of monotonous waiting for something to happen and the almost super-human strain of going up to fight, down to refuel and re-arm and up to fight again all through the long summer day and so for days on end 'till I prayed for cloud and rain. They braced themselves for each engagement with the enemy, expecting to find him in superior numbers and knowing that the penalty for the slightest slackness or slowness was probably death for themselves and possibly disaster to their Squadron"*. Of the Rolls-Royce employees he continued *"...The younger workers were chafing to get into the Services but few could be spared although I am surprised to find that 668 managed to break away into the RAF and of those, three RAF pilots who fought in the Battle of Britain are now working for Rolls-Royce"*. *"...it was customary for the Day Shift to work right through and hand over to the Night Shift and to go on doing that 7 days a week. I remember being told that it was not uncommon for men to put in over 80 hours work a week. Impertinent, Mr Hives, to insist that workers with such a record should feel that they were part of the RAF? On the contrary, the pilots of the Royal Air Force are proud to call such men their comrades"*.

After lunch Lord Tedder inspected the Rolls-Royce ATC guard of honour and then the assembled company of some three hundred gathered round the window in the main entrance hall for the Service of Dedication by the Lord Bishop of Derby. The window depicts a Fighter Pilot standing on the spinner of a propeller while behind him are the buildings of the Derby factory which produced so many of the engines. The inscription on the window reads *"TO THE PILOTS OF THE ROYAL AIR FORCE WHO, IN THE BATTLE OF BRITAIN, TURNED THE WORK OF OUR HANDS INTO THE SALVATION OF OUR COUNTRY"*.

In his address Lord Tedder emphasised the wonderful team spirit between craftsmen, designers and pilots, one of the secrets of the British air power and continued *"... And surely it is of the future that these men we commemorate would wish us to think. Can you not see them looking at this memorial and hear them saying 'Yes, this is a beautiful thing, a fine reminder of what we fought for, ...What have you done, what are you doing, what are you going to do for the cause for which we did all we could? ...Surely this memorial is a challenge as well as an inspiration... May we prove equal to the challenge, worthy of our (sic) trust, and may we achieve the impossible as they achieved it"*. Another speaker made the comment: *"Rolls-Royce employees were always reminded that the difficult had to be achieved yesterday, the impossible took a little longer, but when the Magic failed we were in deep trouble"*.

After touring the factory the guests were given tea then, on boarding the buses for the station, they said farewell to their guides – with one exception. That one was hustled down to the station and frog-marched onto the train. I had the greatest difficulty in extracting myself from the moving carriage as it pulled out for London, much to the surprise of two of the Company's Directors on the platform. I managed to scrounge a lift back to the factory in their chauffeur-driven Rolls-Royce.

Once the war was over, Rolls-Royce had to begin thinking of the

The unveiling and dedication ceremony of the memorial window to the pilots who took part in the Battle of Britain – Marble Hall, Nightingale Road, Derby, 11 January 1949.

inevitable drop in demand for military aero engines – including the new gas turbine engines. At that time, the Merlin and Griffon were still the only engines in full-scale production at Derby. It was realised we would have to enter the civil world and sell against stiff competition – or die. While the motorcar would probably start selling again at almost any price, the days had gone when any product sold itself on excellence alone. The aero engine side of the business was now many times larger than that of the car (the reverse of the 1929 situation when I joined). Everyone was well aware that between the wars aero had been tied to the apron strings of the Government, which had financed virtually all development and production, either directly or indirectly, and now these contracts would be slashed. Sales and marketing had been words and activities that were seldom heard in Derby; that all happened south of the River Trent – a rather fancy business that was left to the London office, a sidekick of the motorcar showrooms in Conduit Street. To me, it was just a place where I reported to collect my tickets, currency, passport and a quantity of 'RR' propelling pencils and pocket knives etc with which to sweeten our overseas customers. Merlins had gained a reputation for reliability and smooth running during the war, so the Company anticipated a further life for them until the gas turbine or 'jet engine' took over. It would be some time before aircraft production could switch from the four-engined heavy bomber to the same sized commercial aeroplane. Broadly speaking this was accomplished in three stages in this country and to some extent in America, while Germany, Italy and Japan were out of the picture, being barred from developing their own aircraft.

Avro had already made the York military transport during the war, using Lancaster wings, undercarriage, power plants, etc married to a large capacity square-sectioned fuselage. After the war they took the Lancaster, stripped it of its bellicose equipment – the nose and tail being faired in where the gun turrets had been housed, and fitted longitudinal passenger seats and renamed it Lancastrian. Avro's third stage was the completely newly designed Tudor – still with Merlin engines. On the other side of the Atlantic, Boeing produced the Stratocruiser using the wings, engines and undercarriage of their B-29 bomber – the Superfortress. The aeroplane that had the edge on all the others was first built in 1938 as a four-engined commercial carrier to augment the smaller twin-engined Douglas DC-3, better known as the Dakota – that veritable workhorse of the war. Douglas initially made a few mistakes with their new venture but redesigned it in 1942 – just at the right time to become a military transport known as the C54 Skymaster. After the war it took little time or cost to convert it back to its original design function and it quickly appeared in airlines round the world as the Douglas DC-4. Its only real drawback was that the cabin was not pressurised for altitude (economic) flying. When a later pressurised version was to be manufactured

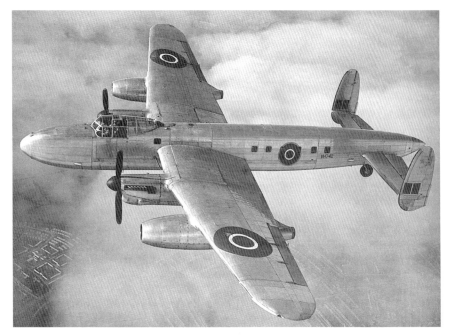

Avro Lancastrians were used by Hucknall for flight testing gas turbine engines such as Avons and Nenes (above).

in Canada for BOAC, Trans Canada and Canadian Pacific Airways, it was quite a sales achievement for Rolls-Royce to obtain the contract to supply Merlins for it in place of the normal Pratt & Whitney engines. Initially the aircraft was known as the DC-4M, but BOAC christened it 'Argonaut'.

In 1950 BOAC invited a few Rolls-Royce personnel to go on Argonaut-proving flights to Cairo for one night and back the following day, and by the time I made the trip the aeroplanes were known as the Juggernauts! My excuse for staying longer in Cairo than one night was that it was time somebody from Derby visited our two resident representatives – Jock Stephens with BOAC and Frank Millward with the Royal Egyptian Airforce to look after the Derwent (turbine) engines in their Gloster Meteors. So once again I was on a commercial aeroplane with Rolls-Royce engines. The trip to Cairo was quite relaxed this time and I didn't really mind what happened, no disaster could cause ninety-six sparking plugs to fail at the same time. The difference was that almost exactly thirteen years previously the passenger aeroplane in which I was flying had only two Kestrel engines and I was certain things were going to drop off the engine installation – and they did – while in an indirect way I had felt responsible. That had been a German aircraft and now this one was American. The years between had shown that we could build war planes second to none and I wondered how long it would be before we could build world-beating passenger aeroplanes as well. As it turned out we beat the world into the 'jet age' with the Comet and Viscount (Rolls-Royce Avons and Darts) and both types were still flying into the 1990s, the former vastly modified and turned into the Nimrod Early Warning Aircraft (EWA) for the RAF. TEMPUS FUGIT- presumably at a constant speed although as one gets older it appears to accelerate at an alarming rate – but aeroplanes have certainly become faster. The Cairo trip demonstrated the civil progress made in speed alone since 1950, but whether one can say the general quality of an in-flight meal has improved, is doubtful.

We left London Airport (it was not Heathrow in those days), at 10.48am on Argonaut G-ALHC 'Ariadne' and were eating an excellent lunch as we cleared the French Riviera. We were over Corsica by 1.04pm and landed at Malta at 3.50pm for a stop of one hour twenty minutes for refuelling and a cup of tea. Passing Alexandria on our port side in the dusk, we were over the lights of Cairo an hour and a half later and came into Farouk Airport, touching down at 10.20pm – no stacking or congestion in those days. Jock Stevens was there and saw that my customs was a mere formality so it wasn't long before we were having a Stella beer in The Helopolis Palace Hotel. Flying time was ten hours twelve minutes, and elapsed time from airport to airport a few minutes under twelve hours – slightly slower than today's schedule! Of the twenty-five or so different aircraft in which I have flown, the Argonaut must have been the noisiest, except perhaps for the Short Sarafand with its six Buzzards.

Travelling in this part of the world was a reminder that great deeds were done in many outlandish places during the war. The conflict was not confined to the European theatre where I had been trying to do my bit. Many will remember George Beardsley of Aero Service, who was attached to the Fleet Air Arm in the Western Desert to look after Hurricanes and Fairey Fulmars in February 1941. About this time the Japanese were threatening India, and there were hardly any effective aircraft in that area, so two Fulmar Squadrons were to be diverted to Ceylon (Sri Lanka) with immediate effect. The only problem was that the Fulmar did not have the range and there was nowhere to re-fuel en route. George did a series of urgent tests of lean carburettor settings, and after many test flights, proved that with careful engine handling, a fuel consumption of 28 gallons per hour could be maintained, sufficient to cover the 3800 miles distance necessary. He got the tests completed, the aircraft and engines prepared and the pilots briefed on the delicate engine handling, all in about seven days. Every aircraft reached Ceylon safely and in time to carry out successful actions against the

Japanese. For this operation and general service to the Royal Navy, George was recommended for an honour. I understand it was never actually offered, on the argument that this sort of initiative was considered to be all part of the day's work for a Rolls-Royce Service Engineer.

Whereas the RAF had given me a Commission into the Volunteer Reserve while I was serving as an Officer in France, the Navy retained George as a civilian. They decided the rig appropriate for him would be an Officer's uniform without any Navy badge of rank. The compromise resulted in a cap badge made up of the RR surrounded by decorative gold braid. The sleeve insignia comprised the words "SPECIAL RN DUTIES". This was hardly consistent with the title of Flt/Lt, RAF which they bestowed upon me for my period on *HMS Indomitable* (Chapter Nineteen).

Another noteworthy enterprise took place in the caves in the Mokattan Hills. Here, in 1942/43, the RAF, together with local talent, had somehow – and almost out of nothing – built an efficient Repair and Salvage Unit where nothing was scrapped and the damaged engines and aeroplanes of the Desert Air Force were repaired and returned to service. There was an amazing story told by one of our repair engineers attached to the RAF at the time. It was

George Beardsley in his Navy civilian uniform – taken in North Africa.

that, being short of Merlin main bearings, replacements were made out of damaged-beyond-repair aluminium propeller blades! Had our hard-won lead-bronze casting technology, which actually originated in Allison, been in vain?

These caves had been created by the hewing of stone blocks for the Pyramids. When they were cleared of rubbish for conversion into bomb-proof workshops, a large block of stone was found already on rollers for dispatch; a 2000 year old 'spare' still in stock, waiting to 'service' one of the ancient monuments! I had not seen the Pyramids for some time so off we went to Gaza. As we travelled along the modern road in the comfort of Frank's car I could not help reflecting on how the same journey had been completed some 130 years previously by a remote relative, Sir Francis Henniker. In

1820 he wrote a book with the rather long but intriguing title of *Notes During a Visit to Egypt, Nubia, The Oasis, Mount Sinai and Jerusalem* (John Murray, Publishers). This is the extract of which I was thinking:

"First December Mr George F Grey of University College and myself with my interpreter hired donkeys and rode to Old Cairo. Here we put our animals on board the ferry boat, the Nile so far diminished that it was impossible to proceed by water to the Pyramids, and not sufficiently so to allow the passage by land we continued to ascend the stream nearly to Sacchara; as we approached the object of our curiosity "What do YOU think of these Wonders of the World?" was the question banded between Grey and myself, to which came the inevitable reply "nothing more than a pile of bricks"

Their journey seemed a little complicated and I wondered why they had not hired camels for the whole trip. Perhaps there were good reasons for this, one of which may have been that the Turks, who occupied the country in those days, were anything but honest dealers and appeared to have the monopoly on camels. The Arabs either favoured, or were left with, the dromedary which was hardly suitable. Incidentally, the Turks were no fools, for the camels were unaffected by cold and high altitude and enabled their owners to make long journeys over mountains into other countries, whilst the dromedary would only operate on hot level terrain. I suppose one hump for ground level – two for high altitude work! In contrast, our excursion now continued, shaded from the hot afternoon sun and in the comparative cool of the car, and taking tea at The Mena Hotel on the way. This hadn't changed, neither had the tea, toast and jam, but since Churchill stayed there during the War, I noticed the price had risen. We then went on to see the last of the Seven Wonders of the World, and having crossed the palm of a guide with a silver piece, we were informed that Cheop's was the tallest of the three Pyramids and had taken twenty years to build. It was no surprise to find it had changed little since I first saw it thirteen years previously on the way to South Africa, though the grin on the face of the Sphinx may have grown slightly more inscrutable!

By 1950 the future of aviation seemed all in Britain's favour. We were the world leaders in gas turbine engines – Rolls-Royce, Armstrong Siddeley, Bristol and de Havilland all had engines at some stage of development and production and there was no doubt that we could build good aeroplanes. The prototype de Havilland Comet (four de Havilland Ghost engines) and the Avro Canada Jetliner (4 Rolls-Royce Derwents) had both flown the previous year, while an Avro Tudor with 4 Rolls-Royce Nenes had flown even the year before, 1948, though the latter two were used for research and never intended for production. The Vickers Viscount (four Rolls-Royce Darts) first flew the same year, and was the world's first turbo-prop to go into quantity production and commenced operation for BEA in 1953. The Comet pioneered the pressurised cabin for high-altitude passenger flight, and then disaster struck.

The cause was determined at the RAE, Farnborough, by immersing a complete fuselage in a specially constructed water tank where it could be put under the equivalent pressure cycles simulating flying at altitude, and the world in general learned of the phenomenon of metal fatigue. The results were published and made known throughout the aviation industry so all could benefit from de Havillands' pioneering work. Twenty-nine years after the introduction of the Comet into commercial use, the Nimrod, a modified version of the basic design, was still in service with the RAF.

To complete the picture of the larger British passenger aircraft, the Vickers VC-10 (four Rolls-Royce Conways mounted in pairs on either side of the tail) was considered by many to be the best commercial aircraft ever built and is still operating in the RAF as a tanker. The de Havilland Trident

The Avro Tudor 8 – or Ashton – flew in 1948 with 4 Nene engines

(three Rolls-Royce Spey engines, also mounted in the tail) and the BAC One-Eleven (two Rolls-Royce Spey engines) were three world beaters and yet none attracted orders large enough to give them profitable production runs. Rolls-Royce was first in series production with the turbo-jet and turbo-prop (not forgetting Whittle, Powerjets and Rover, of course) but true to the British character we then went and gave it all away to our competitors!

I am now in danger of running too far ahead of myself and I must call a halt at the Nene, as this was the last of the original 'centrifugal' family of 'pure' jet engines produced by Rolls-Royce and with which I was familiar. My work was taking me further and further away from the 'hardware' and deeper and deeper into the inevitable IN and OUT trays of the paper world. The mid-fifties found me with the title of Aero Division Service Manager, which – among other duties – entailed sending Service Engineers all over the world – to most of the places I would have loved to have gone myself. The exigencies of wartime collaboration, combined with commercial fancy footwork and a disdain for international patent law, produced the irony whereby Nene battled to the death with Nene over North Korea in the 1950s. The Russians coded theirs RD-45 to power the MiG 15 and the Americans coded theirs J42 to power the Sabre. It would have been exciting if one could have been out there looking after the serviceability of both side's fighter engines. On reflection, perhaps that scenario would be a bit too exciting for a Service Engineer moving into his more mature years.

"I really must be leaving now."
Terry Henniker departing from the September 1998 Sir Henry Royce Memorial Foundation meeting in Paulerspury having been persuaded by Ian Neish to write this book.

APPENDIX

Outline sketches of the careers of some of the better-known Allied fighter pilots encountered in this narrative.

Note: A damaged or unconfirmed or joint 'kill' is counted as a 'half' and halves are accumulated.

Page	Name	Known as	Rank	Victories	Flew	Honours etc	Notes
117	BISDEE, J D	John	Grp Capt	12	Spitfires	OBE, DFC	Cousin of Tony Henniker Started as NCO pilot
174	BOOT, P V	Peter	Flt Lt	6½	Hurricanes	DFC	Died 1984
118	BROWN, M H	'Hilly'	Wg Cdr	18½	Hurricanes	DFC & Bar	Died 1940 Canadian
118	CLISBY, L R	Leslie	F/O	10½*	Hurricanes		Died 1940 Australian * may be as high as 17
144	CLOWES, A V	'Taffy' or 'Darkey'	Sqn Ldr	12½	Hurricanes	DFM, DFC	Died 1949 Started as NCO pilot
249	CORK, R J	'Dickie'	Lt Cdr	16	Hurricanes Sea Hurricanes	DSO, DFC* DSC	Died 1943 FAA pilot Drafted into RAF for BoB emergency *DFC withdrawn by RN and replaced by DSC
	*DEMOZAY, J F						*Refer to MORLAIX, J E F

280

Page	Name	Known as	Rank	Victories	Flew	Honours etc	Notes
177	DRAKE, W	'Billy'	Grp Capt	25*	Hurricanes Spitfires Kittyhawks	DSO, DFC & Bar, The US DFC	*May be as high as 43
184	GOODMAN, G E	George	F/O	14	Hurricanes	DFC	Died 1941
221	GRANT, S B	Stanley	AVM	10	Spitfires	CB, DFC & Bar	Died 1987
118	HANKS, P P	'Ducks'	Grp Capt	18	Hurricanes Spitfires	DSO, DFC, AFC	
90	HUGO, P H	'Dutch' or Piet	Grp Capt	24	Hurricanes Spitfires	DSO, DFC & 2 Bars, Croix de Guerre, The US DFC	Died 1986 South African
144	KAIN, E J	'Cobber'	F/O	16½	Hurricanes	DFC	Died 1940 New Zealander
144	KILMARTIN, J I	'Killy'	Wg Cdr	13½	Hurricanes	DFC	Died 1999 Irish/Australian
254	Le FEVRE, P W	'Pip'	Sqn Ldr	8	Hurricanes Spitfires Typhoons	DFC	Died1944 Huguenot British
90	MALAN, A G	'Sailor'	Grp Capt	41	Spitfires	DSO & Bar DFC & Bar	Died 1963 South African
124	MARTIN, R F	'Dickie'	Wg Cdr	7½	OBE, DFC & Bar, AFC		
173	MATTHEWS, G P H	Peter	Grp Capt	11½	Hurricanes Spitfires Sabres	DFC	Died 1991

Page	Name	Known as	Rank	Victories	Flew	Honours etc	Notes
172	MORE, J W C	'Hank'	Grp Capt	5½	Hurricanes	OBE, DFC,	Died 1944
150	*MORLAIX, J E F	'Moses'	Wg Cdr/ Lt Col	24	Hurricanes Spitfires	DSO, DFC & Bar, Legion d' Honneur, Ordre De Liberation, Croix de Guerre, The US DFC, Czech War Cross	Died 1945 French Real name was DEMOZAY, J F
118	MOULD, P W O	'Boy'	Sqn Ldr	16½	Hurricanes	DFC & Bar	Died 1941 First victorious RAF pilot, 30/10/39
171	ORTON, N	'Fanny'	Sqn Ldr	22	Hurricanes Spitfires	DFC & Bar	Died 1941
125	PALMER, C D	'Pussy'	Sqn Ldr	3	Hurricanes	DFC	Died 1942 American
90	PATTLE, M T St J	'Pat'	Sqn Ldr	58	Gladiators Hurricanes	DFC & Bar	Died 1941 South African Highest score in the RAF
178	PAUL, H G	'Ginger'	Wg Cdr	5½	Hurricanes	DFC	
124	PLINSTON, G H F	George	Sqn Ldr	7½	Hurricanes Kittyhawks	DFC	
180	RICHEY, P H M	Paul	Wg Cdr	14½	Hurricanes Spitfires Vampires	DFC & Bar, Officer of Order of Crown, Belgium, Legion d'Honneur, Croix de Guerre, Croix de Guerre Belge	Died 1998 Author of Best Seller "Fighter Pilot"

Page	Name	Known as	Rank	Victories	Flew	Honours etc	Notes
171	SCOULAR, J E	Ian	Wg Cdr	18½	Gladiators Hurricanes Tomahawks	DFC, AFC	Died 1986 Joined Rolls-Royce after the war
171	SCOTT, D S	Donald	Sqn Ldr	9	Spitfires Tomahawks Kittyhawks	DFC	
144	SOPER, F J	'Marshal Budenny'	Sqn Ldr	13½	Hurricanes	DFC, DFM	Died 1941 Started as NCO pilot
126	STRATTON, W H	'Billy'	Wg Cdr	4	Hurricanes	DFC & Bar	New Zealander
118	WALKER, P R	'Johnny'	Grp Capt	8	Hurricanes	DSO, DFC	Died ? 1982

The Historical Series is published as a joint initiative by the Rolls-Royce Heritage Trust and The Sir Henry Royce Memorial Foundation.

Also published in the series:

No.1   Rolls-Royce – the formative years 1906-1939
        Alec Harvey-Bailey RRHT 2nd edition 1983 (out of print)

No.2   The Merlin in perspective – the combat years
        Alec Harvey-Bailey, RRHT 4th edition 1995

No.3   Rolls-Royce – the pursuit of excellence
        Alec Harvey-Bailey and Mike Evans, HRMF 1984

No.4   In the beginning – the Manchester origins of Rolls-Royce
        Mike Evans, RRHT 1984

No.5   Rolls-Royce – the Derby Bentleys
        Alec Harvey-Bailey, HRMF 1985

No.6   The early days of Rolls-Royce – and the Montagu family
        Lord Montagu of Beaulieu, RRHT 1986

No.7   Rolls-Royce – Hives, the quiet tiger
        Alec Harvey-Bailey, HRMF 1985

No.8   Rolls-Royce – Twenty to Wraith
        Alec Harvey-Bailey, HRMF 1986

No.9   Rolls-Royce and the Mustang
        David Birch, RRHT 1987

No.10   From Gipsy to Gem with diversions, 1926-1986
        Peter Stokes, RRHT 1987

No.11   Armstrong Siddeley – the Parkside story, 1896-1939
        Ray Cook, RRHT 1989

No.12   Henry Royce – mechanic
        Donald Bastow, RRHT 1989

No.14   Rolls-Royce – the sons of Martha
        Alec Harvey-Bailey, HRMF 1989

No.15   Olympus – the first forty years
        Alan Baxter, RRHT 1990

No.16   Rolls-Royce piston aero engines – a designer remembers
        A A Rubbra, RRHT 1990

No.17   Charlie Rolls – pioneer aviator
        Gordon Bruce, RRHT 1990

No.18   The Rolls-Royce Dart – pioneering turboprop
        Roy Heathcote, RRHT 1992

No.19   The Merlin 100 series – the ultimate military development
        Alec Harvey-Bailey and Dave Piggott, RRHT 1993

No.20   Rolls-Royce – Hives' turbulent barons
        Alec Harvey-Bailey, HRMF 1992

No.21   The Rolls-Royce Crecy
        Nahum, Foster-Pegg, Birch, RRHT 1994

No.22   Vikings at Waterloo – the wartime work on the Whittle jet engine by the
        Rover Company
        David S Brooks, RRHT 1997

No.23   Rolls-Royce – the first cars from Crewe
        Ken Lea, RRHT 1997

No.24   The Rolls-Royce Tyne
        L Haworth, RRHT 1998

No.25   A View of Ansty
        David E Williams, RRHT 1998

No.26   Fedden – the life of Sir Roy Fedden
        Bill Gunston OBE FRAeS, RRHT 1998

No.27   Lord Northcliffe – and the early years of Rolls-Royce
        Hugh Driver, RREC 1998

No.28   Boxkite to Jet – the remarkable career of Frank G Halford
        Douglas R Taylor, RRHT 1999

Special   Sectioned drawings of piston aero engines
          L Jones, 1995

Monograph Rolls-Royce Armaments
          D Birch, RRHT 2000

Technical Series:

No.1   Rolls-Royce and the Rateau Patents
        H Pearson, RRHT 1989

No.2   The vital spark! The development of aero engine sparking plugs
        K Gough, RRHT 1991

No.3   The performance of a supercharged aero engine
        S Hooker, H Reed and A Yarker, RRHT 1997

No.4   Flow matching of the stages of axial compressors
        Geoffrey Wilde OBE, RRHT 1999

Books are available from:
Rolls-Royce Heritage Trust, Rolls-Royce plc, Moor Lane, PO Box 31, Derby DE24 8BJ